CAN SOUTH AND SOUTHERN AFRICA BECOME GLOBALLY COMPETITIVE ECONOMIES?

Can South and Southern Africa become Globally Competitive Economies?

Edited by

Gavin Maasdorp
Director and Research Professor
Economic Research Unit
University of Natal
Durban

First published in Great Britain 1996 by
MACMILLAN PRESS LTD
Houndmills, Basingstoke, Hampshire RG21 6XS
and London
Companies and representatives
throughout the world

A catalogue record for this book is available
from the British Library.

ISBN 0–333–65387–4 hardcover
ISBN 0–333–65388–2 paperback

First published in the United States of America 1996 by
ST. MARTIN'S PRESS, INC.,
Scholarly and Reference Division,
175 Fifth Avenue,
New York, N.Y. 10010

ISBN 0–312–16239–1

Library of Congress Cataloging-in-Publication Data
Can South and Southern Africa become globally competitive economies? /
edited by Gavin Maasdorp.
p.   cm.
Includes bibliographical references and index.
ISBN 0–312–16239–1
1. South Africa—Economic policy.   2. Economic forecasting—South
Africa.   3. Africa, Southern—Economic policy.   4. Economic
forecasting—Africa, Southern.   5. Competition, International.
I. Maasdorp, G. G. (Gavin Grant)
HC905.C36   1996
338.968—dc20   96–13147
                                                                                    CIP

10   9   8   7   6   5   4   3   2   1
05   04   03   02   01   00   99   98   97   96
Printed in Great Britain by
The Ipswich Book Company Ltd
Ipswich, Suffolk

To the staff of the Economic Research Unit
1944–94

Contents

Notes on the Contributors   x

Preface and Acknowledgements   xiv

List of Abbreviations   xvii

Overview: Avoiding Marginalisation *Gavin Maasdorp*   1

PART 1   MARGINALISATION IN THE GLOBAL ECONOMY

1. Why is Africa Marginal in the World Economy?
   William Easterly   19

PART 2   REGIONAL AND NATIONAL MARGINALISATION

2. The Changing International Economic System
   Peter Robson   33

3. Can Regional Integration Help Southern Africa?
   Gavin Maasdorp   45

4. Small Countries within Regional Integration
   Michael Matsebula and Vakashile Simelane   53

5. Migration and the Brain Drain
   Oliver Saasa   61

PART 3   MARGINALISATION WITHIN COUNTRIES

6. Income Inequality and Poverty in South Africa
   Mike McGrath   69

7. Public Expenditure and Poverty in Namibia
   Irene Tlhase with Tjiuai Kangueehi   79

8. Provincial Marginalisation: KwaZulu-Natal
   Nick Wilkins   85

PART 4 CHOOSING WINNING POLICIES

9. Asian Lessons in Sustainable Development
   Seiji Naya   95

10. The Real Exchange Rate and Reserve Management:
    Latin America in the 1990s
    Felipe Larraín   107

11. Currency Convertibility and External Reserves
    Laurence Clarke   123

12. Internationalisation of Capital Markets
    S. Ghon Rhee   137

13. Macroeconomic Policy Lessons from Africa
    Anselm London   148

14. Macroeconomics and Marginalisation: the Triumph
    of Hope over Experience
    Tony Hawkins   159

15. Effective Investment and Competitiveness
    Michael Unger   172

16. Improving the Business Environment
    Paul Holden   182

17. Avoiding Corporate Marginalisation
    Millard W. Arnold   196

18. Technology and Unmarginalising
    Roger Riddell   204

PART 5 SOME SOUTHERN AFRICAN ISSUES

19. South Africa's Economic Reforms
    Merle Holden   221

20. The South African Labour Market
    Julian Hofmeyr   231

21. Labour Legislation and the Zimbabwean Economy
    Joe Foroma 245

22. Helping Small and Medium Business
    Marlene Hesketh 251

23. Health, Education and Productivity
    Alan Whiteside 258

Select Bibliography and References 267
Index 276

Notes on the Contributors

Millard W. Arnold is Minister-Counsellor for Commercial Affairs for the Southern Africa region, US Department of Commerce. He previously served in Botswana and Mozambique as policy adviser to government and business on private sector development. A graduate of Howard University, Washington and the University of Notre Dame, Indiana he has also studied in London.

Laurence Clarke was Deputy Governor of the Bank of Botswana from 1990 to 1995 before becoming Director of the Caribbean Centre for Monetary Studies at the University of the West Indies, Trinidad. He held various positions in the World Bank and International Finance Corporation after graduating from the Universities of Guyana and Windsor, and obtaining a doctorate at the University of the West Indies.

William Easterly is Principal Economist, Policy Research Department, World Bank and an Adjunct Professor at the School of Advanced International Studies, Johns Hopkins University. He obtained a doctorate from the Massachusetts Institute of Technology, and has served on missions to various developing countries in Latin America, Africa and Asia as well as Eastern Europe since joining the World Bank in 1985.

Joe Foroma is Chief Economist, Confederation of Zimbabwe Industries. His previous experience was with the Ministry of Finance and Zimbank. He holds an honours degree from the University of Zimbabwe.

Tony Hawkins is Professor of Business Studies and Director of the MBA Programme, University of Zimbabwe. He graduated at the University of Zimbabwe and Oxford where he was a Rhodes Scholar. He was a Fulbright Fellow at Harvard, writes on African business and economic affairs for the *Financial Times* (London) and The Economist Group, and is a Director of the Zimbabwe Investment Centre.

Marlene Hesketh is Senior Manager, Public Sector Finance, Rand Merchant Bank, Johannesburg. She has also been a lecturer in the Department of Accounting and Finance, University of Natal, Durban and visiting lecturer in the Graduate School of Business, University of the Witwatersrand. A graduate of the University of Natal, she has been a consultant to the Sunnyside Group on small business and deregulation.

Julian Hofmeyr was Senior Research Fellow in the Economic Research Unit before becoming Senior Lecturer in the Department of Economics, University of Natal, Durban, at the beginning of 1995. After graduating in engineering at the University of the Witwatersrand, he studied economics at the Universities of South Africa and Cape Town. He obtained a doctorate at the University of Natal.

Merle Holden is Professor of Economics at the University of Natal, Durban, where she also undertook her earlier studies before obtaining a doctorate at Duke University, North Carolina. She was Associate Professor at George Mason University, Virginia, has been attached to the World Bank whilst on sabbatical and has been a consultant to UNCTAD.

Paul Holden is in the Private Sector Development Advisory Group in the Latin America Technical Department of the World Bank. He obtained his earlier degrees at the University of Natal and an MA and PhD at Duke University, North Carolina. He was a senior economist at the IMF before starting a garment manufacturing business in Lesotho.

Tjiuai Kangueehi is a junior researcher at the Namibian Economic Policy Research Unit. She is a graduate of St Olaf College, Minnesota.

Felipe Larraín is Professor of Economics, Pontifica Universidad Catolica de Chile of which he is a graduate, and President of Felipe Larraín and Associates, an economics consultancy. He obtained an MA and PhD at Harvard University. He has been a senior adviser to several Latin American governments and a consultant to, *inter alia*, the UN, World Bank and the Inter-American Development Bank.

Anselm London is Deputy Director, Development Research and Policy Department, African Development Bank. He previously held senior positions with the Bank of Canada and the Conference Board of Canada. After graduating from the Universities at Winnipeg and Manitoba, he obtained a doctorate from Queen's University, Ontario.

Gavin Maasdorp is Director and Research Professor, Economic Research Unit, and Adjunct Professor, University of Pretoria. He obtained his degrees at the University of Natal, joining the ERU in 1964. His research projects have included consultancies to the World Bank, the EC, USAID, African Development Bank and the government of Swaziland.

Michael Matsebula is Associate Professor, Department of Economics, University of Swaziland. He serves on various boards, including that of the Central Bank of Swaziland. After graduating at the University of Botswana, Lesotho and Swaziland, he studied in Canada, obtaining an MA at the University of Manitoba and a PhD at Queen's University.

Mike McGrath is Professor and Head, Department of Economics, University of Natal, Pietermaritzburg. He obtained his degrees at the University of Natal, Durban, where he was Associate Professor, and has also been attached to the Institute of Economics and Statistics, Oxford. He is consulting editor to the *South African Journal of Economics*.

Seiji Naya is Director, Department of Business, Economic Development and Tourism, Honolulu, Hawaii, and was previously Professor and Chairman, Department of Economics, University of Hawaii and Senior Adviser, International Center for Economic Growth. A graduate of the Universities of Hawaii and Wisconsin, he has been chief economist and director of the Asian Development Bank, Vice-President of the East–West Center, Honolulu, and an adviser to the ASEAN Secretariat, UNDP, UNCTAD and USAID.

Ghon Rhee is Professor of Finance and Director of the Pacific-Basin Capital Markets Research Center, University of Rhode Island. He is a graduate of Seoul National University, Rutgers and Ohio State University, and has been a senior adviser to the OECD, IMF, UNIDO and the Asian Development Bank.

Roger Riddell is Research Fellow, Overseas Development Institute, London. A graduate of the Universities of Zimbabwe and Sussex, he was previously chief economist of the Confederation of Zimbabwe Industries, and has worked as a consultant to the African Development Bank.

Peter Robson is Honorary Professor of Economics, University of St Andrews, Scotland, having previously been Head of the Department there as well as at the University of Nairobi. He graduated from the

University of London, and has consulted to the World Bank, EC, and a number of governments in Africa and elsewhere. The author of a standard textbook on economic integration, he was also editor of the *Journal of Common Market Studies.*

Oliver Saasa is Professor and Director of the Institute for African Studies, University of Zambia. He was a Rhodes Scholar at Oxford, and has been a consultant to the World Bank, PTA and SADC.

Vakashile Simelane lectures in economics at the University of Swaziland. She is a graduate of the University of Botswana, Lesotho and Swaziland and of New Brunswick and Connecticut, where she obtained her doctorate in 1994.

Irene Tlhase is senior researcher, Namibian Economic Policy Research Unit. A citizen of Botswana, she has degrees from Utah State University and the American University, Washington, D.C. She was previously with the Bank of Botswana, more recently as Manager of Exchange Control.

Michael Unger is Senior Adviser, Finance and Private Sector, US Agency for International Development, Washington, D.C. and an Adjunct Associate Professor of International Business, George Washington University. He was educated at Ohio State University, Washington University (St Louis), Harvard and Pennsylvania State University. He recently completed a study on the South African financial system.

Alan Whiteside is Associate Professor, Economic Research Unit. He was previously ODI Fellow in the Ministry of Economic Planning and Development, Botswana. A graduate of the University of East Anglia where he is a research associate, he has consulted to the EC, USAID, ADB and the Swaziland government.

Nick Wilkins is Research Fellow, Economic Research Unit. He obtained his degrees at the University of Natal, and has worked in the shipping industry and on various projects throughout Southern and Eastern Africa.

Preface and Acknowledgements

The papers in this volume represent the proceedings of a conference held in Durban on 5–6 December 1994 to mark the Golden Jubilee of the University of Natal's Economic Research Unit. As a forerunner to the ERU, a fellowship was established in 1940 in the Department of Economics at the then Natal University College for a study of the labour resources of Natal. This was the first activity funded by the Durban Economic Research Committee, a body which contained representatives of organised commerce and industry as well as the University, and which played a prominent role in financing research for the next 30 years. The next development was in 1944 when the Department, under Professor H.R. Burrows, undertook to conduct a systematic, long-term economic and social survey of the province on behalf of the Social and Economic Planning Council. This was known as the 'Natal Regional Survey' and necessitated the establishment, in the Department, of a special research section with permanent, full-time staff. Although it was named only in 1980, the ERU (together with the Bureau of Economic Research at the University of Stellenbosch) is the oldest economic research institution in South Africa.

The foresight of the University as well as of the Durban business sector in founding the ERU is remarkable. It is appropriate to pay tribute to the previous heads of the ERU – Professor H.R. Burrows (1944–57), Professor O.P.F. Horwood (1957–65) and Professor G.J. Trotter (1966–81) – for their role in developing and extending the work of the Unit.

The ERU was established, of course, in the midst of World War II when the tide of battle was beginning to turn for the Allies, South Africa was on the 'right side' and its government and prime minister were popular internationally. Little did the founders know that this was soon to change. The early work of the ERU was directed at critical socio-economic issues such as housing, employment and education, and hopes were high of a new, more enlightened South Africa emerging in the post-war period. Disastrously, however, the country took a radically different course after the 1948 elections. The ERU no longer had the ear of government, but it soldiered on, in tandem with other 'liberal' institutions and organisations in South Africa, maintaining the traditions of critical scholarship throughout the heyday of apartheid until the eventual and inevitable demise of that system. The ERU managed to maintain overseas academic links despite the growth of the academic boycott which it naturally opposed, just as it opposed sanctions and disinvestment. The general approach since the inception of the Unit has been a consistently liberal one, that is, it has been opposed to apartheid and in favour of a market-based economy. Whilst its work has been critical of apartheid policies, it has been equally critical of alternative policy proposals, which fail to heed the experiences of countries which have adopted highly regulated economic systems.

Because of its origins, namely, its association with the Social and Economic Planning Council, much of the work of the ERU during the first 25 years of its existence was of a socio-economic nature, studies being conducted both in urban and rural areas of Natal. However, the scope of research began to broaden in the 1960s. Since then, there has been a general concentration in the broad field of economic development, most of the Unit's work today being concerned with national and Southern African rather than provincial problems. Its main fields of interest in recent years have centred on regional economic integration and cooperation, transport, project appraisal, international trade and investment, human capital, economic development, regional and urban issues, and economic systems.

Not all these subjects could be covered during the course of a single conference. However, the title of the conference – 'Avoiding Marginalisation: Can South and Southern Africa Become Globally Competitive Economies?' – appeared apt in that it related to most of the fields in which the ERU had been involved at one time or another since 1944.

After the conference the authors were given the opportunity of revising their papers. Two papers – on investment in emerging markets and small business finance – were not forthcoming, while the papers in this volume were received for editing at various times between January and August 1995. I am grateful to the contributors for their cooperation, and also to Dr William Easterly, Mr Nick Czypionka (Standard Bank), Dr Xolile Guma (Human Sciences Research Council), Professor Merle Holden and Dr Anselm London for serving on the panel which concluded the conference.

The Economic Research Unit expresses its deep appreciation to the following organisations which directly or indirectly contributed to the funding of the conference: African Development Bank, Development Bank of Southern Africa, Fedsure, Greater Durban Marketing Authority, Harvey & Co., Illovo Sugar Ltd, Overseas Development Administration, Royal Norwegian Embassy, South African Department of Foreign

xvi   *Preface and Acknowledgements*

Affairs, South African Sugar Association, Shell S.A. (Pty) Ltd., Standard Bank Foundation, Swedecorp, T. & N. Holdings Ltd, and USAID.

I wish to thank my fellow members of the conference organising committee: Bob Klitgaard (who unfortunately had a prior engagement in the US and thus could not participate in the conference, but who made an invaluable contribution to the formulation of the theme and paper topics), Alan Whiteside and Julian Hofmeyr on the academic side, and to Harry Johnson whose fund-raising ability saved the day and whose perspectives as a former aid official tempered the academic content with reality. John Devlin from the ERU and Pam Clough from the Division of Public Affairs were instrumental in the detailed organisation of the conference, whilst the assistance of Thabo Mpakanyane and Thandi Bengu of the Greater Durban Marketing Authority is gratefully acknowledged.

Finally, in the ERU the skilful typing and patience of Kay Pedley, and the assistance of Madeline Freeman, have been integral parts of the successful teamwork which characterised the conference and the publication of this book. At home, my wife, Jane, and Katie and David, have waited for the completion of this manuscript, and I appreciate their forbearance.

A note on terminology is necessary: in referring to racial groups in South Africa and Namibia, the word 'Black' is applied to Africans, Coloureds and Indians collectively.

Gavin Maasdorp
Durban

List of Abbreviations

In order to avoid repetition and save space in the text, the most common names of organisations and so forth are listed hereunder.

ACP	Africa-Caribbean-Pacific
ADR	American depository receipts
AFTA	American Free Trade Area
ANC	African National Congress
APEC	Asia Pacific Economic Cooperation
ASEAN	Association of South-East Asian Nations
BEM	Big Emerging Market
BLNS	Botswana, Lesotho, Namibia and Swaziland
CACM	Central American Common Market
CARICOM	Caribbean Community and Common Market
CBC	Central Bank of China
CEAO	West African Economic Community
CET	Common External Tariff
CFA	Francophone Africa Franc
CMA	Common Monetary Area
COMESA	Common Market for Eastern and Southern Africa
EC	European Community
EU	European Union
FCA	Foreign currency-denominated accounts
FDI	Foreign direct investment
G-7	Group of Seven
GATT	General Agreement on Tariffs and Trade
GDP	Gross Domestic Product
GDR	Global depository receipts
GEIS	General Export Incentive Scheme
HDI	Human Development Index (United Nations)
HKFE	Hong Kong Futures Exchange
HKFGC	Hong Kong Futures Guarantee Corporation
ICCH-HK	International Commodity Clearing House (Hong Kong) Ltd
IMF	International Monetary Fund
LTPS	Long-term Perspective Study (World Bank)
MFA	Multi-Fibre Agreement
MLL	Minimum living level

NAFTA	North American Free Trade Area
NBFI	Non-bank financial institution
NGO	Non-governmental organisation
NIEs	Newly industrialised economies
NSA	Nikkei Stock Average
NTBs	Non-tariff barriers
ODA	Official development assistance
OECD	Organisation for Economic Cooperation and Development
PTA	Preferential Trade Area for Eastern and Southern African States
PWP	Public works programme
RDP	Reconstruction and Development Programme
ROW	Rest of the world
SACU	Southern African Customs Union
SADC	Southern African Development Community
SAP	Structural adjustment programme
SARB	South African Reserve Bank
SDRs	Special drawing rights
SEC	Securities and Exchange Commission
SMEs	Small and medium enterprises
SMMEs	Small, medium and micro-enterprises
SSA	Sub-Saharan Africa
TNC	Transnational corporation
TSE	Taiwan Stock Exchange
UEMOA	Union Economique et Monétaire Ouest-Africaine
USAID	United States Agency for International Development
WTO	World Trade Organisation

Overview: Avoiding Marginalisation

Gavin Maasdorp

Sub-Saharan Africa was the only region in the world where the population ended the 1980s worse off than at the beginning of the decade. Per capita income had fallen and the region was producing less food to feed its population, which continued to grow rapidly. SSA's economic slide, which has largely continued into the 1990s, is in marked contrast to continued economic progress in South-East and South Asia as well as in Latin America. At the same time, the newly emerging democracies of Eastern Europe have attracted considerable world attention. Thus, global interest and concern have shifted away from Africa, and it is more and more referred to as the 'marginalised continent'.

The challenges to SSA's economic development will intensify as external and internal forces provoke marginalisation: external because of the new world trade order and the growing preoccupation on the part of donors with human rights and political democracy; internal because of continued political instability in many countries. Being marginal usually means being poor and being left out of the dynamics of trade, sectoral specialisation and economic growth. In this sense *marginal* might be thought of as an antonym for *sustainable*. There are several levels of marginalisation, that is to say, in several dimensions African economic development may become less and less sustainable:

1. *Continental*: Already the poorest and most disease-ravaged continent in the world, much of SSA is failing to advance in per capita income, in many cases even after significant economic reforms. The emergence of formal trading blocs and of other countries in need of economic aid, such as those of the former Soviet bloc, may tend to leave SSA even more on the sidelines of the world economy.
2. *Regional*: Lacking any effectively functioning organisation to promote regional integration, specific regions of Africa are themselves becoming marginalised. Southern Africa is more fortunate in that it is at least partially covered by effective arrangements in the form of the SACU and CMA.

3. *National*: Some countries in Africa fear another kind of margin-alisation, namely, that the emergence of a democratic South Africa will reduce their economic sovereignty and political clout.
4. *Sub-national*: Within individual countries themselves, it is not clear how marginalised communities and areas, particularly the poor and the rural areas, can escape from marginality. This is as true of South Africa as it is of other countries in the sub-continent.

Marginalisation entails a dynamic of defeat and domination, and it is not clear that the usual brands of economic advice (more aid, more trade) will be of a magnitude, or even of a direction, to make a differ-ence. The aim of this volume is to examine economic marginalisation and to develop policies to avoid it.

AFRICA'S MARGINALISATION

In the keynote address, William Easterly illustrates that SSA has been conspicuously left out of the worldwide boom since 1960. His com-parison of SSA's share of foreign direct investment and exports with the share of Malaysia makes grim reading. Yet, he makes a point that the decline of Africa was not inevitable but rather was contingent. In fact, in the 1960s Africa had been considered to have a bright econ-omic future. He shows that much of Africa's decline can be explained by poor policy choices: the loss of income due to misguided policies was about four times the total external debt of SSA. But part of Afri-ca's decline cannot be explained by policy choices: ethnic diversity is a factor, and so is the contagion effect, that is, the effect of a particu-lar country's growth on that of its neighbours, and vice versa. Neigh-bours with bad policies drag each other down, and vice versa. Poor growth is explained by poor education, political instability, lack of financial depth, high black market premia, high government deficits, poor infrastructure, ethnic conflict and lack of growth spillovers be-tween neighbours. However, ethnic diversity need not necessarily lead to conflict, whilst the implication for Africa of the adoption of better economic policies in the last ten years or so is that the contagion ef-fect should yield positive results. Africa's poor growth performance is reversible: 'If a political reform movement sweeps the continent, Afri-ca's long exile to the margins of the world economy could finally come to an end.'

REGIONAL AND NATIONAL MARGINALISATION

Africa operates in a changing international economic system. All governments have their domestic problems, but their global involvement determines what can be done domestically, that is, domestic possibilities have to be set against the reality of the global economy. Peter Robson considers three factors, namely (1) the implications of the new world trade order, (2) continuing internationalisation of production, and (3) the resurgence of regionalism. Under the WTO, developing countries have little scope for pursuing protectionist policies other than through customs unions and free trade areas, and may receive few static gains. In order to share in the benefits of international production, they will have to remove obstacles to FDI and facilitate cross-border investments. Regional arrangements (particularly if they provide access to industrialised markets) attract FDI, and north–south links (as in NAFTA and APEC) may prove to be crucial in stimulating investment, trade and development. Africa has tended to resist north–south links, and Robson suggests this might merit re-thinking.

South Africa's complex institutional structure is discussed by Gavin Maasdorp. The establishment of credible regional institutions would help Southern Africa in the eyes of the international investor and donor community, but this requires political will, pragmatism and a rationalisation of institutional functions. The real division in trade integration is between the SACU and the rest of the region, and a relationship between the SACU and the fast-track CBI countries of Southern and Eastern Africa and the islands (all members of COMESA) is recommended, with the important sectoral cooperation arrangements being left to SADC. Most countries are members of the Lomé Convention, and are hence linked with the EU on a non-reciprocal basis, but this north–south link will fall away if (as is likely) there is no Lomé V. South Africa, however, is negotiating a separate trade deal with the EU, possibly in the form of a free trade agreement, and a similar link between the rest of the region and the EU might bear consideration. Another intriguing possibility would be not a north–south link but a south–south link based on the Indian Ocean Rim which would include the NIEs of South-East Asia. South Africa is often regarded as the springboard for investment and development in Southern Africa, and the question as to whether the 'flying geese' would fly in the region is also examined. Here the link with Easterly's contagion effect becomes obvious: if (sensible) macroeconomic policies in the region can converge, so much the better for the flying geese.

None the less, small countries in the region have a number of fears regarding the continued dominance of South Africa. Michael Matsebula and Vakashile Simelane consider the fears of small countries within a regional integration arrangement, namely, the BLNS countries in the SACU, while Oliver Saasa deals with the phenomenon of the brain drain to South Africa and its effect on sending countries.

Matsebula and Simelane argue that small countries have no better alternative but to belong to an economic integration arrangement. Within the SACU, BLNS are peripheral to South Africa in terms of economic size, trade flows, level of industrialisation, influence in tariff-setting, options to diversify trade links, and so on. For their situation to be alleviated, the net benefits of SACU membership need to be distributed more equitably (demanding a continuation of compensation arrangements) and trading relations should be diversified. In addition, they look to the non-orthodox gains from integration to minimise small country marginalisation, mentioning in particular the possibility of monetary union, the importance of a harmonised industrial development policy, improved transport and communications, and political democracy and stability.

Saasa is concerned with the brain drain from countries such as Zambia. Whilst migrant labour movements to the South African mines from neighbouring countries have been continuing for over a century, a recent phenomenon is the movement of skilled individuals (including professionals) to South Africa. The movement of all types of labour is becoming problematic for the sending countries: migrant labour because of decreasing demand as South African gold mining production falls, and the exodus of skilled individuals because of the already critical shortage of high-level manpower. There are also flows of illegal immigrants into South Africa – something that is becoming a political problem as they compete with local disadvantaged communities for access to physical infrastructure and social services. South Africa is the magnet for all types of labour, and the government's decisions will have important consequences for the region as a whole.

MARGINALISATION WITHIN COUNTRIES

The following two chapters deal with marginalised groups in two countries, that is, South Africa and Namibia. Both these countries were scarred by the adoption of apartheid as official government policy and both have a legacy of large inter-racial income and wealth differentials.

Mike McGrath deals with income distribution and poverty in South Africa. He shows that movements in the indicators are not in a uniform direction: overall income distribution has worsened although inter-racial discrepancies have narrowed, and the extent of poverty has diminished slightly. Demographic, economic and social variables are all important determinants of poverty: a household is more likely to be in poverty if it is African; it is large in size with a high dependency ratio; it is in a rural area; and the head has a low standard of education, or is a female, or is in a low-level occupation.

A somewhat similar profile is uncovered in Namibia by Irene Tlhase and Tjiuai Kangueehi, who relate marginalisation to public expenditure especially on education and health. They are concerned about the slow response of government budgetary allocations in the (admittedly short) post-independence period in order to respond to changing needs and reach the most disadvantaged groups and parts of the country.

The final level of marginalisation considered is that of sub-national. Nick Wilkins examines KwaZulu-Natal, one of South Africa's nine provinces, which has an ambiguous developmental status: it contains the second largest urban-industrial region in the country, the two largest ports and the largest tourist industry, but its share of the population exceeds its share of national output and it has the highest unemployment rate, one of the lowest labour force participation rates and the highest incidence of HIV/AIDS. Its quality-of-life indicators, consequently, are comparatively poor, and this is heightened by what is the one feature which clearly sets KwaZulu-Natal apart from the rest of the country, namely, the political conflict which has given rise to (possibly endemic) violence. This, in turn, has led to KwaZulu-Natal being perceived by potential investors as an unsafe area with a risk rating significantly higher than that of South Africa a whole. In addition to the list of development challenges faced by the other eight provinces and, indeed, by neighbouring countries, KwaZulu-Natal has to overcome its political problems if it is to escape a rapid slide towards marginalisation.

CHOOSING WINNING POLICIES

As Easterly demonstrates, the major part of Africa's economic decline can be explained by poor policy choices. An important set of papers, therefore, relates to this issue.

The Asian economic miracle has become something of a legend.

Certainly, there is a stark contrast between Myrdal's pessimism about South-East Asia in the 1960s and the optimistic views of the time about Africa, quoted by Easterly. Yet, each region moved in precisely the opposite direction from that which had been predicted. For Africa, therefore, the lessons of Asia's experience are particularly pertinent. Seiji Naya paints a broad canvas. He argues that there is no such thing as a 'basket case', much in line with Easterly's argument about economic decline being contingent, not inevitable. Naya also points out that there is no single 'Asian model'. For any particular country in Africa, therefore, there is no single Asian strategy which is optimal; rather, it is a case of adapting strategies which have succeeded in Asia to suit individual country circumstances in Africa. Another important point he makes is that economic progress does not occur simply in response to SAPs: more important are factors such as education and training, industrial and technological modernisation, improved governance and efficient economic management. He isolates eight critical determinants of Asia's economic miracle: a long-term vision with the state, private sector and market forces interacting to optimise growth; emphasis on trade, investment and technology improvement; exploitation of a high-growth, high-savings, high-investment cycle; macroeconomic stability; provision of basic human needs; investment in people; sound economic policies; and sensible and efficient government roles.

After appearing to be headed for economic marginalisation, Latin America has made a striking recovery in the last ten years. Felipe Larraín explores some lessons of this experience for Africa, focusing on exchange rate and reserve management policies in the face of large capital inflows. The trade-off facing the authorities has been between stabilisation and competitiveness, that is, between reducing inflation and increasing exports. The real exchange rate is a crucial element in the equation, but large capital inflows tend to cause exchange rate appreciation and thus reserve management policies have an important influence. Latin American countries have tended to move away from fixed exchange rates towards managed regimes and floating currencies, and to accumulate substantial foreign exchange reserves. He considers this a prudent policy since it reduces vulnerability to external shocks, which have been a major cause of macroeconomic instability. A postscript to the paper covers the implications of the Mexican crisis of late December 1994 and points to the importance of avoiding large current account deficits and sharp currency appreciations; of maintaining high local savings; of using capital inflows to accumulate reserves; and of attracting more long-term rather than short-term flows. Larraín concludes by attributing Mexico's débâcle partly to political problems, which harks back to both Easterly and Wilkins in explaining at least part of both continental and provincial marginalisation.

Laurence Clarke's paper follows on from Larraín's in dealing with reserve management and currency convertibility. By contrast to Latin America, Southern African countries generally have low levels of gross external reserves in relation to weeks of import coverage. Because of their foreign exchange constraints, the efficient management of foreign reserves is essential. He favours a move towards currency convertibility and to the progressive removal of exchange control. Countries like Botswana, Mauritius and South Africa, which have full or partial currency convertibility backed by adequate reserves, have most of the necessary ingredients for attracting foreign capital, and consequently abolition of exchange control should not put pressure on their currency. Whilst inflows of equity capital are to be preferred to portfolio capital, the latter is in fact the forerunner to more substantive FDI flows. Full foreign exchange liberalisation, however, would mean that most Southern African countries would be faced with the choice of continued pegs or a freer or free float, with the risks (especially currency risks) for the optimal management of reserves being important for Botswana, Mauritius and South Africa. Clarke concludes that monetary integration should be encouraged: this could be based on the existing CMA (with the Botswana pula rather than the rand being the strongest candidate at present for a unified regional currency), but his preference is for the gradualism adopted in the European Monetary System.

Ghon Rhee is concerned with the internationalisation of capital markets, a subject relevant to the emerging capital markets of Botswana, Namibia, Swaziland and Zimbabwe. He focuses on the important role of government regulators, who frequently fail to recognise that internationalisation is market-driven and that it means more competition among financial intermediaries. Rhee describes the stages of development of a capital market from a closed to an open one, exchange control being abandoned on the path to openness. Governments can impede the process of regionalisation through the incorrect sequence of policy measures, intervention in the market, the lack of real commitment, a fragmented regulatory structure and lack of coordination among government agencies. For governments of Southern African countries with developing capital markets, these lessons from Asia are clear.

The importance of appropriate macroeconomic policies is the subject of the papers by Anselm London and Tony Hawkins. London, following Seers, emphasises the need for policy to produce results that

reduce poverty, unemployment and inequality. South Africa's policy
challenges are akin to those of Africa, and it can learn from the mistakes and experiences elsewhere on the continent. It is important to
avoid or contain monetary and fiscal excesses, overvalued exchange
rates, inflation, price distortions and loss-making parastatals, and to
improve tax administration. Despite adopting SAPs, African economies
are still in trouble, and efforts to relieve poverty have been mere
afterthoughts in SAPs, which have not helped the poor. In attempting
to ascertain why policy reforms have not led to sustainable growth
and development, London focuses on linkages and transmissions mechanisms, especially exchange rate management and the balance of payments, financial liberalisation and regional economic integration. However,
without a sound overall strategy and efficient management of development, the process of growth will be impeded. The lesson for South
Africa is that its policies must be tailored to its particular circumstances.

Hawkins is also concerned with the trade-off between economic efficiency and equity. He points out that in some African countries resource-intensive development unmarginalised the economy but
marginalised the poor; in others, populist policies marginalised the
economy but temporarily unmarginalised the poor. The shortcomings
of both approaches led to the adoption of SAPs; these have not led to
sustainable growth but they have marginalised certain sectors of the
population. Merely getting macroeconomic policies right will not automatically restore growth and reduce poverty; good policy can only
permit good performance, it cannot guarantee it. To achieve good performance requires political commitment and efficient administration.
In particular, governments need to raise the levels and efficiency of
investment with human capital not being neglected as has so often
been the case. The location decisions of multinationals, however, are
influenced more by assessment of the Southern African regional market and its potential within the firm's global operations than by country-
specific macroeconomic considerations. As global economic integration
proceeds, power is moving from governments to global businesses. The
contribution of macroeconomic policy towards unmarginalising the poor
should not be exaggerated, but none the less without sound policy,
sustainable growth will not be achieved nor will the poor be
unmarginalised. An enabling environment is essential.

The question of the effectiveness and competitiveness of investment
is taken up by Michael Unger. It has not been for want of donor assistance that Africa's economic performance has been disappointing. Donors now need to rethink their strategies, especially since governments

are becoming more interested in competitiveness. Levels of investment in Africa have fallen because the continent is not perceived as an attractive location for investment, but even the existing levels of investment should be generating higher levels of growth. That they are not is because of ineffective public sector investment and the absence of an enabling environment. Governments have been slow to discard their devotion to outdated policies, but they must now realise that what investors mainly want is predictability, not cheap labour and special concessions. African firms must become geared to competition whilst donors, apart from encouraging economic liberalisation and privatisation, need to identify bottlenecks to business success and private sector development.

Paul Holden focuses on the business environment: this must be sufficiently conducive to private sector activity in order to promote levels of investment high enough to result in growth rates sufficient to eradicate poverty. He analyses the business environment in Latin America: influencing factors have been macroeconomic, incentive and institutional policies. South Africa's business environment in some respects compares favourably, and in other respects unfavourably, with that of Latin America. Its advantage lies in its institutions (both legal and financial), but its policies and political uncertainty are comparative disadvantages. South Africa needs to do more on fiscal restraint, trade reform, privatisation, abolition of exchange control, labour market efficiency and security. He warns, however, that it will take 10–15 years of rapid growth substantially to improve the incomes of the poor. Populist policies are not a solution, but government needs to spend on security, housing and site development, land redistribution and education.

Millard Arnold's paper on corporate marginalisation picks up some of the themes from the previous few chapters. He is not entirely happy with the notion of the marginalisation and competitiveness of nations: it is firms which compete. However, the success of its firms on world markets is important in determining a country's economic fortunes. He argues that African firms can be successful on world markets, and indeed are in certain niche markets. Whilst macroeconomic policies are important in enabling firms to compete, it is the microeconomic foundations (the behaviour, strengths and capabilities of firms) which are more central. Attracting FDI is important, and Southern Africa needs to improve conditions for foreign investors. Like Unger, he points to donor policies aimed at assisting private sector development, and like Unger he is optimistic: South Africa has been identified as a Big Emerging Market, and this definition in fact extends to all of Southern Africa. The sub-continent, therefore, can look forward to considerable flows of FDI.

A key question for developing countries, and one with implications for job creation and unemployment, is the impact of the technological revolution on their ability to compete on world markets and expand their output and exports. Roger Riddell takes up the relationships between technology, global competitiveness and marginalisation. SSA has not used technology particularly well, nor has it exploited the opportunities provided by recent technological changes: its choice now is not whether to embrace the new technology but how to do so. He warns, though, that the new technologies not only are taking longer to be adopted than had been expected, but their effects are more complex too. In Africa the new technologies have not penetrated further than the modern sector. Productivity improvements are lagging, the reliance on exports of primary products continues and FDI has not been attracted in sufficient amounts. Thus, the new technologies have had little effect on poverty, employment and marginalisation. SSA's technological marginalisation is attributable partly to poor macroeconomic policies and partly to political weaknesses: patronage and corruption, and a general lack of accountability and democracy which means that governments have not worked for national betterment. In developing technological capabilities, gaps in the formal education system will have to be closed and the contribution of the productive and supportive sectors (including large companies, donors and regional networks) must be maximised, whilst the growth of SMMEs needs to be encouraged. Yet, it will be difficult to ensure that the new technologies benefit the poor and marginalised; genuine political democracy can help keep the issue of equity alive, and NGOs could play an important role here.

SOME SOUTHERN AFRICAN ISSUES

The final set of papers covers some specific issues in the Southern African context such as policy reform, the labour market, small business and human capital.

Merle Holden discusses South Africa's attempts to reform an economy in which the allocation of resources was badly distorted by apartheid and sanctions. The economy over the last 20 years has been characterised by slow growth with many key indicators – inflation, fiscal deficit, savings and investment, capital flows, terms of trade and the price of gold – moving in the wrong direction. The government undertook certain structural adjustments, including some trade liberalisation, but the economy, in the face of international and domestic political pressures, continued to perform poorly. The new government's emphasis is on the RDP. However, the success of the RDP is dependent on economic growth, and this requires the maintenance of monetary and fiscal discipline. Like Paul Holden, she is worried about the possibility of macro-populism being adopted by policy-makers.

Julian Hofmeyr, in his paper on the South African labour market, shows how a long period of rapid economic growth (1946–75) was able to create jobs for almost all school-leavers. Once economic growth declined, the rate of job creation fell and today only a small fraction of school-leavers are able to secure formal employment. Yet African wages started increasing at the very time economic growth started falling, and they have continued to rise despite rising unemployment. White wages, by contrast, have stagnated since 1972. Hofmeyr discusses the causes of African wage movements since 1975 and the implications for unemployment and labour market segmentation. The underlying pressure for increased wages must have been institutional in character, and the growth of mass-based unionisation in the 1980s is the most likely factor. This must have led to widening wage differentials and unemployment as well as to re-fragmentation of the labour market into non-competing segments. South Africa's major problem is the marginalisation of a growing section of its population because of rising unemployment: the role of unions, representing an elite in formal employment, is thus a cause for concern. Rapid economic growth with wage restraint is required to avoid further marginalisation, and the economy should be put on a more labour-intensive growth path. In the meantime, however, PWPs could absorb the labour surplus, but they should not compete for labour with the formal sector, and their wages should be at relief levels.

In a companion paper, Joe Foroma deals with the Zimbabwean example, where a new government enacted minimum wage and job security legislation in order to redress pre-independence imbalances. These strategies have well-known adverse effects on the economy and on economic growth: firms become less flexible in response to changing market conditions, productivity declines and capital is substituted for labour. Investor confidence was also hit, but Foroma argues that the most important lesson is that the legislation protects only those already in employment and does not assist the unemployed. Governments need to be cautious in their approach to wage legislation if the effects are not to be counterproductive.

Marlene Hesketh reinforces the points made by Hofmeyr and Foroma.

She shows that SMMEs employ about one half of the economically active population in South Africa and are especially important for African-owned businesses. One problem facing SMMEs is labour legislation, especially legislation that favours the protection of workers in the formal sector. In an economy where some 50 per cent of the economically active population is outside the formal sector, it is clearly advantageous to favour small business and job creation. Among the other constraints facing SMMEs are a general lack of information about, and inability to deal with, laws and regulations in fields such as health, labour and taxation, and the riskiness of training employees. The development of industrial parks and of systems of market information and business advice, as well as the provision of training programmes, could help SMMEs considerably.

Alan Whiteside places productivity in the context of health and education. Investment in education has many benefits, but health budgets are threatened by the continued rapid population growth rates of the region. The high incidence of HIV/AIDS will eventually have a significant adverse economic impact throughout Southern Africa. The level of education is generally poor in the region, and investment in this sector, especially in primary schooling, yields high rates of return. However, technical training has been grossly neglected in South Africa, and companies are not investing sufficiently in human capital. This is of concern given the technological revolution and South Africa's relatively low ranking in international competitiveness: for this ranking to improve, gains will have to be made in productivity.

SOUTHERN AFRICA'S PROSPECTS

When development economics came into its own some 45 years ago, the areas of the world which were of concern were Asia, Latin America and Africa. Many parts of Asia have subsequently undergone a rapid economic transformation to the extent that they have become successful industrialised economies; indeed, the prospect is that the 21st century will be the Asian century. Latin America in recent years has also shown signs of replicating the Asian transformation. If these parts of the world have been able to do it, there is no *ipso facto* reason why Africa should not follow suit: as Easterly points out, the economic decline of SSA is reversible.

One of the threads running through the papers in this volume is that Southern Africa is bound up in a new world order of liberalised trade, regional blocs, global firms and a technological revolution. African countries have no choice but to participate in this world order and hence to open up their economies. This is particularly so given the fact that power in decision-making appears to be moving to global firms and away from individual governments.

There are ample policy lessons from Asia and Latin America for Southern African countries. For South Africa, starting out as it is in a new political era, there are also lessons from other parts of Africa. These lessons from successful and failed approaches alike must be absorbed if Southern Africa is to achieve sustainable growth. They are found in the entire gamut of macroeconomic policies, the commitment of governments to work in tandem with the private sector in achieving high levels of economic growth, a commitment to invest in human capital and technology, an emphasis on trade and the establishment of competitive economies. Although mindful of equity, governments must make economic growth a priority: growth is necessary for greater equity, but governments need to play an active role too, for example, by ensuring access to social services and physical infrastructure and by avoiding policy biases in favour of the urban formal sector.

South Africa is often considered the engine of growth in the subcontinent especially so far as the attraction of FDI is concerned. It is important, then, to assess South Africa's image relative to that of Asia and Latin America among foreign investors. On the plus side, South Africa scores well for the remarkable smoothness (to date at any rate) of the political transformation from apartheid to majority rule. It also has a sophisticated framework of financial institutions as well as an above-average physical infrastructure. However, there are a number of minus factors and danger signals. Consider the following, for example:

1. Continued political violence and an escalating crime rate damage the country's image among foreign investors and as a destination for foreign tourists, thus diminishing flows of FDI and the benefits from further development of the tourist industry.
2. The rapid introduction of an affirmative action policy together with fiscal changes have encouraged the massive early retirement of experienced individuals in both the public and private sectors as well as increased emigration (a particularly worrying aspect being the number of school-leavers and university graduates who quit the country because they see no future for themselves), thereby exacerbating the severe skills shortage and leading to a decline in efficiency especially in the public sector and parastatals.

3. A lack of commitment to maintain internationally comparable standards in government schools and hospitals has also encouraged emigration, with similar effects as in (2) above.

4. A serious decline in ethical standards reflected in a rampant 'gravy train' syndrome in the public sector, growing corruption, non-payment for public services and utilities, and wanton damage to public and private property (as in the vandalising of university campuses and inner-city areas by disaffected students and workers) has led to a loss of public revenue, inefficient and unnecessary public expenditure, and the virtual collapse of local government in certain parts of the country.

5. Continued exorbitant wage demands by trade unions have adversely affected the investment climate, costs of production and competitiveness.

6. An overemphasis on the RDP and some residual admiration for central planning and control in the face of global liberalisation continue to prejudice the enunciation of a clear government economic policy, and hence to retard the decision-making process.

It is clear that the government will have to take firm action on several fronts if South Africa is to achieve a rapid rate of economic growth and fulfil its role as the engine of regional growth. First, it is imperative that the government takes a firm stand on political violence and general law and order. FDI is not going to be attracted to the country in any considerable volumes until the position improves. Secondly, a firm commitment to economic growth as the top priority is required. It is a great pity that the RDP has been allowed to become a set of firm goals instead of merely remaining a set of indicators as it was originally intended to be. In this regard there are now some signs of a greater willingness to place economic growth unambiguously at the top of the priority list.

Thirdly, the government will at some stage have to reconsider labour relations legislation and the operation of trade unions. If South Africa is to have a competitive economy, this will require competitive factor markets. The South African market for unskilled labour is no different from that in less developed countries which have not experienced apartheid, and the government must see the labour market in its global context. Unemployment rates of 40–50 per cent have been reported in many communities, and the overall rate of open unemployment is probably about 25 per cent. Only 20 per cent of the economically active population belong to trade unions, while 50 per cent are in small enterprises. In the circumstances, trade unions are something of an anomaly: an elite club for (largely urban) insiders who have jobs in the formal sector and who are protected against competition from (largely rural) outsiders waiting at factory gates and who are prepared to work at market-clearing wage rates. Unionised workers are not in the poorest 40 per cent of the population. What South Africa needs is a labour market in which market-clearing rates are paid at all levels: for unskilled workers these are likely to be low given the excess supply, while for skilled individuals they will be high, reflecting a scarcity. Over time, however, improved education and training should reduce this scarcity. For professional and managerial ranks, salaries will have to be relatively competitive internationally given the ability of individuals from these groups to emigrate to countries of greater opportunity.

Fourthly, and related to the previous point, South Africa cannot afford to lose its skilled individuals. It is therefore imperative that existing standards of education, health, and so on be maintained, and it may well be that the government will have to reassure minority groups that they do have a future in the country despite their unease at the direction being taken by affirmative action, that is, that South Africa will indeed be a 'rainbow nation'. The way in which the new education policy is implemented could have a major influence on emigration; already, scientists, technicians, accountants, and so on are leaving the country in substantial numbers. Finally, the government will have to grasp the political nettle of reducing the size of the bureaucracy and defusing the rent-seeking component; in particular, the levels of corruption and inefficiency which are being exposed on an almost daily basis in the press cannot be sustained without seriously prejudicing economic growth.

As far as Southern Africa generally is concerned, macroeconomic policy convergence would be a major step in the direction of increased global competitiveness. There is no doubt that SAPs have helped in this regard, but SAPs by themselves cannot provide the entire solution: they require a response from the private sector. SAPs will succeed only when investors believe in their credibility, and thus it is not merely a case of governments adopting SAPs but of maintaining fiscal and monetary discipline. The Zimbabwean example, where a budgetary deficit of 12 per cent of GDP (or more than double the original target) has led to further problems with the IMF, illustrates the point.

Political question marks still remain in relation to several Southern African and adjacent countries, for example, concerning the robustness of the political settlements in Angola and Mozambique, continued instability in Zaire, the genocide in Rwanda and Burundi, the commitment to multi-party democracy in Zimbabwe, the delaying of the inevitable political transition in Swaziland and a possible return to failed policies in Zambia. There is no doubt, though, that the adoption of SAPs in many countries of the region, aided by the collapse of centrally planned economies in Eastern Europe and elsewhere, has made the climate for macroeconomic policy convergence much more favourable than in the 1980s. It is unfortunate, however, that political leaders are still inclined to waste their efforts on initiatives which clearly no future. A recent example is the proposed SADC protocol on the free movement of labour. This would have enormous implications for employment policies in almost every country: even temporary residence permits are notoriously difficult to obtain in most Southern African countries, not to say anything of freehold title to residential land, and it is highly unlikely that there is a single government in the region which would actually implement such a protocol. Yet, it is being seriously considered at a regional institutional level. It would be in the interests of efficient regional cooperation if activities were limited to those in which visible results could be achieved – for example, in sectors such as transport, telecommunications, power, water and tourism.

Despite the reservations in the previous few paragraphs, however, Southern Africa has the potential to accomplish a successful economic transformation, but success will depend upon the ability and political willingness of policy-makers to make the right policy choices as well as on the avoidance of political instability. If any part of Africa can do it, it is surely Southern Africa. Conversely, if Southern Africa fails, the outlook for sub-Saharan Africa is indeed bleak.

Part 1

Marginalisation in the Global Economy

1 Why is Africa Marginal in the World Economy?

William Easterly[1]

Recent slowdowns aside, the last three decades were good ones for the world economy. The average world economic growth rate – both total and per capita – over this period was higher than at any previous time in history. This growth rate translated into huge improvements in the quality of life everywhere, developing countries included. The world rate of infant mortality in 1990 was one third of the rate in 1960; median life expectancy in all countries rose from 50 years to 65 years. Yet there was one region that was conspicuously left out of the world-wide boom of the last three decades: Africa.[2]

THE MARGINALISATION OF AFRICA

Almost all of the countries which had *negative* per capita growth rates over the last three decades, despite the worldwide boom, were in Africa. Africa's average growth rate over the last three decades is close to zero. Although Africa's per capita income was only slightly below that of East Asia in 1960, by 1989 East Asia's income was five times larger. Of the 20 poorest nations in the world, 16 are in Africa.

In the absence of growth, Africa is on the margins of the world economy. In 1990–2, Africa received 1/30th of the net inflows of FDI, and 0.6 per cent of the portfolio equity inflows, to developing countries. Malaysia alone, with a population of about 19 million, received three times as much FDI, and five times as much in portfolio equity, as all of Africa. In 1992, Malaysia exported about the same dollar value of goods and services as all of Africa. For every dollar of GDP produced by the world economy in 1992, Africa produced about 0.7 cent.[3]

At the end of this period of no growth, Africa's infrastructure was in poor shape. In 1988, Burkina Faso had 48 km of paved roads in working order for its ten million inhabitants to traverse its 274 000 sq. km of territory. One out of every ten individuals in Mali had access to safe water. One out of every 100 households in Burundi had electricity.

One out of 1000 people in Chad had a telephone; the likelihood of completing a local call on this telephone was one in ten.[4]

The lack of growth in Africa took a very human toll. Africa's median life expectancy in the 1980s was 48 years. The typical African mother with six children had a 30 per cent chance of having all her children survive to five years of age. The probability of the mother herself not surviving childbirth was 90 times higher in Mali than in Malaysia.

Africa's marginalisation was not preordained and was not predicted. A leading development textbook (Enke, 1963) ranked Africa's prospects ahead of East Asia's in the 1960s, whilst the World Bank's chief economist, A.M. Kamarck, in a book published in 1967, described Africa's economic future as 'bright', and identified seven countries as particularly likely to 'reach or surpass' a 7 per cent growth rate. All of those countries, in fact, had negative per capita growth rates over the last three decades.

The picture of Africa in this presentation thus far has been a grim one. But the very fact that the poor outcome was so unexpected should indicate that the outcome was contingent rather than inevitable. Countries like Côte d'Ivoire and Kenya were African success stories until poor policy choices led to deteriorating performance. Botswana has maintained the highest per capita growth rate in the world for three decades. Throughout Africa, the outcome was contingent on policy choices made; different policy choices today could make for a different future. However, national policy choices explain much, but not all, of Africa's disappointing growth.

HOW MUCH IS AFRICA'S POOR GROWTH EXPLAINED BY NATIONAL ECONOMIC POLICIES?

There is a long tradition in development economics of explaining growth differences between nations by indicators of national economic policies. This literature has grown exponentially in recent years with fresh inspiration from the new views of economic growth suggested by the work of Romer (1986), Lucas (1988), Barro (1991) and others. These new views suggest that national policies can have a strong effect on the long-run rate of growth of an economy, in contrast to the traditional view that national policies affected a country's level of per capita income but not its long-run rate of growth.

Easterly and Levine (1994) examined whether Africa's lagging performance could be explained by a set of policy indicators that have been prominent in previous work on international growth differences. Their paper synthesises results from the huge body of previous work on economic growth in general or African growth in particular, examining the following variables:[5]

1. *Initial income of the country*: Poorer countries grow faster because of the potential for higher rates of return to capital where it is initially scarce. Squared initial income will also be included to capture possible non-linearities.
2. *Initial human capital*: Capital will also have higher returns where there are better educated workers to operate the machinery.
3. *Political instability*: Highly unstable political systems will discourage investment in technology, physical capital and human capital because of the unpredictable rules of the game. The number of political assassinations is used as a crude measure of instability, following Barro (1991).
4. *Financial development*: A deep financial sector will facilitate matching of high-return opportunities with available loanable funds, which will promote high growth.
5. *Black market premium*: A high premium of the black market over the official exchange rate indicates probable diversion of resources to rent-seeking, and inefficient allocation of resources because of distortions of domestic prices away from world prices.
6. *Fiscal surplus*: A high budget deficit indicates likely macroeconomic instability which will create uncertainty for investors as well as the likelihood of future tax increases to restore fiscal balance.
7. *Initial infrastructure*: A well-developed infrastructure of roads, railways, electricity and telephones makes private capital more productive, and hence growth higher. The physical measures of infrastructure tested were kilometres of roads, kilowatts of electricity-generating capacity and numbers of telephones. Only telephones turned out to be significant enough to be included in the final regressions.

In addition to these variables, the study examined an intercept shift variable which takes on the value of 1 for African countries and 0 otherwise. The coefficient of this variable will measure the extent to which Africa's growth is different from the rest of the world, even after controlling for factors 1–7 above.

Decade averages for growth rates and for each of the variables listed above were computed for 1960–9, 1970–9 and 1980–9 (where the

Table 1.1 Can National Policies Explain Africa's Lagging Growth?[a, b]

Variable	Regressions			
	I	*II*	*III*	*IV*
AFRICA intercept shift	−0.0165	−0.0145	−0.0194	−0.0167
variable	(0.0041)	(0.0053)	(0.0046)	(0.0053)
Latin America intercept	−0.0150	−0.0158	−0.0162	−0.0174
shift variable	(0.0032)	(0.0033)	(0.0033)	(0.0032)
Log of initial GDP per	0.0667	0.0957	0.0660	0.1072
capita	(0.0220)	(0.0260)	(0.0215)	(0.0244)
Square of log of initial	−0.0049	−0.0067	−0.0056	−0.0082
GDP per capita	(0.0015)	(0.0017)	(0.0014)	(0.0016)
Log (average years of	0.0115	0.0112	0.0057	0.0087
schooling)	(0.0041)	(0.0051)	(0.0045)	(0.0050)
Assassinations	−17.62	−15.96	−16.74	−20.15
	6.40	6.62	6.66	6.35
Financial depth				
(liabilities of	0.0180	0.0205	0.0120	0.0137
financial system/GDP)	(0.0063)	(0.0066)	(0.0067)	(0.0064)
Black market premium	−0.0237	−0.0187	−0.0245	−0.0176
	(0.0039)	(0.0051)	(0.0045)	(0.0059)
Fiscal surplus		0.1215		0.1985
		(0.0428)		(0.0431)
Log (telephones per			0.0076	0.0074
worker)			(0.0022)	(0.0024)
No. of observations	244	193	222	178
R^2	0.50	0.54	0.52	0.59

Notes: a. Dependent variable is growth of per capita real GDP (decade averages for all countries).

b. Heteroskedasticity-consistent standard errors are reported in parenthesis. Separate decade shift variables were included but not shown.

variables are denoted initial, the first year of each decade is used). Table 1.1 shows the results for pooled cross-section, time-series regressions with several alternative specifications. All of the variables are of the expected sign, and statistically significant.

Countries with lower initial income tend to grow faster, but the effect is non-linear, that is, the catch-up effect is weaker in very poor countries. The coefficients indicate that the catch-up effect is strongest at a per capita income level of about $1600, which is above the income of most African countries. This is consistent with an old idea of Gerschenkron (1962), namely, backwardness is generally an advantage because one can borrow from the technological leaders, but borrowing may become difficult if the technological distance from the leaders is too great. The low saving rates of very poor countries like those in Africa may also inhibit the speed of catching up.

The coefficients on the policy variables indicate that countries that repress financial systems, provide little schooling, create high black market premia through exchange restrictions and overvalued official exchange rates, run large budget deficits and provide little infrastructure will grow more slowly than the average. Political instability also depresses growth.

How much do these variables explain Africa's poor performance? Africa did have worse policies measured by these indicators than the rest of the world. Africa's financial depth (M2/GDP) was half that in East Asia; its black market premia were 50 per cent larger on average than in other developing countries; its level of schooling was 50 per cent lower than in other developing countries; its budget deficits were higher than elsewhere.

Africa's infrastructure problems deserve special mention because they were so severe. Its infrastructure gap existed from the beginning, but has grown worse. In 1960, Hong Kong had more telephones than Nigeria although Nigeria's population was 17 times larger. By 1980, Hong Kong had more telephones than all of Africa. Africa's infrastructure lag accounted for 1 percentage point of its lower growth relative to the rest of the world.

However, even after taking these factors into account, there is still a part of Africa's lower growth that remains unexplained. Table 1.1 shows that the AFRICA intercept shift variable is statistically significant: about $1\frac{1}{2}$ percentage points of Africa's lower growth is not explained by these indicators of national economic policies.

Figure 1.1 shows the explained and unexplained part of the income gap which opened up between Africa and East Asia between 1960 and 1989. The figure compounds the growth difference associated with each East Asia–Africa policy difference to show the effect on the level of income that had been achieved by 1989. About $1050 of the $4100 gap between East Asia and Africa remains unexplained. $850 of the gap in 1989 is due to the original percentage gap in GDP per capita. Initial income and schooling explain $450 of the gap (the disadvantage of lower African schooling more than offsets the advantage of lower African initial income).[6]

Finally, three policy indicators – financial depth, the black market premium and the government surplus – explained $1750 of the 1989 per capita income gap between East Asia and Africa. These three types of policies alone – financial repression, overvalued official exchange

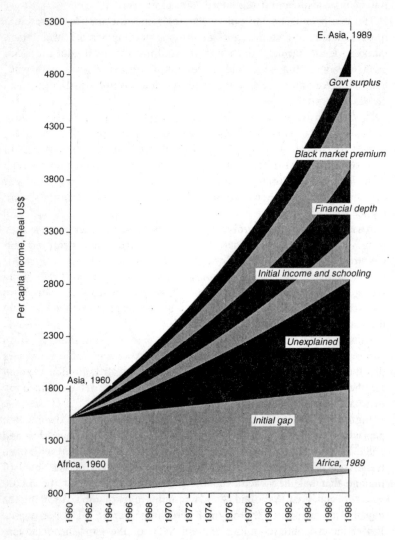

Figure 1.1 Decomposing the Growth Gap between East Asia and Africa

rates and excessive budget deficits – explained a loss of aggregate income equal to about $800 billion for Africa's population (multiplying $1750 by the population of 543 million). The loss of income due to misguided policies was about four times the total external debt of Africa.

TRYING TO EXPLAIN THE UNEXPLAINED PART OF AFRICA'S LAGGING GROWTH

But what about the part that could not be explained? This section examines two other factors which have been discussed in the general growth literature: the effect of ethnic conflict on policies and growth, and the possibility that good or bad growth outcomes are contagious between neighbouring countries.

Ethnic Conflict

Countries disrupted by conflict between ethnic groups may have difficulty agreeing on how much to supply – and who pays for – public goods like infrastructure and education. Ethnically fragmented societies may also be prone to competitive rent-seeking by the different ethnic groups. Policy elites may favour policies destructive to growth like financial repression and overvalued official exchange rates if such policies create rents for 'their' group at the expense of other groups. Ethnic diversity may also be adverse for growth in less quantifiable ways by creating the possibility of explicit expropriation of one group by another, or even overt violent conflict.

Table 1.2 shows the statistical correlations that inspired these suppositions.[7] The measure of ethnic diversity underlying Table 1.2 is a calculation of the likelihood that two randomly selected individuals in a nation will belong to different ethnic groups. The table shows that this measure of ethnic fractionalisation is negatively correlated both with the amount of schooling achieved by society and with three measures of physical infrastructure. A high degree of ethnic diversity is also associated with higher black market premia and lower financial depth.

Table 1.3 shows that adding ethnic diversity to the growth regression improves the explanatory power of the regression. The coefficient on ethnic diversity is statistically significant. This suggests that there is a direct channel by which ethnic diversity lowers growth in addition to its adverse effect on policy variables such as black market premia, infrastructure, education and financial depth. This effect of ethnic diversity

Table 1.2 Correlations of Ethno-linguistic Fractionalisation with Policy Indicators[a]

Indicator	Correlation with ethno-linguistic fractionalisation, 1960	Statistically significant at 1 per cent level?
Log of average years of schooling of labour force (1960, 1970, 1980)	−0.43	Yes
Assassinations per capita (average 1960s, 1970s, 1980s)	−0.02	No
Financial depth (liquid assets/GDP) 1960, 1970, 1980	−0.32	Yes
Black market premium (average 1960s, 1970s, 1980s)	0.21	Yes
Government surplus/GDP (average 1960s, 1970s, 1980s)	−0.09	No
Log of telephones per worker (1960, 1970, 1980)	−0.50	Yes
Log of kilometres roads and railways per worker (1960, 1970, 1980)	−0.31	Yes
Log of electricity generating capacity per worker (1960, 1970, 1980)	−0.45	Yes

Note: a. Correlations are performed over pooled datasets for decade values of variables shown (either averages or initial values as indicated).

on both policies and growth is highly relevant for Africa, as African nations are ethnically diverse (of the 15 most diverse countries in the world, 14 are in Africa). However, the AFRICA shift variable is still statistically significant after including the ethnic diversity variable. Although ethnic diversity helps explain Africa's growth lag, therefore, there is still an unexplained component.

Troubles with Neighbours

The use of an intercept shift variable for Africa's growth implies that the unexplained part of the continent's growth differential is permanent, that is, Africa for any given set of policies will always do worse than the global average, for some unexplained reason. However, there is an alternative view. If economic success and failure spread within regions, then such contagion could lead to strong but temporary unexplained growth differences between regions. There is certainly at least

Table 1.3 Trying to Explain the Unexplained Part of Africa's Lagging Growth[a, b]

Variable	Adding ethnic diversity		Adding neighbour spillovers (two-stage least squares)	
	I	II	I	II
AFRICA intercept shift	−0.0143	−0.0112	−0.0054	−0.0094
variable	(0.0050)	(0.0060)	(0.0060)	(0.0065)
Latin America intercept	−0.0188	−0.0191	−0.0095	−0.0142
shift variable	(0.0032)	(0.0033)	(0.0040)	(0.0039)
Log of initial GDP per	0.0562	0.0869	0.0574	0.1098
capita	(0.0216)	(0.0249)	(0.0220)	(0.0245)
Square of log of initial	−0.0044	−0.0063	−0.0043	−0.0078
GDP per capita	(0.0014)	(0.0016)	(0.0014)	(0.0016)
Log (average years of	0.0119	0.0117	0.0125	0.0163
schooling)	(0.0039)	(0.0047)	(0.0041)	(0.0045)
Assassinations	−14.45	−12.80	−17.02	−15.09
	(6.94)	(8.06)	(9.52)	(8.59)
Financial depth				
(liabilities of financial	0.0135	0.0162	0.0092	0.0136
system/GDP)	(0.0062)	(0.0066)	(0.0062)	(0.0059)
Black market premium	−0.0230	−0.0188	−0.0205	−0.0120
	(0.0038)	(0.0050)	(0.0042)	(0.0046)
Fiscal surplus		0.1211		0.1494
		(0.0442)		(0.0310)
Ethno-linguistic	−0.0164	−0.0170		
fractionalisation	(0.0055)	(0.0061)		
Neighbours average growth			0.5543	0.3364
			(0.1914)	(0.1793)
No. of observations	236	188	234	169
R^2	0.52	0.57		

Notes: a. Dependent variable is growth of per capita real GDP (decade averages for all countries).
  b. Heteroskedasticity-consistent standard errors are in parentheses. Regression includes separate decade dummies not reported above. 'Neighbours' average growth' is the growth rate of per capita real GDP averaged, using 1960 GDP weights, for the neighbours of the country for which data were available, instrumented with the neighbours' right-hand side variables. See Easterly and Levine (1994) for details.

casual evidence for regional contagion: East Asia's synchronised take-off in the 1960s (East Asia was actually performing poorly before 1960) and Latin America's synchronised crisis in the 1980s. In addition to the strong casual evidence, formal statistical evidence of regional contagion has been found in the literature.[8]

Table 1.3 reports a regression from Easterly and Levine (1994) which shows a strong and statistically significant effect of one's neighbours' average growth rate on one's own growth. The neighbours' average growth is computed, weighting each neighbour by its total GDP. Instrumental variables were used to correct for the simultaneity by which neighbours affect one another, using the neighbours' policy variables as instruments. The effect of one's neighbours is remarkably strong: slower growth by one percentage point in the neighbours would reduce the home country's growth by 0.34 to 0.55 percentage points.

What could explain such contagion effects? There is no direct evidence, but one can speculate. The key may lie in demonstration effects. High growth in one country could represent the adaptation of foreign technologies to local conditions, its neighbours can observe what works in local conditions and do likewise. Direct foreign investors may find it easy to move next door once they achieve success in one country. Governments that manage to attain high growth with a given set of policies provide a valuable laboratory experiment for their neighbours, helping show the policy elites and citizenry in the neighbours what works.

What about the transmission of growth *failures* across borders? Unfortunately, governments do not always strive to maximise growth or general welfare. Under some institutional conditions, they may be trying to maximise rent-seeking opportunities. Governments which try out techniques for capturing large rents also provide demonstration effects for similarly rent-seeking neighbours.

Table 1.3 shows that the AFRICA shift intercept is finally insignificant once we add the neighbour growth variable! What's going on? The existence of spillovers between neighbours provides a mechanism which amplifies the effect of policy differences between regions. Neighbouring countries which all have below-average policies will each have poor growth not only because of each individual country's bad policies, but also because of its neighbours' bad policies. This will create a growth differential vis-à-vis the rest of the world that is greater than can be explained by the direct effect of a country's policies on its own growth rate. Neighbours with bad policies were dragging each other down. This is a plausible explanation of what led to the negative AFRICA shift variable, and indeed this variable loses statistical significance once the neighbour growth spillover variable is introduced. In Africa, the whole was worse than the sum of the parts.

The simultaneous interaction between neighbours pulling each other up or down creates a multiplier effect on any policy change in unison.

Easterly and Levine (1994) show algebraically that the multiplier is 1/(1–b), where b is the coefficient on one's neighbours' average growth. Table 1.3 shows that b was estimated at 0.55 in the larger sample, which implies a multiplier of 2.2, that is, a policy change in unison by a set of neighbours will have an effect on growth that is 2.2 times larger than if a single country had acted in isolation. The large multiplier comes because each country is increasing its own growth through its own policy change whilst at the same time providing a favourable spillover effect to all its neighbours. When all neighbouring countries do this in unison, they create a favourable chain reaction: on top of the own-policy effect, my growth increases because yours does, which in turn increases your growth further, which in turn increases my growth again, and so on.

CONCLUSIONS

Poor growth in Africa is statistically explained by low schooling, political instability, not much financial depth, high black market premia, high government deficits, poor infrastructure, ethnic conflict and growth spillovers between neighbours which magnify all of the above.

The strong negative effect of ethnic diversity on policy and growth is troubling, but the outcome is far from inevitable. The economic success of multi-ethnic societies like Indonesia, Mauritius and Malaysia shows that it is possible to transform ethnic diversity from a weakness to a strength.

More research is needed to understand the mechanism of the spillovers of success and failure across national borders. Such spillovers already have very interesting implications for the potential for region-wide improvement. One or more leader economies could provide a strong demonstration effect in Africa of the potential for achieving rapid growth through market-oriented policies. This is not to say that a country need wait for others to act, since one's own policies always have the strongest effect on one's own growth. But if almost all countries improve their policies sooner or later, the continent will get more growth bang for its policy buck.

The strong effects of policies on growth in this statistical analysis indicate that Africa's poor performance is very much reversible. The World Bank's (1994) report on adjustment in Africa found encouraging signs of a growth response when countries have reversed poor policies; these cases are unfortunately still all too few.[9] If a policy reform movement sweeps the continent, Africa's long exile to the margins of the world economy could finally come to an end.

Notes

1. This presentation draws upon Easterly and Levine (1994), available upon request. Views expressed here are not necessarily those of the World Bank.
2. 'Africa' in this paper refers to the region of sub-Saharan Africa as defined by the World Bank. This paper does not attempt to survey the large body of work on Africa's poor economic growth; for some citations to this vast literature, see the companion paper by Easterly and Levine (1994).
3. These comparisons are taken from the SAVEM tables of the World Bank and from the World Development Indicators. The export and total GDP figures for Africa exclude South Africa.
4. Infrastructure data are from the World Development Report (1994).
5. Among the authors who have identified some sub-set of these variables as determinants of growth are Barro (1991), Barro and Lee (1993a and b), Canning and Fay (1993), Easterly (1993, 1994), Easterly and Rebelo (1993), Fischer (1993) and King and Levine (1993a,b).
6. The infrastructure variable was not included in the calculations behind Figure 1.1 because the African sample became too small when it was included.
7. Easterly and Levine (1994) first tried ethnic diversity as a variable because previous work by Canning and Fay (1993) and Mauro (1993) had suggested that it indeed played a role in the determination of policies, institutional characteristics, and/or growth. The data were kindly supplied by Paulo Mauro; the original source of the data was an institute in the former Soviet Union which computed this measure for all countries in the 1960s.
8. Chua (1993) and Ades and Chua (1993) show the effects of a country's investment and political instability on its neighbour's growth.
9. See also the recent update by Bouton, Jones and Kiguel (1994).

Part 2

Regional and National Marginalisation

2 The Changing International Economic System

Peter Robson

The current evolution of the global economic environment presents serious challenges for many developing countries. In the short term, global adjustment to the economic and political turbulence of the past decade has left a legacy that points uniformly to a more adverse international environment for developing countries. In the medium and longer term, the evolution of more deep-seated global structural factors suggests a much more mixed prospect for different developing countries. It is not, however, a prospect that would justify an optimistic prognosis for Southern African countries in the absence of determined and effective policy responses on their part.

The essence of the shorter-term, conjunctural forces is reflected in the fact that by the end of the 1980s, two decades of reasonable growth in the advanced countries of more than 3 per cent per annum had given place to severe recession. The spreading recession in the advanced countries, which reflected their slow productivity growth and their policy responses to inflation and to competition from the NIEs, in turn reduced growth rates and foreign investment in developing countries. Although recovery is now under way, many factors – including expectations of continued slow productivity growth in major economies – seem to point to relatively low investment and growth in advanced countries over the next decade by comparison with their experience of the past 25 years. For one thing, the combined impact of budget deficits in the G-7 countries and their high prospective recovery-induced demand for fixed capital formation coupled with low savings rates suggest relatively high real rates of interest. This tendency will be reinforced by the economic aftermath of political turbulence in Eastern Europe, which manifests itself in a huge additional potential investment demand for restructuring the former Soviet bloc. Furthermore, many Eastern bloc countries constitute locations for foreign investment to serve Western markets that can effectively compete with those offered by developing countries. The conjunctural legacy thus points to relatively depressed prospects of growth for many developing countries. The latest World Bank global forecasts for the next decade nevertheless suggest substantial real GDP growth for developing countries and for sub-Saharan Africa as a whole (3.9 per cent annually).

No consideration of global developments and their significance for developing countries can afford to disregard the conjunctural legacy. In the medium and longer term, however, the implications of a number of more deep-seated global initiatives and structural trends are potentially of far greater importance for the global competitiveness and growth prospects of developing countries. Of these factors, three are currently foremost in the policy debate, partly because perceptions of their implications have fuelled presentiments of exclusion on the part of many developing countries. The factors in question are (1) the implications of the latest initiatives for multilateral trade liberalisation; (2) the continued trend towards the internationalisation of finance and production; and (3) the resurgence of regionalism throughout the world. The rest of this paper looks in turn at these factors and their implications.

MULTILATERAL TRADE LIBERALISATION

Led partly by the effects of previous GATT rounds, the 1980s were a dynamic period for world trade, which expanded by about 50 per cent. Also notable were the substantial increase in the share of product that was traded internationally and the considerable changes in the product composition and pattern of world trade. Mining became of sharply diminished importance, but the share of manufactures rose from rather more than one half to nearly three-quarters of the total. Particularly high annual growth rates were recorded by office and telecommunications products, clothing and other consumer goods, and automotive products. Significant differences in the relative performance of particular countries and groups of countries also occurred. Towards the end of the period the already remarkable growth performance of the Asian region in world trade was reinforced by the emergence of China as a major exporter. Both China and the newly industrialised economies of East Asia experienced major improvements in their merchandise export ranking during the decade. A final notable development is that intra-regional trade in the Asian region has become significant.

The GATT Reforms

In terms of trade policy implications, GATT 1994 is important on several counts. First, it involves the acceptance of the obligation to implement significant tariff cuts in industrial and agricultural products over specified periods. Secondly, quotas and import restrictions have to be converted into tariff equivalents, thus making protection more transparent. Thirdly, the negotiations have involved for the first time the sensitive sectors of agriculture, textiles and clothing. These are of particular concern to many developing countries. Fourthly, the negotiations have also involved non-tariff barriers. Again, it is these which have most constrained exports to developed countries in the past. Thus the Multi-Fibre Arrangement is to be phased out and NTBs should affect only 4 per cent of developing countries' exports to OECD by comparison with the current 18 per cent. Manufactures already amount to 50 per cent of developing countries' exports. Of these, the Asian NIEs have until now accounted for the lion's share. Henceforward, as a result of outward-looking policy reforms, notably in Africa and Latin America, many more developing countries will seek to export to the industrial markets of the rich countries.

The Effects of GATT 1994 on Developing Countries

The implementation of GATT 1994 and the establishment of the WTO will have three main types of effect on developing countries. First, the specific changes in trade barriers will have direct static effects on the value and direction of their trade through their effects on relative prices. The direct partial static gains appear, however, to be modest, yielding an increase of only 3 per cent of export value for developing countries as a whole, with Asian countries gaining most. Indeed, according to Page, Davenport and Hewitt (1991), ACP countries will actually lose, while Goldin et al. (1993) predict that sub-Saharan Africa will itself be $2.6 billion worse off by 2002.

Secondly, the removal or reduction of trade barriers can also be expected to have indirect effects on income levels and growth rates both in industrialised and developing countries through their impacts on resource allocation and increased competition. Some of the dynamic effects on productivity and competitiveness in the longer term could have significant and positive repercussions on the trade and incomes of developing countries, offsetting even for low-income African countries the probably adverse direct static trade effects of GATT 1994. But this potential remains to be actualised. It is comparatively easy to improve static competitiveness, but dynamic competitiveness is both more crucial and more difficult to attain. Moreover, its achievement demands effective responses in other policy areas such as competition. One problem is that there may be a trade-off between static and dynamic competitiveness.

Thirdly, GATT 1994 will result in constraints on the use by developing countries themselves of trade and trade-related policy instruments. Since these countries have become a significant market for most industrial countries, the latter have sought, successfully, to secure improved access to that market and to bring the trade and protection policies of all countries under regulation.

THE INTERNATIONALISATION OF PRODUCTION

The second major change in the international system, and without doubt the most significant one, is the process of the internationalisation of production and business that has been such a striking feature of post-war decades. The increase in the share of product traded, which has been such a marked feature of the last decade and a half, reflects this. Thus, over the period 1983–9, trade grew about 50 per cent faster than output. More recently, it has grown more than twice as fast. The process of globalisation has been stimulated by technological advances which have reduced natural barriers to trade, but also by the acceleration of foreign direct investment (FDI), which began to be marked in 1983 with widespread financial liberalisation and the pursuit of new strategies of investment and production organisation on the part of TNCs.

World Foreign Investment

As a result of these forces, there has been a spectacular growth of world flows of FDI on the part of TNCs since the mid-1980s, at rates far exceeding those of merchandise exports, to reach a peak of $232 billion in 1990. Much has involved mergers and acquisitions. For many developing countries, FDI now constitutes the principal source of foreign capital. Together with the associated flows of technology, training and trade which are bound up with it, it has effectively become the primary means by which a growing number of countries is integrated into the world economy.

The pattern of FDI is, however, extremely polarised. Some three-quarters of flows take place between developed countries themselves, and these are concentrated on the US, the EU and Japan. Even the relatively small (but growing) flows towards developing countries are themselves highly concentrated, some two-thirds being directed to just ten countries. Of these, the Asian NIEs and China take the bulk. In marked contrast, FDI flows to Africa amounted to only $3 billion in the early 1990s.

It is this polarisation of investment that has prompted the question of whether it points to the exclusion of numbers of developing countries from the growth benefits of the globalisation of production. If it does – presumably because spread effects cannot compensate for a lack of FDI inflows – this poses the further question of whether flows can be encouraged to move to those countries and regions otherwise excluded by the market. The results of recent research on the factors affecting transnational investment throw some light on this question, though more needs to be done.

Factors Affecting Transnational Investment

The primary point suggested by a number of recent cross-section studies and case studies is that the prospects of attracting FDI for particular developing countries and blocs are primarily dependent on their over-all economic performance and growth. That is, capital inflows must be expected to be growth-led rather than growth-driving. That seems to underline the importance of successful structural adjustment programmes in preparing the ground.

More specific important and interrelated considerations are brought out by other recent analyses (Oman, 1993; Thomsen and Woolcock, 1993). First, there is some evidence of a tendency for the role of offshore production by US and European TNCs to decline relatively. This seems to be associated in the first place with the diminishing role of unskilled labour in costs. It is unhelpful that this decline should be occurring as more developing countries turn to export-oriented industrialisation strategies, if these have to rely on their attraction as low-wage sites for such offshore production to service markets in rich countries.

A second important and to some extent countervailing consideration is the growing recognition of the importance of the need for flexibility and of distance costs in explaining the investment strategies of TNCs. Distance costs include transport costs but embrace all penalties that arise if producers are far removed from the final market for their products. It is thus the relative importance of economies of scale and distance costs that will influence a firm's strategies. A variety of factors – the growing importance of non-tradeable service industries, preferences of particular markets, the advantages of physical proximity to suppliers which facilitates synergy and non-arm's length relations with suppliers and customers, the need for flexibility and rapid adaptation – is enhancing the role of distance costs. Manufacturing far from the end-user or consumer may be perceived to be risky if flexibility, speed of delivery or some other competitive advantage associated with market proximity is perceived to be important. The outcome is the growing importance of market-based FDI and of regional as opposed to global production and sourcing, focused within the European Economic Area, East and South Asia and North America.

A third consideration not unrelated to the previous one is that the location of FDI appears to be influenced by the existence or prospect of regional integration initiatives and preferential trade arrangements. The mechanism operates by way of the opportunities regional integration presents for investment creation and diversion which alter the balance of scale economies and distance costs just referred to. Not surprisingly, the EU itself has been a notable beneficiary of FDI inflows during the past decade and earlier, in the first place from the US and more recently from Japan. Among developing countries, some of those of Central America and the Caribbean, which enjoy free trade status with the US, have received export-oriented investment in labour-intensive industries that is geared to that market. The Enterprise for the Americas Initiative may extend the importance of such investment in the Western Hemisphere in the future. For a very few countries such as Mauritius, the Lomé Convention has been a spur to such investment for the European market.

THE REVIVAL OF REGIONALISM

The third important international movement which may affect the global competitiveness of economies is regionalism. The recent widespread resurgence of regionalism is partly a response to the factors favouring inflows of transnational investment, but it is also helping to influence the form that globalisation is taking (Robson, 1993a and b). Regionalism itself is currently assuming different forms in the three main areas where it is taking root. In the EU it takes the form of deep, policy-led integration; in the Western Hemisphere, looser free trade areas between North and South, potentially hindered by extra-GATT restrictions, are the mode; while in Asia, informal, investment-led links have been favoured. But in any event, the present context of regionalism is very different from the past, as are its justifications, so that traditional criteria for evaluating its merits have less application. This is perhaps as well since few blocs of developing countries satisfy the traditional structural criteria for success in either the real or the monetary spheres.

In the past few years new regional initiatives have emerged in North America (NAFTA), Latin America (Mercosur), Africa (UEMOA) and Asia (APEC). Several of these aim to achieve high degrees of integration within relatively short periods of time. In the European Union, new deepening dimensions have been adopted while the process of widening has seen its membership expand from 12 to 15 countries in 1995. Additionally, the Union has negotiated a customs union with Turkey and has entered into preferential 'Europe' Agreements with Slovakia, the Czech Republic, Hungary and Poland. These and other countries are themselves in the process of forming the Central European Free Trade Area.

In the Western Hemisphere the new wave in Latin America has in the past been encouraged by the 1990 Enterprise for the Americas Initiative of the US. This offered a fast track to blocs as opposed to individual countries in any negotiation of free trade areas. Other material factors have been the Argentine–Brazil rapprochement and Mexico's accession to NAFTA.

In a major new initiative in 1991, Argentina, Brazil, Uruguay and Paraguay committed themselves to establish a Common Market of the South (Mercosur). This reached the customs union stage at the beginning of 1995, but the programme also includes the coordination of macroeconomic policies and sectoral agreements. The Mercosur initiatives have reinforced the Andean Pact countries' initiatives for the creation of a common market, while the CACM has also taken steps to reactivate itself, making some progress towards re-establishing free trade and reincorporating Honduras.

In further Latin American initiatives, several members of the primary trade blocs have simultaneously entered into other commitments involving the formation of yet more blocs. Thus, Colombia and Venezuela have further developed the special trading relationship they already had with Mexico (the Group of Three). In the CACM, three members (Guatemala, Honduras and El Salvador) have created a sub-grouping (the Triangle of the North) to facilitate closer integration amongst themselves within the framework of the reshaped Central American arrangements. The consistency of such subsidiary arrangements with those of the primary blocs remains unclear.

In addition to these numerous sub-regional commitments, the new enthusiasm for trade liberalisation in Latin America has prompted the conclusion of a series of purely bilateral agreements, of which the Free Trade Treaty between Chile and Mexico is an example. Amongst the Andean Group, difficulties in finalising its CET have led to the conclusion of bilateral agreements between members (involving, *inter alia*, a customs union between Colombia and Venezuela) as well as between members and third countries.

In Africa new regional integration initiatives are manifested in the SACU renegotiations, COMESA, the CBI and the proposed SADC trade protocol. Further north, UEMOA was set up in 1993. It seeks to transform the West African monetary union into an economic union, in the process taking over the role of CEAO which was simultaneously abolished.

In the English-speaking Caribbean, new initiatives for regional integration are reflected in the Grande Anse Declaration of 1989, and by the far-ranging proposals for new dimensions of integration contained in the Report of the West Indian Commission (1992).

In the developing countries of Asia, the only important experience with policy-led regional economic integration is represented by ASEAN, whose foundation goes back to 1967. Although ASEAN's origins lie in political and strategic considerations, economic cooperation has become a central concern. Opposition, notably from Singapore, has hitherto excluded the adoption of significant preferential trade policies, but the formation of a free trade area by 2003 has now been agreed upon. One new initiative concerns the wider APEC forum, which includes the advanced countries of the Pacific Rim, the NIEs and the developing countries of the region. At the end of 1994 the forum adopted an agreement to institute a free trade area by 2020, with the industrialised countries reaching that goal by 2010. It is, however, non-binding.

Although policy-led integration among Asian countries has not yet been significant, there is a substantial and increasing amount of investment-led regional interdependence in the wider Asia Pacific region (intra-group trade in 1990 was 40 per cent of total trade). This is mainly driven by the global strategies of TNCs. The main mechanism underlying it is the transfer of industries such as electronics and components, automobiles and precision machinery from early starters among the NIEs to latecomers in ASEAN, although US TNCs have also played a part. In general, Asia has been unenthusiastic about formal regional integration. Its approach, sometimes termed 'open regionalism', is instead characterised by *ad hoc* efforts to widen markets without tariff discrimination.

Of the numerous 'new' initiatives noted here, EC 1992 is one of the few that is new in character. European experience – not necessarily transferable – suggests that gains several times larger than those from conventional trade creation can be had from non-trade policy measures that reduce, first, the private and, second, the social costs of market fragmentation (EC 1988). Many of these costs are associated with physical, technical and fiscal barriers to market integration. The benefits from overcoming them show up for firms in reduced administrative and transactions costs. For the economy, they show up in increased inter-firm competition which promises a reduction of production costs and monopoly rents. Production integration and cross-border investment through investment creation and diversion should also be stimulated, although there is a danger that resultant rationalisation may reduce competition.

EC 1992 promises substantial benefits. It is, even so, significant that the large single European market it creates is widely perceived to be inadequate in itself to underpin the global competitiveness of European industry. Enterprises in many sectors of industry continue to find it necessary to invest outside Europe through acquisitions and mergers. Strategic alliances, too, are often global rather than purely European.

Of the Western Hemisphere initiatives, NAFTA certainly possesses one novel and positive feature in its North–South link, but recent appraisals suggest that its direct trade benefits may be modest. The inclusion of provisions relating to labour standards and environmental protection could, for one thing, rob the Agreement, and its prospective extension to Chile and other Latin American countries, of much of its trade benefits from their point of view.

What can be said of the numerous other initiatives that involve developing countries alone? It is not yet clear whether these agreements are sufficiently different from the unsuccessful experiments of the 1960s and the 1970s (or can be made so) as to warrant a belief that they will be able to make a significant contribution to enhancing internal and external sources of competitiveness and growth. Many of the old problems seem to be present still in a number of the 'new' arrangements. These include a lack of credibility which will hinder FDI inflows and restructuring; a lack of complementary productive structures and convertible currencies; and sometimes very small regional markets even when integrated. Also, it remains to be seen whether the crucial problem of cohesion and inter-country equity can be adequately dealt with.

It can be said in their favour that most new initiatives among developing countries affect economies that are lowering external trade barriers and that are moving from trying to promote industrial development behind high tariff barriers towards outward-looking policies. These changes reduce the scope for both trade diversion costs and trade creation benefits. To that extent, the direct trade policy effects of integration will be lessened, perhaps greatly. But if so, that seems to pose the question – why bother with regional integration? Why indeed, unless its effects are bound up with other major benefits. In that event, static trade liberalisation gains may not be the decisive consideration.

So far, however, only one new initiative confined to developing countries, CARICOM, explicitly looks to novel non-tariff dimensions of regional integration of the kinds that EC policy has focused on and that affect not just trade but the whole of production. A crucial question for the choice of policy options in developing countries turns on the significance of such gains for them. So far, solid evidence is lacking and research is obviously needed.

Against the background of a polarised globalisation of FDI to which attention has already been drawn, a still more important consideration may be that if regional integration is to justify itself, it must do so largely in terms of its ability to encourage extra-regional FDI inflows. Here the evidence points to the strong positive effect that credible integration can have on FDI. Another pointer which favours integration is that FDI appears increasingly market-based, reflecting the perceived importance of distance costs.

Past regional integration among developing countries rarely succeeded in attracting significant FDI. This resulted partly from self-imposed obstacles against FDI and partly because regionalism lacked credibility. In any event, FDI inflows associated with investment creation and diversion seldom materialised. The lack of credibility also made itself felt in an accentuation of problems of inter-state imbalances. Enhanced credibility may thus be doubly critical for future success. One approach to establishing it is to build in external constraints and incentives. Credibility was given to the African francophone monetary unions by guarantees and guidance from the French Treasury. Current Latin American free trade areas may similarly be enabled to reduce their credibility gap and lock in their trade reforms if the North–South links that are in prospect under an American Free Trade Area (AFTA) should become a significant reality.

But is this, in any case, enough? In particular, can any regional integration initiative be adequate if it is purely reactive and does not directly address the issue of building the South's innovative capacity? This is essentially the laudable perspective of a recent OECD document (Mytelka, 1994). Its message is that to do so it is essential to break with traditional theory and practice concerning the form and function of South–South regional cooperation. The alternative vision offered is of an innovation-driven model of South–South cooperation rooted in regional networking. Unfortunately, inter-firm networks are not like academic networks. Surely, the uncomfortable truth, as Ernst (1994) has argued, is that without improved access to international networks that are dominated by OECD oligopolists who operate important barriers to entry, the chances of viable South–South technological cooperation for innovation may remain very limited. In any case, although encouraging innovation may be a vital element of regionalism, this constitutes no case for abandoning other constructive avenues for cooperation and integration.

CONCLUSIONS: THE POLICY SIGNIFICANCE OF RECENT GLOBAL DEVELOPMENTS

The main points of this paper may be summarised as follows:

1. GATT 1994 offers few if any static gains for many developing countries and reduces their scope for pursuing protectionist policies, except in the context of free trade areas and customs unions.
2. With the growing significance for development of international production and the dangers of exclusion from its benefits, measures to remove obstacles to foreign direct investment and to facilitate cross-border investment assume a particular importance in policy reform initiatives.
3. The evidence suggests that FDI is induced by regional arrangements, particularly those that carry the promise of access to the markets of industrialised countries. In particular, smaller countries that lack such links may find themselves increasingly marginalised in their quest for investment inflows.
4. One of the most significant of recent initiatives, namely that of the EU, has been concerned with deepening or non-tariff measures of integration. Most have an important relationship to the encouragement of FDI inflows, competition and investment creation and diversion. A primary question is whether in Africa these factors are sufficiently important to warrant giving high priority to participation in regional initiatives despite its inevitable cost in terms of reduced policy flexibility. Or would the path favoured by the World

Bank, of unilateral policy reform untrammelled by regional commitments, be preferable? If the latter, what are the indicated solutions to capturing the benefits of FDI?

5. A feature of Western Hemisphere integration initiatives is that they involve North–South links – first, through NAFTA and ultimately, perhaps, through AFTA – on the basis of hemispherical free trade. Similar links are inherent in APEC. The gain to credibility so afforded and the advantage of locking in reforms in developing countries may turn out to be the most important determinants of the ability of these arrangements to stimulate investment, trade and development significantly. So far, Lomé apart, North–South links have not been prominent in Africa, except in the monetary sphere. North–South trade reciprocity has been entirely absent, and strongly resisted by African policy-makers. That approach might merit rethinking – if it is not already too late – if Southern Africa wishes to reduce the risk of marginalisation.

3 Can Regional Integration Help Southern Africa?

Gavin Maasdorp

This paper is written in the context of four recent developments. These are:

1. the establishment of the WTO in January 1995;
2. the commencement, in November 1994, of the renegotiation of the SACU Agreement between South Africa, Botswana, Lesotho, Namibia and Swaziland;
3. the transformation, in December 1994, of the PTA into COMESA; and
4. the decision of SADC, taken in Windhoek in 1992, to transform itself from a body concerned only with sectoral cooperation into a trade integration arrangement.

If this paper had been written a few years ago, it might have discussed the pros and cons of trade integration as compared with sectoral cooperation (or functional integration). In today's climate this no longer seems apt: indeed, it will be argued that there is a role for both. Nor does it seem of any particular use to enquire whether Southern Africa should respond to the growth of regional trading blocs elsewhere by establishing its own bloc (or blocs) when these are already in existence.

The fact of the matter is that there has been a sea change in the international trading environment, and the 'Burma option' is not a feasible one to take for any country wishing to develop: to be protectionist today would be to run counter to global trends. The new, more open international economy also limits the capacity of any country, or region, to control its own destiny, particularly since the economies of Southern Africa are highly open by world standards (ADB, 1993).

The political decision in favour of trade integration has already been made in Southern Africa. The real question for Southern Africa now is how it can use the new WTO rules, and its line-up of regional groupings, to maximise its role in, and its benefits from, the new global economic order. What can integration be expected to achieve, and how can the process best be taken forward?

WHAT INTEGRATION CAN AND CANNOT DO

Southern Africa should be realistic as to what it can expect from regional integration. The record worldwide is not particularly inspiring, and a number of attempts in Africa have failed. As Coussy (1992) points out, arguments in favour of inter-African integration appear to have been borrowed from debates about integration among the developed economies. Few integration schemes among less developed countries have survived let alone made any notable contribution to economic development. Countries in the SADC grouping have been involved in two failed schemes: the East African Community and the Federation of the Rhodesias and Nyasaland. Global political and economic circumstances have changed significantly since then, and the peculiar national circumstances which made for the failure of those arrangements no longer necessarily exist, but none the less it is just as well to begin on a cautionary note.

Southern Africa should also not have an inflated opinion of its importance in the world economy. The total market size of sub-Saharan Africa is slightly smaller than that of Australia; that of the 11 SADC countries is fractionally larger than that of Indonesia; while Eastern and Southern Africa together have a market size smaller than that of Austria.

One of the main goals of economic integration is to stimulate intraregional trade, but the creation of a single Southern African market would not necessarily deflect a large proportion of each member country's trade away from the rest of the world (ROW) (Maasdorp, 1993). Over the last 10 years the original 10 SADC countries have conducted only about 4 per cent of their total foreign trade within the grouping, about one quarter with South Africa, and between 70 and 75 per cent with the ROW. Of South Africa's foreign trade in 1990, only one eighth was with the 10 SADC countries, and this was mainly with its SACU partners. Two SADC countries – Angola and Tanzania – have had insignificant trade ties with Southern Africa. Intra-PTA trade as a proportion of total PTA foreign trade also declined in the 1980s, and was only 4.6 per cent in 1989. Unrecorded cross-border trade is substantial between some countries, so that the official figures are underestimates (perhaps by a percentage point or so). An analysis of transactions through the PTA Clearing House (a mechanism for settling debts) showed that, until 1991, only 12 of the then 18 member countries had used it for trade transactions. COMESA, in fact, contains a number of countries which have had little ability to engage in intra-regional trade, political instability having been a critical factor.

Figures of average annual trade flows during the period 1983–9 show that about 73.8 per cent of intra-Southern African trade consisted of imports from South Africa, and another 15.1 per cent of exports to South Africa, i.e. 89 per cent of intra-regional trade involved South Africa. Intra-regional trade as a proportion of total foreign trade is highest in the SACU. The BLNS countries obtain the bulk of their imports from South Africa or through South African commercial channels, while South Africa is an important market for their commodities. There is relatively little trade among BLNS themselves. South Africa is also a major trading partner of a number of Southern African countries, notably Zimbabwe, Mozambique, Zambia, Malawi and Mauritius, with growing volumes of trade occurring with Kenya and Tanzania. Absolute volumes of trade with the Indian Ocean islands – Comores, Seychelles and Madagascar – are small, but none the less South Africa is an important trading partner for these countries. The balance of trade between South Africa and the rest of the region is strongly in favour of South Africa. The ratio of its exports to imports in this trade is 5.9:1 with the SACU countries, 4.4:1 with the rest of the SADC countries, and 5:1 with COMESA as a whole.

Although most of the intra-regional trade is in fact with South Africa, a number of studies conducted for the PTA and SADC in the past have suggested that the potential for increasing trade among the other countries is larger than commonly supposed. The World Bank (1989) estimated that the share of intra-regional trade in total sub-Saharan African foreign trade could be increased to 18 per cent (Kimaro, 1993), and the ADB (1993) found 'considerable' scope for increased two-way trade between South Africa and the rest of the region. Some 25 per cent of South Africa's manufactured exports go to BLNS, and the Eastern and Southern African market as a whole is an increasingly important one for South African exporters of manufactured goods. The balance of advantage in agriculture, however, lies with the other countries, and this is true too of trade in energy and water. Sanctions seriously affected the growth of two-way trade until just recently, but volumes have been increasing rapidly. Nevertheless, the lack of convertible currencies in many countries remains an obstacle to intra-trade, and trade with the ROW will remain far more important for Southern Africa. The PTA and SADC countries generally are exporters of primary commodities (agricultural and mineral), the markets for which are in the ROW. Their imports consist largely of manufactured goods (especially machinery and capital equipment), the sources also being in the ROW. Thus, the main markets and suppliers will remain abroad.

This raises the question as to whether South Africa, as the largest and most industrialised economy in the region, can act as a spring-board of economic development as, for example, Japan has done in East and South-East Asia. In the 1960s and 1970s the concept of core and periphery was popular in the literature on economic development, the argument being that the core country would draw resources away from the periphery, and hence that growth and development would become increasingly concentrated in the core. The 'flying geese' pattern which has emerged in East Asia, where there was a transfer of industry and technology to the NIEs, and later from them to some of the ASEAN countries, together with the relocation of industry in the EU from the north to the Mediterranean countries, has eroded the credibility of the core–periphery hypothesis.

But will the geese fly in Southern and Eastern Africa, that is, will South African economic growth spill over into the region? South Africa, after all, is hardly a Japan or Germany: it is no more than a semi-developed country with some First World strengths (notably sophisticated financial services and a reasonable physical infrastructure) as well as typical Third World weaknesses (a shortage of skills, high population growth, high unemployment, and so on). It shares many common problems of development with other countries in the region and needs to attract as much industrial investment as possible in order to overcome the massive unemployment problem which has accumulated after 20 years of stagnation in the manufacturing sector. Indeed, its economic health must be a matter of great concern to the rest of the region: many organisations and firms have pinned their faith on the country becoming the success story of Africa. If it fails, this would be a setback to the region since a number of companies are using South Africa as a base from which to launch their African operations (including investments). Although it is not clear at present whether South Africa is on the path to becoming a 'winning economy', the fact is that it is bordered by Zimbabwe, the country with the next most developed industrial sector in Africa, while manufacturing has grown considerably in Botswana, Lesotho and Swaziland in the last 10 years, sometimes as a result of the sanctions and disinvestment campaigns against South Africa. Such a sub-regional juxtaposition of industry does not exist anywhere else in Africa, so that, if there is to be a springboard, it is likely to be found in the southern group of countries. South Africa's importance as a market for BLNS, Zimbabwe and Malawi, and the potential for increased two-way trade not just in goods but also in services (such as tourism) with Mozambique,

Kenya and Mauritius, suggest that there could be a spillover effect from a vigorously growing South African economy.

However, spillovers should not be taken as an indication that equal benefits would accrue to each country from economic integration: by its very nature, integration would benefit some countries more than others. Clearly, though, membership would be worthwhile for a country only if it were better off, or at least no worse off, inside the scheme than it would have been outside it. Because there will be an unequal distribution of the benefits of integration, a mechanism for the transfer of funds to the lagging countries is necessary, as is the case in the EU with the European Regional Development Fund and European Social Fund.

One of the reasons for the poor record of regional integration attempts in Africa is that many countries have not shown the ability to develop economies of scale and hence to overcome the tendency towards polarisation. The congruity between polarisation and the core–periphery argument is obvious. However, the reasons for the failure to develop economies of scale need investigation: one important reason has been the adoption of divergent economic development policies and strategies, for example, between Tanzania and Kenya in the East African Community, which exacerbated the initial disparities in the level of development. By contrast, the adoption of market-based economic policies stressing economic growth in East and South-East Asia encouraged the 'flying geese' pattern of development. The removal of tariff and non-tariff barriers in a regional trading bloc would imply the creation of a single market area, and this could provide opportunities, under certain circumstances, for countries to exploit their competitive advantages and for economies of scale to be developed. However, it is not possible for governments to steer new industrial investment to particular countries: companies, not governments, make investment decisions. The Andean Pact experience shows the futility of attempts to plan an allocation of new industries among countries. A more equitable distribution of industry is best achieved by ensuring that the trading bloc has a common policy concerning incentives and subsidies, including the pricing of utilities and externalities. This would be the economically efficient way of minimising polarisation and ensuring that there is no bias in favour of the core.

It is not just the static but also the dynamic effects of integration which require attention, for example, the opportunities for raising productivity, increasing competition, obtaining better flows of information and technology transfer, achieving savings in transactions costs, and treating education and health (and possibly security too) as regional public goods. Attention to the last-mentioned point would enable small countries to have access, for example, to existing faculties of medicine and engineering in South Africa, which they would find uneconomic to establish on their own.

Integration is not a panacea. What is required is efficiency in the development of human resources, sound national development policies and good governance. In many parts of Africa economic integration has been retarded by declining standards of administration and growing corruption in both the public and private sectors: these societies have been rent- rather than profit-seeking. The determining factor in a country's success is its overall economic and social environment, not whether it is part of a regional grouping. Issues such as the physical infrastructure (especially transport and telecommunications), the social infrastructure, productivity and labour relations are all important. Low wage rates might be attractive to some investors, but total wage costs (which include factors such as productivity) are more important. Perceptions of risk are also critical. To the extent that regional integration can help to improve the physical and social infrastructure and the risk rating of countries, it plays a positive role in their economic development. Foreign investors generally have a negative perception of these factors in sub-Saharan Africa, and it is up to regional groupings in Southern Africa to improve the international image of the region as a good place in which to invest and do business. This is where credible regional institutions can help.

HOW CAN INTEGRATION BEST BE TAKEN FORWARD?

The establishment of credible regional institutions requires political will. One of the reasons for the relative failure of the PTA and SADC in the past has been the lack of political will on the part of all member governments to implement decisions of the particular organisation. There have been other reasons too, of course, but as long as mere lip-service is paid by some governments to regional treaties, they will remain little more than pieces of paper. Governments need to commit themselves to economic growth, the removal of NTBs and currency convertibility. Structural adjustment programmes have helped some countries lower their tariffs, while further tariff reductions and the removal of NTBs will have to be made by WTO members.

The complexity of the institutional structure in Southern Africa at present requires some clarification and rationalisation. In this respect one of the key questions concerns the role of donors: despite considerable overlapping membership of COMESA and SADC, relations between these two organisations have deteriorated, yet donors persist in funding both and refrain from taking a hard line on rationalisation. COMESA was established as a trade body and SADC as an organisation to promote sectoral promotion. However, the optimal geographic area for cooperation in some sectors stretches beyond SADC, for example, Zaire is critical in plans for a regional power grid. Nor is there any reason why an optimal trade area should be limited geographically, and this is evidenced by the progress made under the Cross-border Initiative (CBI). Sponsored by the EU, IMF, World Bank and African Development Bank, the aim is to reduce obstacles to cross-border trade and investment. Membership is open to all COMESA and SADC countries: so far 14 countries are participating, all of which are members of COMESA, while six belong to SADC and three to the SACU. South Africa and Botswana are not participants. Tariff reductions of 60–70 per cent have been made on intra-CBI trade, and a free trade area by 1998 is planned. The position of the CBI countries within the context of COMESA is consistent with the so-called 'variable geometry' approach which allows sub-groups of countries to progress more rapidly than others on the path towards trade integration without excluding the others.

The SACU is the only area of 'real existing integration' (to play on a phrase from the former Soviet bloc) in Southern Africa. Four of the five countries are also linked in the CMA which provides the nearest approximation to monetary integration in the region. In fact, these four countries are close to being a textbook common market. The pragmatic way forward for trade integration would be for the renegotiated SACU to enter into an agreement with the CBI countries, consistent with the provisions of the WTO.

Credible regional integration arrangements could go a long way towards improving Southern Africa's standing in the international investor and donor community. An interesting contrast in this regard is that Southern African institutions consist purely of Third World membership whereas Latin America, through Mexico's membership of NAFTA and the Enterprise for the Americas Initiative, has a potential link with developed industrial countries. Since the OECD countries will remain the main trading partners of Southern Africa, the region could well consider seeking formal links with an economic integration scheme among developed countries. SADC countries are already linked to the EU through the Lomé Convention, and to the EU and US through the generalised system of preferences, but neither covers more than a small proportion of Southern Africa's export commodities. Moreover, there is some doubt about the long-term future of the Lomé Convention. The EU has granted Morocco associate membership, and a similar agreement on the basis of reciprocal trade could be important for the region's exporters in order to gain access to the markets of the world's largest trading bloc. Such an association could make a real difference in helping Southern Africa avoid marginalisation in global trade. Another possibility would be to join an Indian Ocean grouping: this would include, *inter alia*, Australia and four ASEAN countries, and would provide a unique opportunity for trade on a so-called South–South basis between some of the NIEs and less developed countries (Maasdorp, 1995).

CONCLUSION

The presence of efficient and credible institutional structures for trade integration and economic cooperation would be beneficial for Southern Africa. This is not so much because economic integration is a good thing: the alternative for any individual country would be to implement its WTO tariffication bindings and engage in freer global trade on its own. However, any such country would be part of what has generally been considered as a fairly unstable region. Credible regional institutions would help to attract investors from abroad and stimulate intra-regional investment by winning the confidence of investors. This would be one of the best guarantees of a regional spread of investment, something that has been well demonstrated in the EU where the (poorer) Mediterranean countries have attracted relatively more investment than the (richer) northern member countries because of confidence in the organisation. This is perhaps the main reason why trade integration would be beneficial for the smaller and poorer countries in Southern Africa. However, realism must prevail in expanding the area of integration and in the time frame: if Asia and the Pacific are considering 20–5 years, Southern Africa should also exercise patience. The sub-continent can avoid marginalisation in the global economy, but it must play its cards correctly, and that includes not only its institutional but also its general macroeconomic policy framework.

4 Small Countries within Regional Integration

Michael Matsebula and Vakashile Simelane

This paper is concerned with the determinants and alleviation of marginalisation in the context of regional integration in Southern Africa. The working premise on which the analysis is based is that there is no superior alternative for small countries but to belong to an economic integration arrangement.[1]

CONCEPTUAL FRAMEWORK

The core–periphery framework will be used to indicate how small countries in a regional economic integration can become marginalised. An understanding of how marginalisation occurs is necessary in order to appreciate not only the genuineness of the fears that small countries may have, but also what can be done to alleviate the problem to the long-term benefit of all partners.

The core–periphery framework has global, regional, national and subnational dimensions. This paper is interested in the regional dimension (alternatively referred to as international economic dualism). In this context, the core refers to the country or group of countries experiencing a conspicuously high degree of economic activity. The periphery is essentially the antithesis of the core, its very label reflecting the fact that it is at the fringe of mainstream international economic relations.

The models which attempt to explain the determinants of increasing divergences between core and periphery can be divided into three broad categories:

1. *Cumulative causation:* International factor and product movements are such that the core experiences favourable changes in an almost exponential fashion whilst the periphery grows at a relatively modest rate. This process is reinforced through economies of agglomeration which amplify the multiplier-accelerator effect.
2. *Trade-related growth:* The core produces and exports secondary

products to the periphery in return for primary products. Secondary products tend to have higher price and income elasticities of demand and supply than primary products. Thus, gains from trade will accrue disproportionately between the core and periphery with the core getting the lion's share.

3. *Unequal exchange:* In the Marxist-Leninist tradition, the core is always in a dominant position vis-à-vis the periphery; simultaneously, the periphery is dependent on the core. The outcome of bargaining at different levels will typically be to the greatest advantage of the core because of its superior economic power.

Small countries in Southern Africa are peripheral to two cores comprising the relatively more industrialised countries within the region (Core I) and in the rest of the world (Core II) respectively. As Core I intensifies its linkages with Core II, the periphery in Southern Africa will become even more marginalised. In particular, as the new South Africa re-enters mainstream international economic relations, international focus will tend to shift away from the periphery. This is compounded by the competition for attention from the emerging market economies in the former Soviet bloc. All of this presents a real problem of marginalisation for the small countries, hence their fears.

The relationship between the core and periphery can be analysed at the aggregate (or economy-wide) and sectoral (or sub-national) levels. Both levels are associated with what are referred to as orthodox and non-orthodox gains from economic integration. Orthodox gains, in turn, can be explained in terms of trade creation and diversion.[2] Trade creation tends to have a positive impact and trade diversion a negative impact on welfare, the difference between the two determining the net effect on welfare.

If any member experiences a trade diversion effect that more than offsets the trade creation effect, then there is a need for some compensation from those members which have become better off. Marginalisation will occur where this compensation either reduces the recipient country to a dependency status (at times perpetuated by the usage of the compensation to finance public consumption instead of investment) or the recipient country is made to feel grateful for, rather than entitled to, the compensation. It is in this context that trade plays an important role in the assessment of marginalisation.

The trade creation and diversion effects are referred to as static efficiency gains because they involve a more efficient allocation of existing resources. In the long run, however, there are dynamic effects which come into play and result in the augmentation of resources. These effects have come to be regarded as non-orthodox (to distinguish them from the conventional effects just described). They are associated with accelerated industrialisation stemming from internal and external economies of scale generated under the expanded market; foreign exchange savings where the union involves a common currency or some trade mechanism which involves the usage of domestic currency; improvement in terms of trade; and reduction of dependence on the core. Ultimately, they induce higher investment in both infrastructural and directly productive projects. The marginalisation of the periphery will occur if these dynamic effects are appropriated disproportionately by the core. Hence, regional economic cooperation based on an equitable distribution of benefits can go a long way towards reducing marginalisation.

MARGINALISATION AT THE AGGREGATE LEVEL

On the basis of population, the BLNS countries can be considered as small: Botswana has 1.3 million, Lesotho and Namibia 1.8 million each and Swaziland 0.8 million inhabitants, as against South Africa's 41 million. The rest of the countries have populations ranging from 8.1 million (in the case of Zambia) to 15.7 million (in the case of Mozambique). Until recently all the BLNS countries also have had lower per capita incomes and degrees of industrialisation, but Botswana's per capita income now slightly exceeds that of South Africa ($2790 as against $2670 in 1992) while the share of manufacturing in total output for Swaziland is now about 36 per cent compared with 26 per cent for South Africa and Zimbabwe. But Botswana's national income is dependent on minerals, whilst the high manufacturing share for Swaziland is the result of a few agro-based industries (mainly sugar and woodpulp) and one large beverage concentrate producer. Neither Botswana nor Swaziland has anything like the diversified economies and industrial sectors of South Africa and Zimbabwe.

For the purposes of this paper, therefore, BLNS are regarded as the small countries in the periphery whilst South Africa and Zimbabwe are in Core I. Because of their common membership of SACU, BLNS and South Africa will form the primary focus of analysis.

In the context of the *cumulative causation* framework, South Africa had an early start in the development process. European settlers from the seventeenth century onwards brought with them capital and expertise which generated an economic surplus, most of which was reinvested, resulting in increased demand for complementary inputs including labour and capital. Labour flowed in from BLNS. Similarly, the economic surplus generated in BLNS found its way into South Africa where returns were higher. The result was a divergence in the stages of development between South Africa and BLNS.

In the context of the *trade-related growth* argument, three points should be noted. First, the economies of the small countries are highly open in terms of the relative size of the trade sector (ADB, 1993), and the high ratios of trade to GNP imply that a given change in the rest of the world would have a considerable amplified effect on the BLNS economies.

Second, most of BLNS trade is with South Africa, and they have a net trade deficit vis-à-vis South Africa. To the extent that most of their imports are products which have been manufactured inside the SACU tariff wall, it can be inferred that BLNS have been subsidising industrialisation in South Africa. This justifies some form of compensation to ensure an equitable distribution of the gains from economic integration within the SACU. Indeed, such compensation has been forthcoming under the 1969 SACU Agreement. If this compensation is removed (as some quarters in South Africa are arguing for), then an alternative compensatory mechanism has to be found otherwise future trading relations in the region will be strained.

Third, BLNS exports are predominantly primary in nature whereas their imports are predominantly secondary. The problem with primary commodities is that they tend to have low price and income elasticities of demand. This is further compounded by low price elasticities of supply due to long gestation periods, poor infrastructure and shortage of various inputs. As such, it would take a considerable expansion in Cores I and II just to produce a modest expansionary effect on the BLNS economies. At the same time, the imports have high elasticities of demand and supply because of their secondary nature. Moreover, some of them are vital intermediate products which have to be imported even under rising prices. As such, a given expansion in the BLNS economies will tend to induce a proportionately higher increase in imports. This is partly why the South African manufacturing sector has benefited significantly from BLNS markets, for instance, McFarland (1983) estimated that over the period 1970–9, exports to BLNS contributed 19.6 per cent of the increase in South Africa's manufacturing output and 11.3 per cent of the increase in its overall GDP.

In the context of the *unequal exchange* model, the country that industrialises first will naturally wish to protect its position. This desire is reflected in a variety of relations. First, the periphery is used as a backyard market to serve the interests of the core. This has tended to be the case for BLNS: instead of receiving due recognition for contributing significantly to South Africa's industrialisation, they have been perceived as unfairly benefiting from the SACU arrangements, hence the calls for removing the compensation element in the revenue-sharing arrangements. This ignores not only the original justification (which is still valid) of the revenue-sharing formula, but also the fact that BLNS have experienced both faster economic growth and greater structural transformation over the period since 1969. This is the price of being marginal in the scheme of things.

Second, there is the dominant role played by South Africa, through its Board of Tariffs and Trade, in the setting of common external tariffs. In practice, this has worked to the disadvantage of BLNS in setting up any large industries that would compete with existing South African industries. Essentially, South Africa's reaction, when faced with the prospect of new competing industries setting up in BLNS, has been to protect its own, using almost any device. Of course, economic efficiency considerations would require that any South African industry unable to compete with new industries in BLNS simply be shut down.

Third, any of the smaller countries has a limited number of options to divest itself of the trading links with the more developed partner even where net costs are incurred. For instance, Leith (1992) demonstrates that Botswana incurs a net cost of up to 3.3 per cent of GDP as a result of SACU membership. Even in the realisation of such a cost, the option of withdrawal is not feasible. In a sense, the smaller countries are locked into a peripheral position from which it is impossible to pull out. The only solution is for the more developed partner to adopt a more accommodating attitude, which will enable more equitable relations for mutual long-term advantage.

How can the problem of marginalisation as evidenced in the above analysis be alleviated? There are three possible solutions. First, the principle of compensation for the small countries in the SACU must be upheld. This need not be implemented in the form of cash transfers as has been happening under the 1969 Agreement: alternatives could be conditional financing targeted at industrial development or freer labour mobility. Second, the trading relations of the small countries must consciously be diversified so as to reduce the cost of risk-bearing and dominance dependence. Third, the issue of industrialisation for the small countries must be handled in the context of equitable regional development without sacrificing the principle of comparative advantage.

The fact that most of the countries in the periphery have similar trade patterns has been interpreted by some scholars as indicating very limited opportunities for trade. Whilst this may seemingly be the case from an aggregative perspective, it is not necessarily the case when the focus is on individual products. It is at this level that issues of comparative advantage and transportation cost assume significance. For instance, Swaziland is already exporting significant amounts of secondary products to South Africa and has the potential to supply not only similar products, but also highly processed agro-based products, to other countries in the periphery.

AVOIDING MARGINALISATION THROUGH SECTORAL COOPERATION

Marginalisation may be minimised through sectoral cooperation, which provides significant net gains (part of the non-orthodox gains from economic integration mentioned above) because of its ease of implementation relative to formal integration issues at the aggregate level. Several areas of cooperation are basic to trade enhancement.

1. *Finance*: BLNS together with South Africa were in a *de facto* monetary union until 1974, when Botswana withdrew and introduced its own currency (the pula). Lesotho, Swaziland and Namibia are members of the Common Monetary Area (CMA) with South Africa. However, the rand also has the heaviest weighting in the currency basket used in the exchange rate determination for the pula. Thus, the ground is already fertile for a monetary union in the SACU. To generate some of the gains in this connection, a mechanism for monetary policy coordination could immediately be introduced. For instance, the Governors of the Central Banks could informally make it a habit to contact each other by telephone before introducing monetary changes. Such contact would be intended to discuss the implications of the changes being contemplated and how positive effects can be maximised or adverse consequences be ameliorated.

2. *Industrial development*: A harmonious and coordinated approach towards industrial development entails, *inter alia*, a region-wide policy on measures and incentives directed at attracting both domestic and foreign capital. This is an important point given the likelihood of the new South Africa attracting the great bulk of FDI flowing into the region. However, once firms have established themselves in South Africa, they are likely to open subsidiaries in the neighbouring states, and it

is thus critical that these countries provide an environment conducive to investment. In this regard, a number of countries, including Swaziland, are working towards a simplification of investment procedures in the form, for example, of the 'one-stop shop' – an arrangement whereby all investment applications are decided upon quickly without being referred from one government agency to another. Another measure is the attempt to promote cross-border investment under the CBI. By not restricting private capital to domestic markets, it is argued that an investment culture will be developed for exploiting investment opportunities regionally. It is thus crucial for the smaller states not to engage in competitive behaviour on industrial incentives because this is costly and inefficient. Instead, they should harmonise industrial incentives and place heavy emphasis on an environment of political stability and good industrial relations.

3. *Transport and communications*: That efficient and harmonised transportation is a *sine qua non* for trade (internal or external) is indisputable; that several countries in the region rely on South Africa for their major transportation needs is a fact. With South Africa now in SADC, and greater political stability in Mozambique, regional transportation problems should be solved more easily, but the telecommunications network in most of Southern Africa is of major concern to the business community. One country's efforts at improving telecommunications will not bear fruit if neighbouring countries are not exerting similar efforts, and it is imperative that the improvement of these services now be accorded top priority.

4. *Other sectors*: Small economies in particular, and the region in general, would gain significantly from improved cooperation in fields such as water and energy, tourism and wildlife, and human resource development. There are already elements of cooperative efforts in these fields, but much more can be done. For example, the establishment of a regional electricity grid system would benefit all countries; whereas tourism is Kenya's largest foreign exchange earner, this resource has not been efficiently tapped further south, and joint advertising campaigns would not only be cost-effective but would portray the region as one entity, thereby forging greater regional identity; and a rationalisation of specialised and costly research and training facilities in education and health would enable economies of scale to be realised.

All this cooperation, however, would be nullified unless there is greater political democracy and stability. Illustrations abound of the failure by political leaders to realise that it is their uncontrollable greed for power that has destroyed the economies of the entire continent. They include the post-1992 election war in Angola and the recent Rwandan genocide. In all these cases, it is the quest for political power that is to blame. None of these acts will lead to economic progress; instead, they merely perpetuate the state of marginalisation. Until there is political calm, all other efforts will be in vain. The region should, therefore, work together towards ensuring a stable political environment. It is encouraging to observe that the quick return to normality in Lesotho was instigated by a cooperative effort of, primarily, the leaders of South Africa, Botswana and Zimbabwe. Through pressure from the same group of leaders, RENAMO in Mozambique promised never 'to go back to the bush'. All of these efforts are vital in ensuring an escape from the undesirable state of marginalisation.

CONCLUSION

The solution to the problem of marginalisation for small countries lies in a restructuring of trading relations, innovative strategies and a change of attitude among the partners. Emphasis should be laid on long-term mutual net benefits rather than on short-term net benefits accruing disproportionately to the stronger partner(s).

NOTES

1. The case for integration in general (together with the associated literature) is presented in Simelane (1994: 15–44). The case for integration in Southern Africa (together with the associated literature) is presented in ADB (1993, Vol. 1: 33–203).
2. Trade creation occurs when production is reallocated from high- to low-cost member countries after formation of the union, whereas trade diversion occurs when imports are switched from low-cost sources in the rest of the world to high-cost sources within the union (induced by the tariff wall).

5 Migration and the Brain Drain

Oliver Saasa

A democratic South Africa brings with it new challenges and opportunities to the political and economic relations that have prevailed for decades in Southern Africa. The nature of inter-state alignments during the apartheid years reflected both the general political determination of the region's states to isolate the minority-ruled South Africa and, ironically, the economic realities that obliged the less developed economies to maintain closer economic ties with the despised regime in Pretoria. With respect to labour migration, considerable numbers of people, mainly unskilled, had traditionally trekked to the South African mines for wage employment. Botswana, Lesotho, Mozambique, Malawi, Swaziland, Zimbabwe and, to a lesser extent, Zambia maintained this type of relationship with South Africa both before and after their political independence.

With a democratic government in South Africa, new opportunities are emerging that amount to a peace dividend. Among these are the possibilities of a better organised and reciprocal intra-regional movement of people within Southern Africa, thus departing from the more uni-directional migratory patterns that have dominated the scene up to now. However, there are also peace costs from the new dispensation, namely, the possible restraint that the new government in South Africa may be forced to apply on the movement of people, particularly unskilled labour, into that country at a time when the demand for jobs by the largely marginalised African population there is mounting. Under this new politico-economic scenario, the cost to countries such as Lesotho, Mozambique and Swaziland in terms of the loss of a large labour market for their own citizens could entail significant socio-economic disruptions.

At another level, the emerging hospitable regional climate is expected to ignite the consolidation of another type of labour migration that has up to now been restrained by a number of factors. This refers to the migration of the more specialised professionals away from the less-rewarding states to the 'greener pastures' of Southern Africa, particularly South Africa. While such movement of skilled labour may be seen as a peace dividend in the receiving country (and, thus, be conceived of as positive 'brain circulation'), it could have far-reaching peace costs for these countries which are already in a relatively poor economic condition. The latter group of countries could rightly see such a development as an unacceptable negative 'brain drain'.

Against the above background, this paper attempts to highlight the magnitude of Southern Africa's peace costs and dividends vis-à-vis intra-regional skilled and unskilled labour migration. The aim of the paper is to identify the new challenges at this level of regional cooperation. Due to space restriction, however, no serious effort is made to find answers to the main issues and challenges posed.

UNSKILLED LABOUR MIGRATION

Labour migration within regions is an international phenomenon that is not unique to Southern Africa. Worldwide, in regions where there are marked developmental disparities among the countries, labour has a general tendency to gravitate away from the less to the more developed economies. What makes the Southern African migratory pattern unique is the long period of time over which the system has persisted, with workers being recruited in neighbouring countries on time-limited individual contracts which involve long separations from their families and accommodation in single-sex hostels under apartheid conditions.

From the late nineteenth century until 1976, the majority of workers in the South African mines were recruited from the rest of the subcontinent, but between 1971 and 1986 the proportion fell from 78 per cent to 40 per cent as a result of a campaign to reduce dependence on foreign migrants. In 1994 Lesotho (8700) and Mozambique (51 000) together supplied 83.3 per cent of the 166 000 foreign migrant miners in South Africa (Chamber of Mines, 1995). The last year in which a comprehensive record of foreign migrants in all sectors of the South African economy was kept was 1986, the number standing at 378 126 (Esterhuysen et al., 1994: 71). It is worth noting, however, that a large number of illegal workers, recently estimated at over one million (ibid.), are said to have migrated to South Africa especially from Lesotho and war-torn Mozambique.

Given the above state of affairs, what are the main implications for unskilled labour migrants in the post-apartheid regional context? First, contrary to the general hopes and expectations that South Africa will be the saviour for the region in terms of economic opportunities, it is clear now that, at least in terms of the country's potential as the major employer of regional labour, the new government has to face daunting internal challenges with respect to reserving and creating jobs for its own nationals. One likely possibility – and the signs are already there – is for the government to tighten its immigration laws to make it difficult for foreign unskilled labour to penetrate the limited market. For countries like Lesotho and Mozambique, this could entail serious additional pressures on their formal employment sectors given their heavy dependence on South Africa in this field.

Similarly, the heavy dependence that some of the countries have on mineworkers' remittances could entail a serious decline in economic and social welfare should the situation emerge where a significant cutback on the number of migrant workers is effected by the new government in South Africa. The Lesotho case is a good example in this regard. The remittances of Basotho migrant workers have continued to account for a considerable portion of their country's GDP (73 per cent in 1990). In that same year, approximately 42 per cent of GNP was generated by migrant earnings. Indeed, Lesotho has depended very much on South Africa as the main source of formal sector employment. For example, in 1990, whereas only 45 000 persons were employed in the formal sector within Lesotho itself, a total of 150 000 migrants, mainly men, found employment in South Africa.

The changed political climate in the region, particularly South Africa's entry into the SADC, the democratic transition in Malawi, and the achievement of peace in Angola and Mozambique, has led to the emergence of new challenges and possibilities for organised labour, not least being the workers' pursuit for improved conditions of employment within the regional context. In a region that has been dominated by the migrant labour system, calls for the adoption of harmonised regional labour policies (expressed in terms of the elimination of discrimination, occupational safety, and so on) are becoming more frequent from organised labour. For example, in 1990–1, trade union organisations from all Southern African countries came together to draw up the 'Social Charter on the Fundamental Rights of Workers in Southern Africa'. In this respect, the peace dividend has enabled trade unions to bring to the fore labour issues in the region with a view to facilitating the harmonisation of labour laws, rights and standards, as well as employment conditions.

MIGRATION OF PROFESSIONALS

A recent trend is for increasing numbers of professionals from African countries to emigrate to South Africa. Until recently, a number of factors have militated against the uninterrupted movement of professionals (mainly doctors, lecturers, teachers and engineers) into South Africa. First, relatively few professionals were able to move freely to South Africa in view of the restrictions that were linked to the frontline states' call for economic sanctions against that country. Secondly, the fairly limited opportunities for Black South African professionals during the apartheid period meant that the recruitment of professionals from the region was limited. Thirdly, it is not unreasonable to assume that professionals from the largely anti-apartheid states were perceived by both the minority government and private business as destabilising elements whose freedom of movement to, and settlement in, South Africa could have undermined the apartheid status quo. This is because the more educated people, particularly university academics, have a higher propensity to question and challenge unacceptable systems than their less enlightened counterparts.

Notwithstanding the above, however, there was a sizeable degree of emigration of professionals from Southern Africa to the Bantustans such as Transkei and Bophuthatswana during the period before apartheid was eliminated in South Africa. This type of movement started quietly several years ago when skilled professionals from Africa in general and Southern Africa in particular began to accept jobs in the Bantustans. The universities, hospitals and other specialised bodies in Zambia and Zimbabwe, for example, have experienced serious difficulties due to the steady loss to South Africa of lecturers and professors, engineers, accountants, architects, secondary school teachers and nurses. Zambia, in particular, continues to suffer from this 'brain drain' whereby professionals stream not only to South Africa but also to the other comparatively better paying universities in the region such as those in Botswana, Lesotho and Swaziland. As long as these 'greener pastures' enjoy comparative prosperity, this type of migration is likely to be accentuated in years to come. The major reasons for this brain drain to the more developed parts of Southern Africa include poor salaries, absence of appropriate facilities and equipment, political pressures and the generally poor working environment in the countries losing skilled labour.

Those countries which are affected by the brain drain of high-level manpower have continued to suffer serious damage. They lose their investment in the costly training of professionals, and the contributions of such professionals to the countries' development is forgone. The situation is quite serious in some countries. In Zambia, for example, the loss of lecturers has resulted in the closure of several important programmes, particularly at the post-graduate level. Zimbabwe has lost 75 per cent of its graduate veterinarians since 1985, and 200 of its medical doctors migrated to South Africa and Botswana in 1992 alone (Esterhuysen et al., 1994: 73). It is noteworthy that the brain drain into South Africa also originates from further afield. For example, the South African press reported that, between April 1990 and June 1992, some 2300 foreign doctors were granted limited registration in South Africa. Out of this total, 31 per cent came from Eastern Europe and 24 per cent from Asia, but medical graduates from African countries such as Uganda, Nigeria and Zaire had also been granted limited registration during this period (*Cape Times*, 31 July 1992). An increased demand by South Africa for specialised manpower is likely as more facilities for the Black population are created.

The migration of highly skilled individuals in Southern Africa is by no means one way. A major and quite interesting change has been taking place, beginning just before majority rule in South Africa. This relates to the considerable interest exhibited by South Africans, particularly farmers, in migrating to the less politically turbulent areas of the region in search of a secure investment climate. A number of 'fleeing' South African farmers, evidently unsure of the turn of political events in that country just before the multi-racial elections of early 1994, found their way to countries like Zambia where the agricultural potential is considerable. An organisation has now been formed, with intergovernmental support, to promote the settlement of South African commercial farmers in countries such as Mozambique, Zambia and Gabon, and such movements could compensate for the loss of professionals in the other fields. If sustained, such migration, bringing with it a number of valuable skills in agriculture, could be seen as an intra-regional brain circulation rather than brain drain, a phenomenon that enhances the much sought-out cooperation and integration in Southern Africa.

CONCLUSIONS

It is evident from this brief analysis that countries in Southern Africa are being confronted with new challenges and opportunities which call for a serious effort in addressing the region's imbalances. The democratically elected government in South Africa has to make difficult decisions pertaining both to its internal challenges and the expectations of its much less developed regional partners. Foremost on the agenda is the need to arrive at mutually acceptable – and yet realistic – solutions to a number of regional developmental problems that found their origin in the apartheid system itself. Many such problems have emanated from the form and magnitude of the migrant labour system, and the South African government's policies on immigration could have far-reaching positive or negative consequences for those countries which have depended on the South African labour market for employment. For unskilled labour, restrictive immigration laws could have adverse effects on the region, but a more liberal policy towards the immigration of professionals may have an equally disastrous effect for those countries which will continue to lose their trained human resources. Notwithstanding this paradox, there is increasing agreement among governments in the region that an enabling environment for the free movement of labour and capital should be encouraged under the current liberalised geopolitical and economic conditions. The major challenge thus becomes one of recognising the demerits of protectionism while at the same time acknowledging both the post-apartheid internal challenges in South Africa (mainly the creation of jobs for the marginalised Blacks) and the demands of those countries which have been dependent on the migrant labour system and which have been used by apartheid South Africa as cheap labour reserves.

Part 3

Marginalisation within Countries

6 Income Inequality and Poverty in South Africa

Mike McGrath

In the context of the South African economy, where the apartheid system existed as a malevolent invisible hand which severely distorted the distribution of income, an encompassing perspective of marginalisation is best given by examining those households which are marginal to the economy in terms of their incomes. This paper describes the distribution of income and then examines the extent of poverty before analysing the characteristics of households in the lowest deciles of the income distribution.

INCOME DISTRIBUTION

Income distribution among races is especially significant in South Africa since inequality has historically had a strong racial aspect. Previous research showed that between 1917 and 1970 there was a remarkable constancy in the White share of total personal income. Whites earned about 70 per cent of total income yet constituted less than 20 per cent of the population. This historical constancy was broken between 1970 and 1975 when the White share of income decreased significantly. Analysis of 1991 data showed that this share continued to decline from 1980 and 1991 while the African, Coloured and Indian shares increased.[1] It should, however, be emphasised that this change in income distribution among population groups has been gradual and that the distribution is still heavily skewed in favour of Whites. In 1991 Whites comprised just over 13 per cent of the population yet earned more than 60 per cent of total income, while Africans, who comprised 75 per cent of the population, earned a little over one quarter of total income. It is predictable, therefore, that the majority of marginalised households are likely to be found amongst the African population.

The real economic growth of the South African economy slowed in the decade 1970–9 to an average annual rate of 3.3 per cent, and declined further in the following decade to average 2.2 per cent per annum.

Table 6.1 Per Capita Incomes and Racial Disparity Ratios

	Per capita income (constant 1991 prices)		Per capita income growth p.a. 1980–91 (%)	Disparity ratio White: other		Absolute income gap White: other	
	1980	1991		1980	1991	1980	1991
African	1 742	1 710	–0.2	12.9	12.3	20 810	19 411
White	22 552	21 121	–0.6	–	–	–	–
Coloured	4 295	3 885	–0.9	5.3	5.4	18 257	17 236
Indian	5 742	6 945	1.7	3.9	3.0	16 810	14 176

In the first three years of the 1990s, GDP declined at an average annual rate of 0.6 per cent. In the 1960s over 80 per cent of new entrants to the labour market obtained wage employment, whereas in recent years less than 10 per cent have managed to do so. The reasons for this can be attributed to a slowing of economic growth, capital deepening and annual growth rates of the labour force in excess of 2 per cent over the period 1980–93. Despite substantial growth of the informal sector, the unemployment rate has soared whilst the proportion of the African labour force not in wage employment is estimated to have increased from 37 per cent in 1980 to 55 per cent in 1992.[2] Table 6.1 shows per capita incomes for 1980 and 1991 (in constant 1991 prices) as well as the real annual growth in incomes over that period for each population group, and illustrates the effect of the stagnating economy on incomes per head.

The Indian population group is the only one in which income growth exceeded population growth during the low growth years of the 1980s, and all other groups showed small decreases in their per capita incomes. There was a slight decline in the per capita income disparity between Whites and Africans, but the gap was still enormous, the ratio being over 12:1.

The shares of total income accruing to the poorest 40 per cent, the next 40 per cent, next 10 per cent and the richest 10 per cent of households are shown in Table 6.2. The figures show a worsening income distribution with the poorest 40 per cent of households earning less than 4 per cent of total income in 1991, down from over 5 per cent in 1975.

The Gini coefficients for summarising income inequality for 1975

Table 6.2   Income Shares of Households (%)

	Poorest 40%	Next 40%	Next 10%	Top 10%
1975	5.2	23.9	21.7	49.2
1991	3.9	25.6	19.3	51.2
Change	−25.0	7.1	−11.1	4.1

Table 6.3   Gini Coefficient According to Population Group

Population group	1975	1991
African	0.47	0.62
White	0.36	0.46
Coloured	0.51	0.52
Indian	0.45	0.49
All groups	0.68	0.68

and 1991 are shown in Table 6.3. These coefficients reveal stark increases in inequality amongst African and White households and smaller increases in inequality within the Coloured and Indian communities. At the economy-wide level, the widening income inequality within population groups was almost balanced by the narrowing between groups, resulting in the overall Gini coefficient being unchanged. The increasing inequality within the African community can be explained in terms both of decreasing incomes of the poorest and rising incomes of the richest households. Poorest urban households have been affected by rising unemployment, and rural households by several seasons of severe drought. Wealthy African households, by contrast, have benefited from the erosion of apartheid in the economy resulting in rising incomes of upwardly mobile professionals, skilled workers and entrepreneurs. However, the poor growth performance of the economy has meant that relatively few African households have benefited from economic changes, whilst at the same time many have suffered as a result of rising unemployment and low agricultural output.

Wide income gaps are emerging within both the White and African communities, and together these gaps are gradually taking over from the Black–White income gap as a major explanation of income inequality in South Africa. However, there should be little solace in the finding that the country's maldistribution is increasingly shifting from being race- to being class-based for, irrespective of the racial dimension of income inequality, the gap between rich and poor is so wide as to militate against long-term social stability.

POVERTY

In 1991 48.9 per cent of households in South Africa were estimated to be living in poverty, i.e. with incomes below the 'minimum living level' (MLL). The level of poverty in the four so-called independent homelands (or TBVC states) (76.7 per cent) was substantially higher than that in the rest of the country (43.3 per cent) with the Transkei, Ciskei and Venda having exceptionally high levels. Almost one half (3.4 million) of all households in the country as a whole, containing 17.3 million people, were living below an income level which has been calculated as the minimum on which a household should be able to survive in the short term. Two-thirds (67 per cent) of the African population was living below the poverty income line as against 38 per cent of Coloureds, 18 per cent of Indians and 6.7 per cent of Whites.

Tentative comparisons of the extent of poverty over time can be made by comparing McGrath's 1975 estimates with 1991 data. In order to make the estimates comparable, the 1991 estimates of poverty given above had to be recalculated using the MLL for the average-sized African household as the poverty line. The results show that decreases in poverty within the Coloured and Indian communities have been substantial. The incomes of the fifth decile of Coloured households increased between 1975 and 1991, and this led to a decrease in poverty in this group from 52 per cent to 38.6 per cent of households. Similarly, the mean income of the third decile of Indian households increased, drawing these households out of poverty. The overall poverty level of Indian households thus decreased from 30 per cent to approximately 19.6 per cent. A comparison of the 1975 and 1991 results show that the poverty level within the African community fell slightly from 68 per cent to 67.2 per cent. Incomes of the eighth decile of African households declined, yet this decline was probably insufficient to lower many of these households to below the poverty income. Households in deciles 1 to 7 were already in poverty in 1975, and have suffered substantial decreases in real income per head since then, indicating that poverty has deepened; that is, the households already in poverty have been pushed further into poverty over this period. The results also show an opposing trend within the White population group, the extent of poverty more than trebling from 3 per cent to 9.5 per cent between 1975 and 1991. The mean real income of the lowest decile decreased almost five-fold, and this brought almost all households in this decile to below the poverty income level.

DETERMINANTS OF THE INCOME DISTRIBUTION

This section analyses important determinants of the distribution of household incomes based on data from the 1991 Population Census. The tapes of the Census contain data on 20 household income classes split into urban/rural residence, economically important characteristics of the household head and limited data about the composition of the household such as its size and the number of earners and unemployed members. There are data on age category, education level, sex and occupational status for the household head only.[3]

The characteristics of a random sample of households drawn from the census are shown in Table 6.4. The sample exhibits the large income disparities which typify the racial distribution of income in South Africa. Average household sizes vary significantly by race group with White households averaging 3.25 and African households nearly 5 members. Although White households are markedly smaller, the mean number of earners per household considerably exceeds the figure for Indian and African households, whilst the mean number of dependants in White households is nearly 50 per cent smaller than in Coloured and Indian, and over 60 per cent less than in African, households. African and Coloured households exhibit much higher average levels of open unemployment than for the sample as a whole, with one household in four having an unemployed member compared to approximately one in six for the sample as a whole. Predictably, the mean urbanisation rate for African households of 28.8 per cent is far below the rate for the other racial groups.

The characteristics of the heads of households also yield valuable insights: a much larger proportion of African households are headed by women, reflecting *inter alia* the ravaging effects of migrant labour, urbanisation pressures and a high illegitimacy ratio. African households also have the highest proportion of households headed by a member whose age exceeds 60 years, and by a member who is not economically active. The distribution of occupations and levels of education reflect the historically unequal distribution of opportunities and employment between races.

Table 6.4 Characteristics of South African Households (excluding TBVC areas)

	All households	White	Coloured	Indian	African
N	3826	1405	507	178	1736
Characteristics of All Members					
Income per capita (R)	8790	19 120	4051	6 540	2066
Size (no. persons)	4.25	3.25	4.72	4.31	4.91
No. of earners (W)	1.64	1.95	1.97	1.77	1.28
No. of unemployed (U)	0.17	0.05	0.27	0.15	0.23
No. of dependants[a](D)	2.44	1.25	2.48	2.39	3.40
Area: Urban (M_1)	0.621	0.925	0.801	0.955	0.288
Non-urban (M_2)	0.379	0.075	0.199	0.045	0.712
Characteristics of Household Heads (%)					
Sex: Male (S_1)	69.3	79.9	78.5	83.7	56.5
Female (S_2)	30.7	20.1	21.5	16.3	43.5
Age group (years)					
< 21 (A_1)	2.8	2.6	2.2	1.1	3.3
22–9 (A_2)	12.9	13.7	13.6	9.6	12.4
30–9 (A_3)	24.7	22.1	28.0	30.9	25.2
40–9 (A_4)	21.7	22.8	22.9	28.7	19.7
50–9 (A_5)	16.1	17.6	16.0	15.7	15.4
60+ (A_6)	21.9	21.7	17.4	14.0	24.1
Level of Education (years completed)					
0 (E_0)	21.6	0.4	16.4	5.1	41.9
1–7 (E_1)	19.8	1.7	34.7	13.5	30.7
8–10 (E_2)	25.3	29.3	34.3	44.9	17.5
11–12 (E_3)	28.8	58.0	13.8	32.0	9.1
13+ (E_4)	4.6	10.6	0.8	4.5	0.9
Occupational Status					
Professional and managerial (0_1)	14.2	29.2	4.7	18.0	4.6
Clerical and service workers (0_2)	10.9	18.0	10.1	22.5	4.1
Farming (0_3)	10.5	3.5	15.6	1.1	15.6
Artisan (0_4)	8.5	13.9	11.0	11.2	3.2
Not economically active (0_5)	32.4	21.0	21.7	24.2	45.5
Production workers & unskilled (0_6)	22.4	13.8	34.7	21.3	25.9
Unemployed (0_7)	1.1	0.6	2.2	1.7	1.2

Note: a. Dependants = household size − (earners + unemployed). A household head who is not an earner or unemployed will be classified as being dependent.

The data-set provides the opportunity to examine the distribution of household per capita incomes divided into quintiles. This classification is convenient because the bottom two quintiles of households correspond very closely to households below the MLL.[4] The lowest quintile of households in the per capita distribution lie below R400 per annum. This represents households in chronic poverty (with per capita incomes approximately 25 per cent of the MLL).

The mean characteristics of households in the quintiles of the distribution of household per capita incomes are shown in Table 6.5. It is noteworthy that the size of households falls almost monotonically from 5.31 to 3.11 from the poorest to the most affluent quintile, while the number of earners rises steadily from 0.46 to 2.11 per household (again ranged from the lowest to highest quintile). The lowest income households (that is, in the first quintile) have 4.56 dependants per household, including the unemployed members who average 28 per 100 households. In sharp contrast, households in the highest quintile have a smaller number of unemployed members (a mere 3 per 100 households) and average only one dependent member per household. The poorest households are concentrated in rural areas, with 80 and 57 per cent respectively of households in the lowest two quintiles being resident there, while the upper quintile contains an overwhelming predominance of urbanised households.

The sex of the head of household also appears to be important in determining income levels. Of those households in rural areas in deep poverty, 63 per cent are headed by females, and thereafter the proportion of female heads of households falls as one moves upwards in the quintile distribution. These data show too that the incomes of the poorest households are clearly related to a lack of employment and income-generating opportunities in rural areas where individuals often bond in household structures around the pensioner breadwinner.

The educational and occupational status of heads plays a major role in determining household income. Heads who are professionals or managers account for 42 per cent of occupations in the top quintile of incomes, whilst the lowest 40 per cent of households are headed by individuals who are not economically active or who fall into the farming or the residual occupational categories. The returns to education are clearly displayed by the high proportion of poor households headed by individuals with primary school education or lower (levels E_0 and E_1), whilst in the upper quintile 78 per cent of heads have completed secondary or tertiary education.

The racial dimensions of the distribution are also striking for African households account for 91 and 71 per cent respectively of the

Table 6.5 Mean Characteristics of Households in the Distribution of Household per capita Income by Quintile (excluding TBVC areas)

	1st quintile (lowest)	2nd quintile	3rd quintile	4th quintile	5th quintile (highest)
Mean per capita household income (R)	130	961	3304	9246	29 956
Characteristics of Households:					
Racial Group(%)					
White	0.02	0.06	0.18	0.64	0.91
Coloured	0.04	0.21	0.28	0.12	0.02
Indian	0.02	0.02	0.10	0.08	0.02
African	0.91	0.71	0.50	0.16	0.05
Size of household (no.)	5.31	5.12	4.19	3.53	3.11
Earners (no.)	0.46	1.71	1.91	1.98	2.11
Unemployed (no.)	0.28	0.25	0.49	0.07	0.03
Dependants (no.)	4.56	3.15	1.86	1.48	0.97
Characteristics of Household Heads (%):					
Education level					
E_0	49.1	39.1	16.8	2.9	0.6
E_1	29.2	35.0	23.7	6.1	0.5
E_2	14.8	18.3	34.9	38.3	20.1
E_3	6.8	7.5	18.6	48.6	61.4
E_4	0.1	0.1	1.0	4.3	17.3
Age group					
A_1	7.1	1.5	1.8	2.3	1.2
A_2	12.2	9.9	12.0	15.0	15.4
A_3	21.1	27.4	25.5	26.7	22.8
A_4	20.2	18.3	23.0	22.4	24.5
A_5	15.3	15.8	15.9	14.6	19.0
A_6	24.2	27.2	21.9	19.0	17.2
Sex					
Male	37.0	69.0	77.0	78.8	84.4
Female	63.0	31.0	23.0	21.2	15.6
Area of domicile					
Urban	19.9	40.9	68.6	88.5	91.6
Non-urban	80.1	59.2	31.3	11.5	8.4
Occupational status					
O_1	0.9	2.0	6.8	18.9	42.1
O_2	1.6	4.9	11.5	18.8	17.4
O_3	8.9	24.9	12.3	3.3	3.2
O_4	1.6	4.9	9.2	15.1	11.7
O_5	75.5	32.2	23.2	18.9	12.3
O_6	9.0	30.5	35.6	24.3	12.9
O_7	2.5	0.7	1.3	0.8	0.4

marginalised group (the lowest two quintiles). White households make up a mere 2 and 6 per cent respectively of these two quintiles. At the upper spectrum of the distribution, the picture is radically different, with African households accounting for a mere 5 per cent of households in the top quintile whilst White households account for almost 92 per cent. In total, 85 per cent of White households are found in the fourth and fifth quintiles.

CONCLUSION

Even though the African share of personal income increased after 1970, and the per capita disparity ratio between White and African incomes narrowed, the share of income accruing to the poorest 40 per cent of households declined, and by 1991 the poorest 40 per cent earned less than 4 per cent of total income. Notwithstanding this worsening of income distribution, an estimate for 1991 showed that the extent of poverty had diminished slightly since 1975, although the proportion of African households in poverty had remained unchanged.

An analysis of household characteristics indicates that demographic, economic and social variables all contribute to the process of depressing the incomes of those households in the bottom 40 per cent of the income distribution. Higher educational attainment and higher skilled occupational status are associated with raising household incomes, whilst transfer payments are important sources of income for poor households. Attention is also focused on the depressing effects on household income of domicile in a rural area, higher unemployment and dependency ratios, and a lack of human capital. The high proportion of poor households headed by females is vividly shown.

This analysis can contribute to determining priorities in the Reconstruction and Development Programme. The creation of human capital must be given a high priority, as must measures to increase earnings and economic participation in rural areas. Rebuilding the family in African society will also play a major role in combating marginalisation. The high dependency ratio of poor households plays a major role in determining household per capita income, and policies to slow the growth rate of the population and to increase the growth of employment are essential if income inequality, poverty and marginalisation are to be reduced.

Notes

1. The data and analysis of sections 2 and 3 draw extensively on McGrath and Whiteford (1994) and Whiteford and McGrath (1994).
2. The estimate for Whites is 21 per cent and for Indians/Coloureds 34 per cent (Fallon and da Silva, 1994).
3. A random 0.05 per cent sample of the households was drawn from the tape of the 1991 Population Census, yielding a sample of 4280 households. However, the records for 454 households could not be used because they had missing data for at least one of the variables to be analysed. After omitting the households with missing data, the final sample which resulted contained 3826 households.
4. On a per capita basis for 1991, the MLL was approximately R1580 per annum. The per capita income dividing the bottom two quantiles of the distribution was R1711, and only 0.8 per cent of the population of households lay between the MLL and this income.

7 Public Expenditure and Poverty in Namibia

Irene Tlhase with Tjiuai Kangueehi

This paper examines the Namibian case of marginalisation, relating it to government expenditure particularly on education and health. This is done in the realisation that Africa still suffers from domination in the psychological sense: Africans behave as an appendage of the Western system, economically, culturally and socially. The designs of political leaders differ from the needs, expectations and aspirations of the people, and this weakness is partly responsible for Africa's marginalisation. This situation will not be corrected until the direct involvement of the people is apparent through participatory democracy. If sub-Saharan Africa is to ensure economic security and sustainable livelihoods for its people, it needs to follow social and economic policies which address the most fundamental needs of the people, particularly vulnerable groups like women, youth, children and the rural and urban poor. The overall message of the Namibian experience of marginalisation is that patterns of public expenditure in the post-independence period largely fail to address these needs.

INEQUALITY

The Namibian economy is characterised by its small size, relative openness and its reliance on the production of primary commodities both for its export earnings and national output. It is sensitive to, and dependent on, developments both in neighbouring countries and in the world economy, being particularly influenced by external demand for its three most important exports (diamonds, fish and meat products) and by conditions in the South African economy.

Namibia's real GNP at constant 1985 prices grew at an annual average rate of less than 0.3 per cent during the 1980s. With a population growth rate of 3.5 per cent per annum over that period, real per capita incomes declined in the aggregate by nearly 22 per cent over the decade. Real GDP grew at an average annual rate of only 0.1 per cent during the decade as a result of declining investment caused by political uncertainty. After independence, however, real GDP grew rapidly in 1991 and 1992 (by 6.9 per cent and 7.5 per cent respectively) before declining by 1.6 per cent in 1993 and recovering to record a growth rate of an estimated 5.5 per cent in 1994.

The inherited inequalities of opportunity and material wealth from the previous apartheid regime are commonly considered to be among the most extreme in the world. Economic and social change, therefore, holds the key to transforming Namibia from a country of extreme inequality to one of general prosperity since no society can look forward to a stable and prosperous future while social and economic indicators show highly skewed income and wage differentials between races. In 1988, it was estimated that 5 per cent of the population (mostly Whites) earned more than 70 per cent of the national income, whilst the poorest 55 per cent (mostly Blacks) earned a mere 3 per cent. Per capita GDP for Whites was 22 and 233 times higher than for Blacks in the wage and traditional sectors respectively (Gaomab, 1994: 1).

Namibia also inherited an inequitable system of law, education, health and taxation. During the past five years of independence, government has been changing discriminatory laws and regulations, but it is faced with the task of striking a balance between welfare spending and spending which increases productivity and future revenue. Clearly, there is a need for redistribution, but this must not endanger the most productive areas of the economy on which the country's future depends. Policies to improve the quality of living of all on a sustainable basis must not only focus on the poorest in the society but, for long-term development, must assist those parts of the economy which are already successful so that they can benefit a growing number of people.

There has been no increase in total consumption expenditure as a proportion of GDP. Because of rising inflation, an increased personal tax burden and limited growth in salaries of civil servants, Namibia is faced with a downward drift of real personal disposable income per capita. This has led to a levelling off in real private consumption expenditure and to increased indebtedness and reduced savings rates by households. The policy has been to restrain government total expenditure whilst redirecting its composition away from infrastructural development and other expenditure benefiting mainly the elite groups towards spending on social services, in particular education and health.

The pre-independence period was characterised by a highly unequal allocation of expenditures across regions: it favoured regions such as Windhoek (the capital) at the expense of the north where more than

50 per cent of the population lives. This bias has not yet been overcome. For example, there was extreme inequality in the education system at independence: separate systems for each racial group concentrated resources on the education of a small (mainly urban) minority to the neglect of the majority of the population. This inequality still persists today, despite much of the focus of post-independence policy being on strengthening access to primary education and improving its quality. Thus, Windhoek has 15 per cent of the primary school population but receives 22 per cent of the budget, while Ondangwa East with 26 per cent of the primary school population receives only 15 per cent of that budget. Windhoek also dominates the secondary school budget. The differences between the regions in education expenditures are accounted for primarily by differences in personnel costs, school capital costs and boarding costs.

The pre-independence health system showed extreme inequalities of provision, and therefore of expenditure, across the regions. Altering these allocations is not a straightforward or rapid process. The issues regarding health expenditure, therefore, are similar to those of the education sector. There has been a consistent growth in expenditure in all regions except the north-east, while the north-west remains seriously disadvantaged compared to the rest of the country when per capita expenditure is compared across the regions. Yet, since the northern regions contain the largest share of Namibia's population, any major expansion of primary health care must be focused on them. A major constraint impeding a swift reallocation of resources towards disadvantaged regions is the continued urban bias which favours the best-endowed facilities. The health sector has taken on average 14 per cent of the national budget over the past five years, which is high by international standards. Although this reflects the government's aim to improve health, an analysis of the composition of health expenditure does not reflect a balance between community and specialised services. A bias towards spending more on specialised services is clearly evident through examining health status indicators alongside the composition of spending.

According to recent surveys, the poor are mainly rural but with a significant peri-urban component in Windhoek and smaller towns. Households are more likely to be in poverty if they are female-headed and if the head has had no (or very little) education (Namibia CSO, 1994). The majority are dependent on subsistence farming and remittances from relatives, and are more dependent on pensions than the average Namibian.

Namibia is one of the few countries in Africa to operate a universal state pension scheme. This is non-contributory and is the most important component of social services expenditure. The scheme started before independence and was characterised by the unequal provision for different racial groups. The government has decided to equalise pensions but, because it cannot afford the rate to be at the level paid to Whites, it has adopted a policy of freezing pensions for Whites at current levels and allowing other pensions to increase through gradual adjustments. In 1994 the maximum pension was N$382 per month for Whites as against N$120 per month for Africans.

A preliminary survey (CSO, 1994) indicates pensions as the most important source of income for poor households. The scheme currently covers 61 per cent of the eligible population (those aged over 60 years and the disabled). Coverage varies significantly between regions, for example, from 30 per cent in Kavango to 80 per cent in Ovambo, reflecting differences in administrative efficiency among the defunct second-tier authorities. The administration and disbursement of pensions is cumbersome and costly: with pensions being paid out in cash, substantial sums of money have to be transported for long distances. However, efforts are being made to pay urban pensioners by means of transfers to their bank accounts. Reducing the costs of disbursing rural pensions is more problematic given the much lower frequency of savings accounts in such areas.

SECTORAL STRATEGIES AND POLICIES TO ALLEVIATE POVERTY

Although imbalances in resource allocation were inherited from the apartheid period, the marginalisation of disadvantaged groups has persisted because the practical implementation of policies to narrow income gaps has proved difficult.

The government's commitment to spending more on the social sectors assumes that the completion of secondary school education is the principal strategy for achieving equality. However, whilst education is a necessity, it may not be a sufficient part of a redistributional strategy. This is already evidenced by the numbers of Namibians with completed secondary schooling who are unemployed because the modern economy has no space for them. Despite the policy changes since independence poor households devote considerable amounts of their resources to education to make up shortfalls in state provision. The poor still receive the lowest allocation per capita of the education budget and pay the highest proportion of their income towards education.

The analysis of household living standards shows that pensions are an important source of income for the poor. However, it does not follow from this that the state pension scheme is an effective means of targeting the poor given its universal coverage (all pensioners receive the same amount regardless of their income) and its high administrative costs.

In agriculture, certain services of the Department of Agriculture and Rural Development, notably fertiliser subsidies and credit programmes, have ceased to favour the large commercial farmers. However, they now favour the middle-income farmers rather than the poor, as the latter do not have the resource base to enjoy the benefit of these services. Rural infrastructure has been receiving much more attention in the post-independence period, although there remains much to be done. In particular, an augmented programme of rural road construction in the poorer regions should be effected through the increased use of labour-intensive methods in road construction and maintenance.

Public expenditure, when combined with appropriate policies, has a significant role to play in the reduction of poverty. Ensuring access to primary education and primary health[1] care is especially important for the poor, but investments in agriculture and transport can also play major roles by providing supporting infrastructure. For example, the incomes of small farmers are influenced by the availability of transport, storage and irrigation infrastructure. The key to poverty reduction in this respect is achieving labour-intensive growth which is critical to poor households whose major productive asset is their labour. This encompasses self-employment both in agriculture and in micro-enterprises.

The sectoral strategies and policies for education, health and agriculture indicate the extent to which the government is committed to reduce poverty in the medium term. These policy statements (Namibia National Planning Commission, 1994) are positive steps towards reducing the inequalities existing across regions and racial groups. Reflecting even more commitment from the government to address distributional issues is the current joint World Bank Expenditure Review which not only aims to ensure an improvement in public finance but also attempts to redress the inequities of apartheid.

A number of policy recommendations arise out of the analysis in this chapter. First, the optimal strategy for economic development is to take public measures necessary to accelerate growth in the agricultural sector. This is the dominant sector, and the poor are located largely in the rural areas. This point needs emphasising at a time when foreign aid agencies are turning away from assistance to the agricultural sector and the institutional development which is so essential to its progress.

Secondly, government expenditure policy should be reviewed in order to ensure that it is responsive to the country's changing needs. The government should avoid the risk of spending on the social sectors at unsustainable levels and underspending in the most productive areas of the economy. Social services expansion should, therefore, be balanced by government expenditure which encourages production and the provision of employment, for example, investment in housing.

Thirdly, Namibia needs to slow down its population growth in order to reduce poverty within the shortest possible time. In addition to aggravating poverty, the growing population has adversely affected the environment by increasing the encroachment on forests and by intensifying farming, resulting in soil erosion and stagnating yields. It is, therefore, imperative that government develop rational family planning programmes.

Finally, women have a pivotal role to play in poverty alleviation both because of their strategic position in the household and the productive work they do outside. Although there has been much recognition of this role, there remains a great deal of tokenism in supporting and strengthening their activities. The close interdependence between what women produce and earn and the size of the family, whether a family has sufficient food to eat, or whether daughters go to school, implies that there can be no stable, long-term response to the problems of poverty if the productivity and incomes of women are not improved.

NOTES

1. Since output is raised by human capital investment, the problems of a 'trade-off' between economic growth and poverty reduction is less significant than is often supposed, provided that poverty reduction strategy is implemented through concentrating public resources on those services that are most important for the poor.

8 Provincial Marginalisation: KwaZulu-Natal

Nick Wilkins

This paper discusses marginalisation and strategies to overcome it at the provincial level in South Africa, focusing on KwaZulu-Natal. The paper discusses the developmental status of KwaZulu-Natal and outlines possible strategies for the promotion of sustainable development.

IS KWAZULU-NATAL MARGINALISED?

In order to assess the level of development of KwaZulu-Natal relative to the other eight provinces and the rest of the country, its output, labour and quality-of-life indicators are compared with the national averages in Table 8.1. It is clear that KwaZulu-Natal is below the national average on all indicators except for average real annual growth in GGP during the 1980s, and the latter achievement is of little comfort since its economy is growing from a low base. Moreover, it ranks among the four least developed provinces on five of the indicators. Only in contribution to GGP can KwaZulu-Natal be rated among the three leading economic performers in the country, having overtaken the Western Cape during the 1970s to contribute 14.5 per cent to South Africa's real GGP in 1988, second only to Gauteng's 37 per cent.

KwaZulu-Natal had the largest population (8.55 million) and the second highest density in 1993. However, its labour force participation rate was the third lowest in 1991; despite this low rate, the province experienced the highest unemployment rate in 1991. This apparent anomaly may be due to the fact that perceptibly high unemployment discourages prospective work-seekers from looking for jobs. Dependency ratios are usually inversely related to participation rates; KwaZulu-Natal registered the third highest overall dependency rate in 1991, largely because juvenility (the proportion of the population aged 0–14 years) was higher than the national figure. Hence, with low labour force participation rates, a high rate of unemployment and high dependency rates, it can be inferred that a comparatively large proportion of the

Nick Wilkins

Table 8.1 Comparison of Output, Employment and Quality-of-Life Indicators for KwaZulu-Natal with the National Average, 1988

Indicator	KwaZulu-Natal	Total SA	KZN rank (n = 9)
Nominal GGP per capita	70	100	7
Nominal GGP/worker	79	100	6
Real annual GGP growth rate (1980–8)	135	100	4
Unemployment rate	130	100	9
Labour absorption	90	100	7
Dependency ratio	121	100	7
Literacy rate (1991)	94	100	5

Source: Calculated from Development Bank of Southern Africa (1994: 18).

population of KwaZulu-Natal is excluded from the formal economy and in effect, therefore, is economically marginalised.

Although it is clear that the province compares poorly with most of the others in terms of quality-of-life indicators, Table 8.2, which contains a breakdown of provincial GGP by economic sector, shows that the economy is very similar to that of Gauteng and the Western Cape in terms of the importance of the sophisticated secondary (manufacturing) and tertiary (finance and commerce) sectors. Indeed, KwaZulu-Natal makes the second highest contribution to national GGP, it has the second largest manufacturing output, its industry contributes the largest share to provincial GGP (followed by non-primary sectors), and it contains the second largest metropolitan region (Durban) in the country as well as South Africa's two largest ports (Durban and Richards Bay). These factors are all characteristic of a relatively high level of development. In addition, it enjoys ample water and tourism resources. However, while KwaZulu-Natal contributes 15 per cent of the country's economic output, it houses 26 per cent of the population, a statistic which highlights the ambiguity in the developmental status of the province.

A recent workshop noted that KwaZulu-Natal has inherited a socio-economic and spatial imbalance which is deep and difficult to overcome (Hindson, 1994: 2). This imbalance has to do with race, gender and the spatial allocation of resources within the economy, and causes glaring problems of unemployment, poverty, and so on. The contrast between economic and social performance in KwaZulu-Natal is, therefore, explicable in terms of the fact that the majority of the population

Table 8.2   Contribution to GGP (at Factor Cost, Constant 1985 Prices) by Economic Sector, 1988 (%)

Sector	Gauteng	West Cape	KZ-Natal	Mpumalanga	Free State	North West	East Cape	North Cape	Northern	Total SA
Agriculture	0.7	8.9	7.8	10.9	12.9	7.5	8.1	12.4	15.0	6.3
Mining	10.9	0.3	2.6	22.5	30.8	51.9	0.2	30.3	14.8	13.4
Manufacturing	28.0	24.9	30.2	22.1	13.3	10.4	24.4	4.6	8.8	23.7
Electricity	2.3	3.5	2.2	23.0	5.3	0.9	3.0	3.7	6.5	4.5
Construction	3.2	3.5	3.5	1.8	2.7	3.1	3.7	1.8	4.7	3.2
Commerce	13.6	15.4	12.2	4.8	6.7	6.4	12.9	8.5	9.1	11.6
Transport	8.6	10.0	12.6	3.4	6.5	3.6	10.8	13.2	4.4	8.5
Finance	15.4	14.1	10.3	3.5	7.3	5.8	9.9	7.3	6.5	11.4
Community services	17.3	19.6	18.6	8.1	14.5	10.5	27.0	18.3	30.1	17.5
Total	100.0	100.0	100.0	100.0	100.0	100.0	100.0	100.0	100.0	100.0

Source: Development Bank of Southern Africa (1994: 116).

are disadvantaged and are generally excluded from the formal economy which generates the vast bulk of output. Particularly in rural areas, the African population tends to suffer from low skill levels and poor access to resources, education and employment. As in the rest of South Africa, most resources and skills are concentrated within a small section of the population. Thus, impoverished communities experience a serious capacity mismatch: they face the most severe developmental challenges, yet lack the resources with which to harness the will towards self-improvement.

The socio-economic vulnerability of KwaZulu-Natal is worsened by the fact that much of its industry is highly capital-intensive. Moreover, given relatively high labour costs and low skills, the more labour-intensive sectors remain internationally uncompetitive. Critical manufacturing subsectors such as clothing and textiles are becoming increasingly vulnerable to foreign competition in domestic (let alone export) markets as a result of tariff reductions on imports in terms of South Africa's commitments to the WTO.

A major threat facing the province is the HIV/AIDS epidemic: KwaZulu-Natal has consistently recorded the highest levels of HIV prevalence in South Africa; the latest survey of women attending antenatal clinics in late 1994 showed that over 14 per cent were HIV-positive. This was nearly double the national average of 7.57 per cent and higher than the next most badly affected province, Mpumalanga, which recorded 12.16 per cent HIV-positivity. These figures are cause for great concern since the prevalence of HIV amongst antenatal clinic attenders is a reliable guide to the level of HIV infection amongst sexually active adults in general. The socio-economic burden imposed by the HIV/AIDS epidemic on KwaZulu-Natal will take several forms, including the removal from the labour force of workers who will typically only recently have completed their education and training, and will not yet have repaid the social investment in their upbringing. The removal of skilled and semi-skilled workers will have a more direct impact on industry in the province due to the serious skills shortages already experienced in several sectors.

Further complications are that local authorities in many areas of the province are not functioning, which is a serious obstacle to the implementation of the RDP, and roles for national, provincial and local government in the facilitation of development have yet to be clearly defined (Hindson, 1994). These political and administrative difficulties will not only hold up development programmes in KwaZulu-Natal, but will continue to have a serious impact on private investment. The province needs to project a positive image to potential overseas investors, but the mood of domestic corporate investors is even more critical as they are responsible for the bulk of new fixed investment in South Africa.

Given the socio-economic weaknesses mentioned above, it is clear that KwaZulu-Natal is threatened with economic marginalisation in several respects. Strategic manufacturing sub-sectors are threatened with the loss of domestic and foreign markets, investors regard the province as a high security risk, and communities which are themselves already economically marginalised are likely to experience increased difficulties.

KwaZulu-Natal is no different from, and may be better off than, several other provinces since many of the disabilities listed above are not peculiar to it alone. However, there are signs that recent economic activity is concentrating in Gauteng and the Western Cape, and that KwaZulu-Natal, despite its geographic, climatic and resource advantages, is being sidelined. The major reason for this is the levels of political violence and instability which have become more or less endemic: the major party in the provincial government and the ANC (the major national party) are at loggerheads. It is clear that an immediate priority must be the ending of political violence which has a debilitating effect on people who could otherwise be channelling their energy into constructive work. Violence, the political impasse (which has been manifested *inter alia* in a struggle over the choice of a provincial capital and in political rivalry between the provincial government and the Greater Durban Metropolitan Authority) and the worsening crime rate are severely undermining confidence within the province and with respect to prospective tourists and investors. It is feared that the HIV/AIDS epidemic might cause even further political instability since it has a disproportionately heavy impact on economically marginalised communities.

STRATEGIES FOR SUSTAINABLE DEVELOPMENT

Clearly, the highest priority in reviving socio-economic development in KwaZulu-Natal is the eradication of political violence and the stabilisation or 'normalisation' of political activity. Furthermore, a solution to the rising crime rate must be found, which itself is exacerbated by socio-economic imbalances which cause conflict around scarce resources in disadvantaged communities. It has been recognised that 'without growth redistribution is limited by resources; without redistribution growth is limited by instability' (Morris, 1994: 3). It is therefore crucial that the Reconstruction and Development Programme (RDP) launched by the national government soon begins to have a positive impact on KwaZulu-Natal. The two central objectives of the RDP are the improvement of the quality of life and economic growth to ensure the sustainability of the programme.

It is clearly essential for successful development that employment creation be a high priority, but this requires an increase in the real economic growth rate, possibly to above 5 per cent per annum. Manufacturing, transport and tourism have traditionally been the growth sectors in the provincial economy and have considerable potential for further expansion. For example, the province has advantages with regard to the promotion of export industry, being ideally situated to exploit opportunities offered by markets in the Indian Ocean Rim; KwaZulu-Natal's strong advantage in the transport sector could be consolidated by current plans for harbour expansion at Durban and Richards Bay, which should improve the competitive position of these ports; while tourism (based on ocean, mountain and wildlife attractions) could grow strongly.

In addition, KwaZulu-Natal has considerable surplus water resources, and the development of infrastructure to deliver water to the proposed Tugela-Vaal Transfer Scheme, for example, would yield many benefits to the Tugela Basin and ultimately to the province as a whole (Hofmeyr and Wilkins, 1995). The construction of a large complex of dams and pipelines in the Tugela Basin, installed largely at the expense of consumers in the Vaal Basin, would provide benefits not only when the

Nick Wilkins

infrastructure has been paid for, but also immediately. The presence of the dams will provide water for additional irrigation, as well as for piping to rural communities presently without a regular water supply. Those dependent on the rivers of the basin below the proposed dam sites would receive an assured supply of relatively clean water. There are opportunities for the conjunctive use of water between the Umgeni and Vaal Basins and for electricity generation via existing and proposed pumped storage schemes. The considerable investment required over a substantial period will generate not only an increased direct demand for labour and resources from the local economy, but will also have large multiplier effects, which could provide a major long-term boost to the provincial economy. Even in terms of the most conservative option, the Tugela-Vaal Transfer Scheme offers clear net economic gains to KwaZulu-Natal.

However, the implementation of the RDP in the province has already encountered problems. First, the central government has seen its primary task as the restructuring of national, provincial and local government budgets to free funds for development projects. The central government's RDP Fund was intended *inter alia* to help the different tiers of government to achieve economic growth through strict fiscal discipline: key development programmes identified by such bodies would initially be financed only through the restructuring of their own budgets. Not surprisingly, this proposal has met with resistance from officials at all levels of government.

Furthermore, the inevitable reliance of the RDP on the provincial administrations themselves to propose development projects has run into capacity constraints in several provinces. It has been reported that substantial sums from the RDP Fund, long earmarked for the 'topping up' of development programmes in KwaZulu-Natal, have not yet been allocated due to the inability of the provincial administration to plan and implement the projects concerned effectively. It is not surprising that the major recommendations from a recent workshop concerned the speeding-up of the integration of provincial and local government bureaucracies, and the clarification of the roles and functions of the various levels and forms of government.

The private sector maintains that provincial government should consider funding the development of an industrial policy. Those elements of industrial policy on which there is consensus should be implemented as soon as possible so that there are visible signs of progress. One immediate priority is seen to be the nurturing of small, micro- and medium-sized enterprises (SMMEs), which are not necessarily merely a survival strategy adopted by the economically marginalised, but offer a path to formal business development for those with entrepreneurial aptitude. Priorities in SMME development include the rehabilitation of small businesses devastated by violence and left insolvent, assistance in gaining access to formal sector markets and opportunities for SMMEs to become integrated into the major formal business clusters. Provincial government has a major role to play in these initiatives.

As an interim measure to provide temporary jobs to as many unemployed as possible, it is clear that labour-intensive methods should be used for infrastructural development wherever economically viable. Labour-based construction programmes could have a significant positive impact on disadvantaged communities, alleviating unemployment in the short term through the provision of public infrastructure such as roads, schools, clinics and low-cost housing, and helping to liberate many from the cycle of poverty in which they appear to be trapped. Research has highlighted the socio-economic benefits of implementing a labour-based public works programme in South Africa (ERU, 1993), and guidelines for the planning and implementation of such a programme at national level have gained broad consensus (NEF, 1994). The way is clear for provinces to reap the benefits of such programmes if the capacity constraints described above with respect to the implementation of the RDP can be overcome.

Given the serious skills shortages and the general capacity mismatch in KwaZulu-Natal, education and training are obviously of vital importance to the province's development. However, because the formal education system will take several years to restructure, adult basic education and training, including industry training, has been proposed as the appropriate strategy to facilitate economic and social development at a sufficiently rapid pace in the short to medium term. A crucial constraint here is financing, and it will be necessary to tap the private sector and foreign aid donors.

There is little new or surprising in the list of development initiatives which should be undertaken in order to redeem KwaZulu-Natal from its apparently growing marginalisation both within South Africa and internationally. What is new in KwaZulu-Natal is the volatile political environment in which these initiatives have to be planned and implemented, and the political structures which must oversee them. It is these aspects of development which offer the biggest challenge to the province if it is to avoid marginalisation and realise its economic potential.

Part 4

Choosing Winning Policies

9 Asian Lessons in Sustainable Development

Seiji Naya

The sharp contrast in recent decades between the accelerated growth of economies in East and South-East Asia and the apparent economic retrogression in much of sub-Saharan Africa has drawn much analytical and policy-making attention. Although it is important to understand why this wide disparity has occurred, the more pertinent question may be: are there any lessons from the Asian experience which may prove relevant for African policy-makers as they seek to promote development and to avoid marginalisation?

This paper attempts to answer this question by focusing on the 'critical determinants of Asian development performance' against which development experiences in Africa and Asia may be evaluated. The role of governments in initiating, implementing and managing development policies is stressed, as well as the impact of cultural and external factors on domestic economic performance. The concluding section highlights some of the most urgent requirements for renewed African development and identifies some potential areas for Asian–African cooperation as well as for external economic and technical assistance. Policy recommendations are put forward with the strong caveat that whatever actions are taken must conform with an African vision of Africa's future development.

RELATIVE ECONOMIC PERFORMANCE IN ASIA AND AFRICA

The high growth and developmental progress of economies in East and South-East Asia are well known. Over the past decade, these economies have grown at an average rate of 6 per cent p.a. as compared with worldwide growth of only 1.2 per cent. In stark contrast, sub-Saharan Africa recorded a negative 1.2 per cent p.a. rate over the same period.[1] Continued Asian dynamism is evident in recent growth performances, particularly if the spectacular growth rates of China – exceeding 10 per cent p.a. – are considered. By contrast, the outlook for much of Africa appears bleak indeed. Declines in real income are accompanied inevitably by increases in mass poverty, deterioration in health and living standards and environmental degradation. And with increasing global interdependence, the deleterious consequences are not confined to the immediately afflicted regions. It is incumbent on the international community to stimulate the means for renewed growth and progress in Africa.

To further this goal of African development, the Asian experience merits careful scrutiny. In assessing the latter and its relevance for Africa, three important elements stand out.

(1) There are no 'basket cases' in development annals. No matter how depressed the outlook may appear, it should be remembered that such currently dynamic Asian performers as Taiwan and South Korea were once viewed as economically hopeless. Singapore was regarded as Asia's Cuba. Yet these economies were able to beat the odds. Today, they consistently rank amongst the world's highest growth economies. With Africa's abundant natural and human resources, the potential for sustained growth should be no less.

(2) There is no single 'Asian model'. Growth and development have taken place in countries of different cultural and religious backgrounds and under a wide range of political regimes, from democratic to authoritarian. In terms of population size, climate, resource base and culture, the diversity among the countries of Asia is as great if not greater than that in Africa.[2] Despite the great diversity of Asian experiences, one should not lose sight of the commonalities of these economies' development strategies. Some recent studies, by focusing exclusively on East Asian experiences, seem to overemphasise the differences between the Asian high performance economies. If focus is turned instead on contrasting the Asian experience as a whole with that of other developing regions such as Africa and Latin America, the common features of the Asian experience stand out.

In Asia, there has been a 'demonstration effect' of development success, sometimes also called the 'flying geese' pattern or the 'contagion hypothesis' (Petri, 1994). Japan's early export success motivated the adoption of similarly outward-oriented strategies by the NIEs and ASEAN countries. Each of the latter countries proceeded to reshape the strategy to meet its own conditions, requirements and priorities. Hong Kong and Singapore as traditional entrepôts were quick to follow Japan's lead. South Korea and Taiwan, with limited natural resources but strong rural-based labour forces, moved into labour-intensive exports. More richly resource-endowed, Thailand, Malaysia and Indonesia nevertheless faced increasingly adverse commodity terms of trade; with the spectre of rising labour costs haunting the NIEs, these three South-East Asian economies reassessed their development strategies and moved toward more active cultivation of manufactured exports.

Just as no single strategy was applicable to Asia, no single strategy drawn from the Asian experiences should be considered optimal for any specific African country. The relevant 'lesson' is that of reshaping successful strategies to suit domestic development circumstances and priorities.

(3) Development is a continuing long-term process; societies do not change overnight. Progress does not occur simply in response to structural adjustment policies. It depends more fundamentally on human capital formation, industrial and technological modernisation, improved governance and strengthened capacity for economic management.

CRITICAL DETERMINANTS OF ASIAN ECONOMIC PERFORMANCE

Several explanations have been put forward for the 'Asian miracle'. The neoclassical, structuralist, culturalist and regionalist approaches each single out different aspects of the Asian experience – market-based policies, government leadership, Confucian traditions and regional interactions – as key determinants of growth (Petri, 1994: 4). Although often cast in stark contrast with one another, these views are not mutually exclusive. Nevertheless, some elements of the Asian experience have more explanatory power than others. This section summarises what is seen to constitute the critical determinants of Asia's spectacular economic performance.

(1) *Successful Asian economies viewed development as a continuing long-term process, guided by the state, but with reliance on openness, market forces and the private sector.*

A question that has been repeatedly raised is why Asian economies were able to attain high economic growth rates when, over the same period, other developing countries were less successful. Obviously, there are many contributing factors, but few would dispute the importance of the outward-looking, market-oriented policies that were followed in the region. Yet there was no single path to successful market orientation. Korea followed a model resembling Japan's, featuring reliance on large conglomerates (known as *chaebol*) to spearhead industrial growth. Taiwan, by contrast, relied primarily on small and medium-sized enterprises to pursue international markets. The common thread was that, in both cases as well as elsewhere in Asia, governments were able to direct economic policies toward highly visible and acceptable objectives with a powerful national purpose and long-term vision.

(2) *Asian dynamism was propelled by openness to trade, investment, and technological improvement.*

Although patterns of development strategy varied widely among Asian economies, one commonality that set them apart from other developing regions was their overriding emphasis on trade as the engine of growth. Country after country followed export-led growth strategies because domestic markets were not large enough for efficient import substitution.

Rapid export growth enabled the NIEs as a group (Korea, Taiwan, Hong Kong and Singapore) to increase their share of world trade dramatically from 2 per cent in 1960 to 10 per cent currently. Export growth far exceeded income growth with export: GDP ratios doubling over the past two decades, reaching 25 per cent in Indonesia, 34 per cent in Korea, 36 per cent in Thailand, 50 per cent in Taiwan and 74 per cent in Malaysia. Import ratios were even higher in most cases despite the retention of relatively high import barriers in all but Singapore and Hong Kong.

Asian economies adjusted well to changing market conditions. Taiwan's small and medium-sized trading firms, for example, proved adept in finding market niches (early dominance in footwear and sporting goods being a case in point). China, a relative latecomer but now a market force in all types of consumer goods, dispersed its traditional foreign trade monopolies into thousands of semi-autonomous trading firms for easier entrée into global markets. Exchange rates as well as factor and input prices were adjusted by Asian governments to maintain export competitiveness and to increase market share.

Asian economies have also been successful in attracting FDI. Here too, patterns varied. Singapore, for example, has relied quite heavily on foreign investment. Hong Kong, Malaysia, Indonesia and Thailand have also drawn in considerable FDI as an important channel for receiving and absorbing foreign knowledge, including management skills and technology. By contrast, South Korea followed more closely the Japanese example of borrowing technology through such means as licensing agreements, allowing little FDI until recently.

Although fiscal incentives such as tax holidays and accelerated depreciation allowances are widely used to attract FDI, the host country's political and macroeconomic stability are paramount. In the late 1980s, for example, Indonesia did not offer incentives, but attracted much more foreign investment than the Philippines, which did.

(3) *Dynamic Asian economies were able to exploit a virtuous cycle in which high growth led to high savings which financed the investment needed to sustain high growth.*

This virtuous cycle of savings and growth is reflected in the sharp increases of savings ratios in the Asian economies. For example, from the early 1960s to the 1990s, Korea's savings rate rose from 5 per cent to 37 per cent, Singapore's from 10 per cent to 45 per cent, and Indonesia's from almost nil to 37 per cent. The key lay not in arbitrarily forcing the rates upward, but in establishing an environment conducive to accumulation through efficient resource use and rapid productivity and income growth. This process was facilitated by the encouragement of various forms of financial intermediation, ranging from informal curb markets to full-fledged institutions; establishment of regulatory systems which focused on maintaining financial soundness; and perhaps most important, by a political commitment to macroeconomic stability.

More specifically, successful mobilisation of domestic savings in dynamic Asian economies resulted from: (a) positive real interest rates which gave the populace incentives to save; (b) availability and convenience of savings institutions, such as the postal savings system in Japan, which encouraged savings and pooled resources; and (c) the profitability of investment opportunities which promoted domestic savings.

(4) *Maintenance of macroeconomic stability enabled Asian economies to weather both internal and external shocks with minimal disruption while sustaining their long-term growth momentum.*

By contrast with much of the African experience, Asian governments were ever vigilant in controlling inflation. The detrimental effects of inflation were acknowledged to be numerous, ranging from inhibiting access to basic needs and human resource improvement to encouraging capital flight.

To control inflation, a country must manage money supply growth and the budget deficit. Monetising a large budget deficit has been the

primary cause of double-digit inflation in developing countries. By
following conservative monetary policies and holding fiscal deficits to
manageable levels, Asian governments were able to keep inflation under control, that is, at below a 10 per cent rate over the past 20 years.
They have been willing to forgo economic expansion and reduce expenditures to squeeze out inflationary tendencies. In a few cases – the
Philippines, South Korea and Thailand – excessive borrowing ignited
inflationary pressures, but prompt remedial action was taken, at least
by the latter two countries.

In fact, policy flexibility in the face of policy-induced as well as
exogenous shocks has been an extremely important, albeit under-
emphasised, feature of Asian development. Asian governments have
shown a readiness to recognise mistakes and correct defective policies.
Singapore, for example, tried to raise wages excessively in the mid-
1980s, but soon realised the folly of trying to hasten a market process.
South Korea also retracted policies designed to speed up the development of chemical and heavy industries in the late 1970s and early
1980s, once it was recognised that the policies were driving beyond
market and infrastructure capabilities.

The Asian experience has demonstrated that maintenance of macro-
stability even in the face of political and socio-economic crises has
been the basis for systemic continuity and long-term economic sustainability. This was evident most recently in Thailand, where the economy
maintained its growth momentum despite major political upheavals.
In the opposing case, macro-instability in the Philippines contributed
to political disruption.

Such policy responsiveness enabled the Asian economies to weather
internal and external shocks over the decades with minimal disruption
of their long-term development strategies. Exports and incomes of Asian
countries continued to expand through the high growth and commodity price boom of the 1960s, the exchange rate realignments, inflationary bouts and energy shocks of the 1970s, and the high interest rates,
debt crises and slow industrial growth of the 1980s.

During this period, the rapidly growing Asian economies generally
drew in modest resources from abroad – about 2–5 per cent of GDP.
At these levels, 'crises' were manageable, as evidenced by Korea's
rapid readjustment from the second oil shock in 1980. Indonesia and
the Philippines faced more serious debt crises in the mid-1980s, but
were able to surmount them in each case through reform measures
designed to restore investor confidence and flexible adjustment consideration on the part of donors.

In many respects it was not difficult for Asian economies to adopt structural adjustment policies since such policies are consistent with those that were already in place. When actions advocated by the World Bank and other institutions conflicted with Asian prerogatives, policies were tailored to fit domestic conditions.

Rather than increasing vulnerability to external shocks, the policy mix in Asia seemed to promote adaptability to changing circumstances in the global economy. The source of this adaptability lay in the interaction of far-sighted human resource development, competent bureaucracies and openness to information and technology from abroad.

Adherence to macro-stabilisation also enabled some flexibility in the sequencing of reform policies. Taiwan's development experience provides one example of a reasonable and effective sequencing of reforms: after stabilisation was achieved, the next steps were interest and exchange rate reforms. Taiwan liberalised the commercial account prior to its capital account. Trade policies shifted from quantity controls to tariffs, maintaining a significant level of domestic protection while building international competitiveness through export processing zones; only later did Taiwan liberalise imports (Winrock, 1991: 30–1). This sequence of structural adjustment policies was logical and obviously worked quite well. By contrast, Indonesia has for the past quarter-century maintained an open capital account and intervened in its domestic markets whenever necessary to defend its exchange rate. Thus, sound macro-policies can enable different economies to institute variations in sequencing more appropriate to their conditions and capacities, rather than simply following academic or externally imposed directives.

(5) *Asian economic success has been characterised by early attention to the provision of basic human needs – food and shelter – and continued support of agricultural and rural development.*

Although the accelerated growth of dynamic Asian economies is widely attributed to their emphasis on manufactured exports, the fundamental role of agricultural development in all but the city-states of Singapore and Hong Kong cannot be overlooked. The sharp rise in agricultural productivity resulted in (a) the release of labour to manufacturing activities in the cities; (b) the provision of foreign exchange (either directly through exports or through savings on food imports); and (c) the lowering of urban food prices which reduced pressure for wage increases.

In Japan, South Korea and Taiwan, the implementation of land and agrarian reforms laid the foundation for sustained development and more equitable distribution of the fruits of economic growth. Taiwan's integration of agricultural development and industrialisation is perhaps the most successful in the world (Winrock, 1991). The developmental benefits of enhanced agricultural productivity extended beyond the Asian NIEs. The three largest increases in food production per capita among all low- and middle-income developing countries from 1979 to 1989 were in Malaysia, Indonesia and China where policies conducive to agricultural growth were instituted or strengthened.

(6) *Human resource development – investment in people – has been a key to successful Asian development.*

Frequently one hears that social development and economic growth are conflicting goals, but Asian experiences show that this need not be the case. With early attention to enhancing agricultural productivity, the Asian NIEs and neo-NIEs were able to meet basic human needs and to shift resources to labour-intensive industries. Increases in the demand for labour in turn raised income levels and spread the benefits of growth relatively equitably throughout the society. High rates of public sector spending on human resource development were augmented by considerable private spending, especially for education. Although educational investments in less successful regions (such as Latin America, Eastern Europe and the Philippines) have been in many cases comparable to those of successful Asian developing countries, the latter stand out for the quality and technical orientation of their educational spending and in their broad-based private commitment to learning (Petri, 1994: 17).

Effective infrastructure and institutional development enabled services to be delivered at reasonable cost, and no major segments of the population were passed over for reasons of ethnicity, gender or geography. Thus, a virtuous circle was formed in which human improvement facilitated economic growth, and growth afforded the means for further improvement. However, this phenomenon was by no means universal throughout the Asian continent; departures occurred particularly in South Asia and less-developed border and island areas of South-East Asia.

(7) *Cultural factors are often cited as instrumental to Asian development success, but sound economic policies are more basic.*

It has been argued that Confucianism, which encourages hard work, saving and education, has been an influential ingredient in Asian economic success. High rates of savings permitted domestic expansion without large external debts. The emphasis on education created a large pool of literate and skilled workers able to meet the needs of an industrialising economy. But these characteristics are not confined to those with the Confucian ethic.[3] Moreover, culturalist explanations of Asian success fail to explain 'why economies with traditions that are so conducive to development have only recently embarked on rapid growth' (Petri, 1994: 26). Improvements in economic performance following policy changes in countries with widely differing cultural backgrounds (India in the late 1980s, Indonesia in the mid-1980s, China in the late 1970s, and Korea and Taiwan in the early to mid-1960s) invalidate the claim that economic success in Asia is due to a common, homogeneous culture. Economic policies, by contrast, can explain why long-term growth rates have differed among countries with relatively similar endowments and in a given country during different periods. Yet it may also be true that cultural factors determine how responsive an economy is to economic policy changes.

(8) *Asian governments played activist roles in shaping and guiding economic development and reform in ways that generally promoted rather than inhibited private activity and market decisions.*

Government intervention was not inconsequential, but focused on establishing and requiring adherence to sound macroeconomic policies, building developmental infrastructure, and providing safety nets for industries that were dislocated in the transitional reform process. Several East Asian countries have implemented industrial policies, utilising tools of financial control, tariffs and quotas, forbearance towards cartel and oligopolistic arrangements, favouritism in government procurement and administrative 'guidance' by such institutions as Japan's Ministry of International Trade and Industry and South Korea's Economic Planning Board. Outward-looking policies performed a vital function by providing built-in limits to policy distortions and signalling corrective action when needed.

The unique feature of Asian governance was that it went beyond an autonomous bureaucracy to one of close partnership between government and business. Instead of the adversarial relationship often found in the West, close collaboration between public and private sectors helped to ensure that appropriate policies were adopted and that a constituency supporting these policies existed. Although business–government relationships that are too close can invite corruption and neglect of the public interest, Asian economies generally have been the beneficiaries of relatively efficient and disciplined government bureaucracies. The high degree of professionalism in the ranks of the civil service (the technocracy) has been critical not only in sustaining growth-oriented development strategies, but also in assuring continuity despite political upheavals.

In short, the 'Asian miracle' was not really a 'miracle'. Concrete and identifiable factors underlay Asian success. Hard work combined with growth-stimulating policy choices made spectacular economic performances possible. It is in this sense that the Asian development experience is most relevant for Africa.

CONCLUSIONS AND RECOMMENDATIONS

Unlocking Africa's potential requires effective economic policies, but these policies must be African-generated and implemented, not imposed by external authority.

The Asian development experience points to a number of critical policy areas for sustainable development: (1) macroeconomic stability; (2) agricultural development; (3) human resource development; (4) mobilisation of savings, development of financial intermediation and incentives for productive investment; (5) outward-orientation and attraction of FDI; (6) effective management of foreign exchange resources and incentives to potential producers of foreign exchange; (7) proper sequencing of structural adjustment policies; (8) institutional capacity-building and improved governance; (9) development of the informal sector; and (10) encouragement of a dynamic private sector working in cooperation with government toward a society-wide vision of development.

In the light of the Asian experience, the following policies are suggested as being particularly important for preventing marginalisation and promoting renewed African development:

1. African policy-makers need to be given leeway to engage in long-range development planning.

2. Structural adjustment programmes should become more long-term growth-oriented and be broadened to embrace industrial restructuring, institutional reform, capacity strengthening and human resource development, in addition to dealing with important short-term balance-of-payments or macro-deficit issues.
3. Closer accommodation should be accorded the informal sector as a means of mobilising savings and facilitating government–private sector interaction.
4. Regional economic cooperation ought to be encouraged as a basis for broadened development, beneficial policy interaction and political cohesion.
5. The debt overhang must be resolved in ways that do not abort recovery programmes or misuse governance capacity, and total forgiveness should be a viable option for the most heavily burdened, lowest-income countries.
6. Donors need to help Africa build capacity for effective economic management. Although humanitarian aid and short-term assistance are necessary, there is also urgency in building institutional capacity.[4]

In terms of closer and fruitful Asian–African cooperation and interaction to achieve some of these objectives, the following are suggested:

1. Programmes should be established to foster direct contact between Africans and Asians. This paper has pointed to the commonalities between African reform efforts and experiences of three South-East Asian nations – Indonesia, Malaysia and Thailand – which began their development acceleration some two decades ago under economic circumstances roughly similar to those in Africa today. Development of training and professional visitation programmes for African policy-makers and scholars to these as well as other dynamic Asian countries can provide first-hand information and insights on development experiences. Attention should be given not only to initiation and implementation of government policy but also to private sector dynamism and how the two sectors have worked in partnership for development.
2. A more closely structured collaborative research and policy outreach programme on structural adjustment and policy reform has recently been instituted for India and the Philippines by the International Center for Economic Growth under funding by USAID, and could well serve as a prototype for African country programmes.[5]

In the long-term process of economic development and the prevention of marginalisation, multilateral institutions such as the United Nations and the World Bank as well as the western partners in African development (in Europe, North America and elsewhere) can and should play a supportive role. But ultimately African development depends upon the African people. Just as Asians have turned economies that were seemingly 'basket cases' into dynamic and even 'showcase' developing countries, Africans face the challenge of putting into practice their own vision of development. It will inevitably take time and determination to make the economies grow, adjust and develop. But with sound policies and Africa's abundant natural and human resources, a more prosperous future is not out of reach.

Notes

1. In the interests of brevity, references to the 'Asian' experience will focus on Japan, the NIEs of East Asia, South-East Asian countries and post-Mao China, while references to Africa will be mainly to the sub-Saharan region. However, it should not be forgotten that there are many poor countries in Asia, as well as countries like Mongolia, Vietnam and Laos that are in the early stages of a transitional process.
2. See the annual *World Development Report* and *African Development Outlook* of the World Bank and Asian Development Bank respectively for data on these indicators as well as on savings and investment ratios and inflation rates.
3. As Petri (1994: 26) points out, 'while clearly consistent with fast growth, Confucianism appears to be neither sufficient nor necessary for it'.
4. Support could be extended through such efforts as the African Capacity Building Foundation, a joint initiative of the United Nations and concerned African institutions, which intends to focus, at least initially, on the key areas of policy analysis and development management.
5. The Asian endeavours call for an integrated programme of seminars by distinguished international authorities on relevant policy issues such as privatisation, trade liberalisation, financial reform, institutional capacity-building and human resource development; collaborative research on selected policy-oriented topics by in-country research institutes and outside specialists; visits by researchers and policy-makers to other Asian research centres or government ministries; and international conferences where results and recommendations would be deliberated before audiences of key policy officials and donor agency representatives. Based on this experience, such a programme could be readily implemented at minimal cost for interested African countries.

10 The Real Exchange Rate and Reserve Management: Latin America in the 1990s[1]

Felipe Larraín

The ending of apartheid in South Africa has led to the start of a new era. The obstacles to integration into the world economy have been removed and the ability to take advantage of this opportunity depends mainly on what South and Southern Africans can do for themselves. The Latin American experience of the 1990s, with large capital inflows and appreciation of the currencies, offers some pertinent lessons.

INTRODUCTION

Latin American economic authorities have faced important policy dilemmas arising from the heavy capital inflows of the 1990s. A basic trade-off has existed between stabilisation and the competitiveness of the tradeable sector. Most economies in the region are attempting to reduce inflation, some from quite low levels (even single-digit rates in Argentina, Mexico and Bolivia in 1993 and 1994). At the same time, they aim to maintain export competitiveness. The real exchange rate is a crucial element for both goals, but acts in opposing directions: an appreciation helps to reduce inflation but hurts competitiveness, and vice versa. And large capital inflows tend to appreciate the exchange rate.

This dilemma has major policy implications. On the one hand, the aim of defending export competitiveness requires that the domestic interest rate not be allowed to deviate 'too' far from the world rate so as to prevent further inflows of capital which would appreciate the local currency. On the other hand, the aim of preserving macroeconomic stability requires a domestic real interest rate consistent with a path for aggregate demand that would allow for a gradual reduction in inflation.

In a context of increasingly integrated financial markets, it is no easy task to reconcile these two objectives.

Another important aspect of capital flows is their composition. After the scarcity of foreign resources that followed the debt crisis, countries in the region are happy to receive significant net inflows of long-term capital, much needed to supplement the local saving effort in the financing of higher levels of investment. But they are much less happy to have to cope with massive flows of short-term speculative capital which may lead to excess volatility in key economic variables such as domestic interest rates and the real exchange rate.

Pursuing stabilisation, aiming to maintain export competitiveness in the face of abundant capital inflows and trying to attract the 'right' kind of capital are difficult tasks. To attain these goals, economic authorities have carried out measures on several different fronts, such as exchange rate policy, reserve accumulation and sterilisation of capital inflows, restrictions on particular capital inflows and selective liberalisation of capital outflows. This paper is focused on exchange rate and reserve management policies in Latin America.

EXCHANGE RATE POLICY

After the collapse of Bretton Woods in 1973, many countries, especially in the industrialised world, moved to flexible exchange rate regimes. But this did not happen in Latin America and, as Table 10.1 shows, by the end of the 1970s the overwhelming majority of countries in the region were under fixed exchange rate schemes pegged to the US dollar.

Since the early 1980s, however, there has been a progressive move away from fixed exchange rates towards managed regimes and even floating currencies. This was to some extent a result of the greater flexibility needed in exchange rate management to cope, first, with the foreign debt crisis, and then with large capital inflows. In other cases, increased flexibility has been sought after the initial stage of stabilisations with fixed exchange rates that have prompted significant appreciation of the local currencies. Chile, Mexico and Colombia, for example, have favoured exchange rate bands with some form of crawl.

By the late 1980s, floating rates continued to gain ground and have become the most popular exchange rate arrangement during the 1990s. Interestingly, by March 1994, 13 out of 17 countries in Latin America were classified as having flexible exchange rate regimes, eight of them

Table 10.1   Exchange Rate Arrangements in Latin America

Currency pegged to US dollar	Adjusted according to a set of indicators	Managed floating	Independently floating
		As of 31 March 1994	
Argentina	Chile	Ecuador	Bolivia
Panama	Nicaragua	Mexico	Brazil
		Uruguay	Costa Rica
		Venezuela	El Salvador
		Colombia	Guatemala
			Honduras
			Paraguay
			Peru
		As of 30 September 1989	
El Salvador	Brazil	Argentina	Bolivia
Guatemala	Chile	Costa Rica	Paraguay
Honduras	Colombia	Ecuador	Uruguay
Nicaragua		Mexico	Venezuela
Panama			
Paraguay			
Venezuela			
		As of 30 November 1984	
Bolivia	Brazil	Argentina	Uruguay
El Salvador	Chile	Costa Rica	
Guatemala	Colombia	Ecuador	
Honduras	Peru	Mexico	
Nicaragua			
Panama			
Paraguay			
Venezuela			
		As of 30 November 1979	
Bolivia	Brazil	Argentina	Uruguay
Chile	Colombia	Mexico	
Costa Rica		Peru	
Ecuador			
El Salvador			
Guatemala			
Honduras			
Nicaragua			
Panama			
Paraguay			
Venezuela			

Source: International Financial Statistics, IMF, various issues.

independently floating schemes, with the other five under managed floating.[2] Among the major countries, only Argentina and Brazil (since the inauguration of the 'Plan Real' in July 1994) today have a fixed exchange rate scheme. This progressive move away from fixed exchange rates is quite clear in Table 10.1.

Conceptual Aspects in the Choice of an Exchange Rate Regime

The dispute between competing exchange rate regimes has not been settled in economics, reflecting the basic trade-offs involved in this choice. Thus, many different exchange rate regimes coexist in the world. Latin America attests to this wide variety. Table 10.1 presents four basic regimes, but in reality the choice is much richer since considerable differences exist within each of them. A comprehensive analysis of the elements behind this choice is clearly beyond the scope of this paper.[3] The purpose here will be merely to discuss some of the main issues involved.

Alternative Regimes

A wide agreement exists at least on a basic point: it is impossible to sustain a fixed exchange rate in an economy with a significant money-financed fiscal deficit. But even if the fiscal deficit has been eliminated, inflationary inertia may doom a scheme where the exchange rate is used as an anchor to stabilise prices. In such a case, the resulting appreciation of the real exchange rate may lead to an unsustainable current account deficit, and could result in a speculative attack against the local currency (just as in the case of a significant fiscal deficit). This was precisely the experience of Chile in 1979–82, when a fixed exchange rate collapsed whilst the public budget was in surplus.

Fixed exchange rates have been advocated as a way of imposing discipline on, and bringing credibility to, economic authorities (Calvo, 1978). By reducing discretion in exchange rate management, the argument goes, the economy may avoid unexpected devaluations aimed at reducing real wages and expanding output. Edwards (1992) has presented empirical evidence suggesting that the adoption of a fixed exchange rate has introduced discipline in countries with a history of stability (but, unfortunately, here is precisely where the fixed rate is less necessary).

Conceptually, however, there are several drawbacks in this view. First, credibility will only be attained under a regime in which economic authorities somehow tie their hands to move the exchange rate (such as the case of Argentina since 1991, as discussed below); merely fixing the exchange rate will not do. Secondly, the exchange rate may be correctly used as a response to changes in its fundamentals, such as in the terms of trade, and not merely as a device to reduce real wages. And thirdly, credibility may be gained with instruments other than the exchange rate, such as the money supply (Edwards, 1993).

The alternative to a fixed rate scheme is a floating exchange rate or some kind of crawling peg regime. Crawling pegs were pioneered in Chile and Colombia in the 1960s and have become quite popular since. In an active crawl, the exchange rate is adjusted according to a table so as to achieve some nominal target such as a reduction in the rate of inflation. A passive crawl aims to maintain the real exchange rate and adjusts the nominal rate by the difference between domestic and international inflation. Crawling pegs may also be used in a band that allows some fluctuation of the exchange rate according to market forces.

Williamson (1982) has been a leading advocate of crawling peg regimes whose main advantage is that they may be used to protect the real sector of the economy from the volatility of financial flows and other outside shocks. Crawling pegs, however, have the drawback of creating inflationary inertia and thus tending to perpetuate inflation. This is especially the case for passive crawls with backward-looking rules.

Monetary Policy and Exchange Rate Stability

In a small and financially integrated economy, as the larger Latin American economies may be characterised today, there is a basic trade-off between the choice of exchange rate regime and the effectiveness of monetary policy, on the one hand, and exchange rate stability, on the other.

Under a fixed exchange rate regime, perfect asset substitution and free capital mobility, domestic authorities of a small economy lose total control over monetary policy. This is the basic Mundell–Fleming result. In other words, such a scenario precludes the authorities from simultaneously setting the interest rate (or the money supply) and the exchange rate. The ineffectiveness of monetary policy is complicated when fiscal policy is inflexible in the short run, as it happens to be in general.[4]

If assets are not perfect substitutes or capital movements are not totally free (as in practice), monetary policy maintains some of its effectiveness under a fixed exchange rate regime. Kouri and Porter

(1974) studied this issue for Australia, Italy, Netherlands and West Germany in the 1960s at a time when these countries were operating under fixed exchange rates; they found a surprisingly high degree of effectiveness in monetary policy.

A flexible exchange rate (or a wide band) is also a way of maintaining control over monetary policy, but at the cost of increased exchange rate volatility. Increased nominal exchange rate volatility leads to higher real exchange rate volatility, which is of special concern.

Most countries in Latin America have turned to development strategies based on the expansion of exports and efficient import substitution within the context of an (increasingly) open trade regime. Maintaining a stable and competitive real exchange rate (RER) is an intermediate objective which must receive central priority in achieving this goal. Such is the lesson from the experience of the East Asian economies that have been successful for decades with outward-oriented strategies.

The exchange rate, however, is both the price of an asset, subject to the volatility that is common to financial markets, and a variable which plays a central role in medium-term resource allocation. A stable path for the RER means an evolution for this variable which is more related to medium-term fundamentals than to short-run financial flows.

Growing theoretical and empirical evidence suggests that excessive instability of the RER has a depressive impact on exports (Caballero and Corbo, 1990) and private investment (Larraín and Vergara, 1993). Krugman (1987) and others have suggested protecting the tradeable sector from short-run stabilisation policy and other transitory shocks, due to the more permanent effects that these can have on the tradeable sector through changes in the RER.[5] In the same direction, excessive instability on the RER and/or real interest rates caused by short-run speculative capital flows can have a negative impact on productive investment of the reversible type, and thus on economic growth (Tornell, 1990).

On the other hand, both economic theory and international evidence indicate that the process of economic development may bring a strengthening of the domestic currency and, thus, a sustainable increase in welfare (Dornbusch, 1989). Therefore, it may be 'too' costly to try to sustain the RER over its 'long-run' equilibrium for a long period of time, not allowing it to reflect these structural changes. A country would also suffer a higher inflation rate if it tries to sustain the RER over its equilibrium value.

A More Detailed Look at some Latin American Experiences

The major Latin American countries have suffered a significant real appreciation of their currencies since the mid- to late 1980s, a trend that has continued in 1994.[6] Real exchange rate appreciation since 1988 in the five main countries of the region ranges from almost 50 per cent in Argentina to 23–4 per cent in Brazil and Mexico to 16–17 per cent in Chile and Colombia. Since its peak in the second half of the 1980s, the RER has appreciated 53 per cent in Argentina, 39 per cent in Mexico, 32 per cent in Brazil, 27 per cent in Colombia and 18 per cent in Chile. Not only has Chile's RER experienced the lowest appreciation among the five countries, but it has also been the most stable: the coefficient of variation for 1985–94 reveals that Argentina's RER was 3.5 times, Mexico's and Brazil's around 2.5 times and Colombia's twice as volatile as Chile's.

The RER has many determinants, some of them largely exogenous to a country (such as the terms of trade) and others under the direct control of the authorities (such as fiscal policy and nominal exchange rate management). This section looks more closely at the experience with exchange rate management in three of these countries: Argentina, Chile and Mexico. Other than Brazil, these are the countries that have experienced the largest inflows of foreign capital in the region. They also provide an interesting comparison of strategies: Argentina has a totally fixed exchange rate; Chile and Mexico have bands of fluctuation where important differences exist.

Argentina is today the only major country in the region (other than Brazil since July 1944) that has a fixed exchange rate. A brief look at the country's past experience helps to explain this policy. Argentina suffered extreme exchange rate instability in the 1980s and tried several different forms of exchange rate management. Maxi-devaluations were used extensively – and unsuccessfully – to stem capital flight and as part of stabilisation programmes. By the end of the 1980s, the country had reached hyperinflation and economic chaos, and Argentines had lost all confidence in their currency.

In March 1991, the government implemented several dramatic economic changes through the 'Convertibility Law'. This eliminated all restrictions to buy and sell foreign exchange, fixed the exchange rate to the dollar and established the validity of contracts denominated in any currency. The Central Bank was allowed to increase the money base only as a result of reserve accumulation, thus practically eliminating monetary financing of fiscal deficits. Moreover, the value of the

Felipe Larraín

exchange rate was set by law, so that changing it would require congressional approval.

The policies of early 1991 represented a dramatic departure from the recent past. Their rationale was the belief that something radical was necessary to regain the lost confidence in the currency and stabilise the economy. Thus, the recovery of credibility is the main element that explains the uniqueness of Argentina's exchange rate policy. Fixing the exchange rate was not enough because it had been tried and failed repeatedly in the past. Full convertibility and legislative approval to change its value were added.

Argentina's exchange rate policy – supported by the structural reforms implemented – has scored important successes. The economy has been stabilised, the inflation rate has been reduced to single-digit levels (7.4 per cent in 1993 and around 4 per cent in 1994), and the authorities have defeated speculative attacks against the currency, most prominently that of late 1992. The trade-off, however, has come in the form of a sharp appreciation of the exchange rate, coupled with a significant deterioration of the current account. In fact, the real exchange rate has declined by more than 50 per cent since its peak in 1989. Although the 1989 RER is considered an 'overshooting', the appreciation is still very considerable measured from more 'normal' years.

This does not mean, however, that an exchange rate crisis is bound to occur. A number of policy measures (on trade, labour markets, transportation and infrastructure) have deregulated and liberalised the economy. They provide increased competitiveness to the tradeable sector which at least partly offsets the losses from the exchange rate appreciation. The risk still exists, however, that the competitiveness gained from these measures may not be able to offset the exchange rate losses. A key issue here is how soon the country's inflation converges to international levels which it seemed to be approaching; in the meantime, the real exchange rate will keep appreciating.

Chile's exchange rate was tied to the dollar in a narrow band whose amplitude started at +2 per cent of the central rate and was progressively raised, reaching +5 per cent in June 1989. The central rate has been (generally) adjusted monthly in the difference between domestic inflation and an estimate of international inflation.[7] In essence, this policy has aimed to maintain the real exchange rate while allowing some breathing space for monetary policy.

The combination of macroeconomic adjustment in January 1990 (when *ex-ante* real rates on long-term Central Bank bonds reached 9.7 per cent) and increased capital mobility due to a lower perception of country risk,[8] prompted massive capital inflows which quickly moved the exchange rate to the bottom of the band. At that point, and with further downward pressure on the exchange rate, the country operated *de facto* under a pegged exchange rate regime, and the band was sustained only by Central Bank intervention. After a significant increase of reserves in 1991, the Central Bank revalued the central rate by 5 per cent and widened the band to +10 per cent in January 1992. Again, in spite of the Bank's efforts, the exchange rate quickly converged to the lower point of the band.

Part of the pressure on the real exchange rate was attributed by the authorities to transitory factors such as low interest rates in the US, but another part was thought to come from permanent (that is, structural) factors. Among the latter were the consolidation of the export sector, the reduced burden of foreign debt and the increase in net foreign investment. In other words, part of the capital flows were attracted by a reduction in Chile's perceived country risk.

Hoping to add more 'market uncertainty' to capital movements, the Bank not only increased the amplitude of the band in early 1992, but also changed the peg of the central rate to a basket of currencies in July 1992 (with weights of 50 per cent for the dollar, 30 per cent for the Deutschmark and 20 per cent for the yen). At the same time, the Bank announced that it would intervene within the limits of the band.[9] This is the scheme that prevails today, and this means that the relevant international interest rate for arbitrage operations is no longer the US rate but rather a combination of the German, Japanese and US rates. This reduces vulnerability of the Chilean economy to fluctuations in US interest rates which reached record lows in the early 1990s.

Chilean exchange rate management has been more worried about the competitiveness of the tradeable sector than in Argentina or Mexico. Of course, the Central Bank controls just the nominal exchange rate, which may affect the real exchange rate only during the short to medium term. But exchange rate management helps to explain why Chile's real exchange rate appreciation has been more moderate than in Argentina or Mexico.

At the same time, Chile's current account deficit has been quite moderate (it even had a surplus in 1990). Only in 1993 did this deficit increase significantly (to 5.2 per cent of GDP), but this was mostly the result of a substantial terms-of-trade deterioration, and it declined to around 2.5 per cent of GDP in 1994. The trade-off, however, is reflected today in Chile's inflation rate which, after declining significantly since 1990, ended 1994 still in double digits (around 11 per cent). De-indexing the exchange rate from past inflation would help to reduce inflation further, although running the risk of significant real exchange rate appreciation.

Mexico started using its exchange rate policy as a stabilisation device in the mid- to late 1980s. In 1988, the exchange rate was fixed to the dollar, and in January 1989 the scheme moved to a crawl, with a pre-announced rate of devaluation. More precisely, the exchange rate depreciated by 1 peso per day in 1989, 80 cents per day in 1990 and 40 cents per day in 1991. Since then, Mexico's exchange rate management has become more flexible after large capital inflows started to come into the country.

A major overhaul in the exchange rate regime occurred in November 1991, when the scheme of exchange controls implemented in 1982 was eliminated. In the new environment of large net capital inflows, the regulations placed to deal with a shortage of foreign exchange had clearly become obsolete. At that time, the free and controlled exchange rates had virtually converged.

The scheme to determine the exchange rate also changed in November 1991. The band in which the rate was allowed to fluctuate was widened, allowing the band's ceiling a continuing depreciation of a fixed nominal amount per day, but fixing the floor at 3.06 pesos per dollar, the level that it had reached on that date. And intervention inside the band by the Central Bank (dirty float) became normal. Almost one year later, in October 1992, the path of depreciation of the ceiling accelerated, while the floor remained fixed.

By widening the band, the changes implemented since 1991 have added flexibility to exchange rate policy, thus buying breathing space for monetary policy. Mexico's exchange rate scheme, however, has not been primarily aimed at maintaining the real exchange rate (such as Chile's). Rather, it has been more concerned with stabilisation. The trade-off is, once again, extremely clear. The Mexican peso has appreciated 39 per cent in real terms since its peak in 1987. The effects have been felt on the current account, whose deficit soared to $22 billion, on average, in 1992–3. In these years, about 90 per cent of the capital account surplus was used to cover the current account deficit.

Mexico's scheme has some common features with the Chilean system, but there remain important differences: the floor of the band is fixed in Mexico, while it moves upward in Chile according to a pre-set rule; the width of the band is constant in Chile (+10 per cent of the central rate) while it moves up in Mexico; the Mexican peso is pegged to the dollar while the Chilean peso is pegged to a basket of currencies in which the dollar has only a 50 per cent weight; and there is no central rate in Mexico, just the upper and lower limits of the band.

INTERNATIONAL RESERVES AND STERILISATION

Reserve Accumulation

Capital inflows have not only financed current account deficits in Latin America, but also have allowed for a major build-up of foreign exchange reserves. This has been a welcome development for the region. Foreign resources have allowed both the increase of investment rates well above the saving capacity of countries, and the recomposition of foreign exchange reserves from the low levels attained during the 1980s.

All major countries in the region have accumulated significant amounts of foreign exchange reserves in the present decade. Relative to the size of each country's economy, the largest accumulation of reserves has occurred in Chile which increased its foreign exchange holdings by more than 10 per cent of GDP between 1989 and 1994. Reserve accumulation during the same period was 7.1 per cent of GDP in Colombia, 4.2 per cent in Brazil, 3.8 per cent in Mexico and 3.5 per cent in Argentina. (Note that these figures are measured relative to each year's GDP, and that significant growth has occurred in real GDP, as well as a substantial appreciation of the local currency.)

Another comparative measure of reserves is related to a country's annual import bill. Reserves have grown much more than imports in all these countries, the ratio of reserves to imports typically doubling in Argentina, Brazil and Chile since the late 1980s. Increases in this indicator are more modest, but still significant, in Colombia and Mexico.

Six months of imports is a rule-of-thumb of what is considered a prudent holding of foreign exchange reserves for a country. By 1993, all these economies – with the exception of Mexico – had surpassed this level. In fact, Brazil and Chile had one year of imports in reserves while Argentina and Colombia had some 10 months. Mexico, at the lower end of the scale, still had five months of imports in reserves.

The use a country makes of foreign capital inflows has a number of interesting economic implications. Take two polar cases. If the complete capital inflow is accumulated as reserves at the Central Bank, no change in the net foreign debtor position of the country is registered. In this case, the economy would be better prepared to face external shocks, which has been a major source of macroeconomic instability in Latin America. If, on the other hand, the inflow of capital is used to finance a current account deficit, there would be an increase in the net debtor position of the country, a rise in its vulnerability to external shocks and a sharper appreciation of its real exchange rate (through some combination of nominal exchange rate appreciation and higher inflation). Nevertheless, if the larger current account deficit reflects higher capital formation, this supports future growth.

The countries examined here have used capital inflows both to cover current account deficits and to accumulate reserves, but in quite different proportions. Argentina and Mexico have used most of the inflow to cover current account deficits, while still accumulating substantial reserves. Brazil, Colombia and Chile have mainly used the resources to accumulate reserves.[10]

In spite of these differences, the overall trend is a significant accumulation of foreign exchange reserves in all major countries. This is quite prudent policy, especially after the low levels of reserves reached in the 1980s. Today, however, the issue in some countries seems to be whether the level of reserves attained may be too high. Although the 'optimal' level of reserves for a country is hard to determine, it is reasonable to think that one year of imports in reserves may be on the long side: there are alternative uses for them such as the pre-payment of debt at a discount (an option that is still available for some countries in the region), and there is a public finance consideration in the accumulation of reserves when this is accompanied by sterilisation.

Sterilisation

Several countries in the region have tended to sterilise, through open market operations, the monetary effects of foreign reserve accumulation so as to control inflation and prevent a sharper appreciation of the local currency. The most notable examples of this trend in the 1990s have been Chile and Colombia.

As a result of sterilisation, the composition of the Central Bank's balance sheet changes, with more reserves on the asset side and more domestic bonds on the liability side. Because the interest rate on Central Bank bonds has been substantially above the rate that could be earned on foreign exchange reserves, the Central Bank's financial position has worsened. Rodriguez (1991), for example, has estimated that the operating loss attributable to sterilisation in Colombia was half a percentage point of GDP in 1991. In Chile, the accumulated loss during the period 1990–3 has been slightly higher than 0.5 per cent of GDP (Labán and Larraín, 1994).

Clearly, sterilisation is no panacea on other grounds, too, as it tends to maintain the differential between domestic and foreign rates, thereby perpetuating the capital inflows. Calvo et al. (1992) report that the reduction of local interest rates in Latin America has been much slower in countries that have sterilised vis-à-vis those which have not. Theoretical analyses have also shown that sterilisation may reduce social welfare (Calvo, 1991).

SUMMARY AND CONCLUSIONS

Over the last 15 years, a major shift has occurred in Latin America's exchange rate policy, away from fixed rates towards managed regimes and floating currencies. This has been largely a result of the greater flexibility needed in exchange rate management to cope, first, with the foreign debt crisis, then with large capital inflows, and finally, with appreciation after the initial phase of stabilisation programmes. Among the major countries of the region, only Argentina and Brazil (since the Plan Real of July 1994) had fixed exchange rate regimes as at December 1994.

Fixing the exchange rate helps to stabilise, but the resulting appreciation may ultimately undermine the exchange rate scheme. Also, a fixed exchange rate cannot be sustained in an economy with a significant money-financed fiscal deficit. Crawling pegs are a popular alternative to fixed rates, aiming to protect the real economy from the volatility of financial flows and other outside shocks. But passive crawls with backward-looking rules increase inflationary inertia, and thus tend to perpetuate inflation.

Faced with large capital inflows, all major Latin American countries have experienced appreciation, the extent of which is significantly influenced by the choice and purpose of exchange rate policy. In Argentina, a fixed exchange rate set by law with full convertibility has been used as the main instrument to achieve credibility and stabilisation. Inflation has successfully declined to levels of around 4 per cent in 1994, but the real appreciation has surpassed 5 per cent since 1989, and the current account deficit has increased. Mexico, too, has used the exchange rate to stabilise, and has suffered both a real exchange rate appreciation of 39 per cent since 1987 and a large increase in its current account deficit.

Chile and Colombia provide an interesting contrast. Both countries have privileged real exchange rate stability and have suffered milder – although still significant – appreciations (in the order of 18 per cent and 27 respectively since the late 1980s). But they have made less progress on the inflation front, especially Colombia whose inflation rate is still above 20 per cent. At the same time, their current account deficits have been much smaller than Argentina's and Mexico's during the 1990s.

All major countries in the region have accumulated substantial foreign exchange reserves in the 1990s. Relative to the size of the economy, Chile and Colombia present the largest accumulation of reserves. The countries which have used most of the capital inflows to accumulate reserves have also suffered the lowest real exchange rate appreciations. Reserve accumulation also reduces the vulnerability of a country to external shocks which have been a major source of macroeconomic instability in Latin America.

To offset the monetary effects of reserve accumulation, several economies have used sterilisation, thereby changing the composition of the Central Bank's balance sheet towards more low-yielding assets (reserves) and more high yielding liabilities (domestic bonds). As a result, operating losses mount, as attested by both Chile and Colombia in recent years. Sterilisation also tends to maintain the differential between domestic and foreign interest rates, thereby perpetuating the capital inflows.

POSTSCRIPT

This paper was written and presented before the Mexican crisis of late December 1994, the consequences of which spread to the rest of Latin America in what became known as the 'Tequila effect'. In early 1995, foreign investors did not make much distinction between countries. Capital outflows were widespread in the region, stock markets plunged and exchange rates depreciated or came under heavy attack if they were fixed (as in the case of the Argentine peso). With time, however, the situation of the different countries started to diverge, providing several interesting lessons both for Latin America and for Southern Africa as well.

First, large current account deficits and sharp currency appreciations are to be avoided. As pointed out in this paper, Mexico had the largest current account deficit in the region (in the order of 8 per cent of GDP in 1994) and suffered one of the largest currency appreciations in recent years. Argentina, the economy most affected in the region by the Tequila effect, had the sharpest currency appreciation and a current account deficit in the order of 4 per cent of GDP. Chile, widely perceived as the country that suffered least from Mexico's crisis, had one of the lowest current account deficits in the region (less than 1.5 per cent of GDP in 1994), and suffered a milder appreciation.

Secondly, behind a low current account deficit in a fast-growing economy lies a strong domestic saving effort. The crisis has also served to reappraise the value of high local saving. Chile's saving rate, at 27 per cent of GDP, is the largest in the region. High saving results from macroeconomic stability, fast growth and institutional reforms such as the privatisation of pension fund administration.

Thirdly, capital inflows and their uses have also come into question during the recent crisis. Although all major countries attracted large inflows, some of them used the inflows to accumulate reserves (as in Chile and Colombia) rather than financing a large expenditure boom (as in Mexico and, to a lesser extent, Argentina). The composition of capital inflows also matters. Roughly, out of every 3 dollars that went into Mexico, 2 were short-term and 1 long-term; the proportion was exactly the opposite in Chile. No consensus has appeared, however, on the right policies needed to attract long-term capital and discourage shorter-term flows.

One final and important lesson is that economic shortcomings are only part of the problem. Political issues are as important. Mexico suffered in 1994 the assassinations of two prominent political figures, namely, the leading presidential candidate and a reformist party chief. This added to the uncertainties posed by the rebel Zapatista Army of National Liberation, with strong following in the south of Mexico. Political stability is also an essential part of any successful development process.

Notes

1. This paper draws on previous research by the author for the Group of Thirty in Washington, D.C. The author thanks Pablo Garcia for efficient assistance and Gavin Maasdorp for insightful suggestions.
2. Additionally, one may wonder why Chile's is not classified as a regime of managed floating by the IMF.
3. A more detailed treatment of these issues is provided, for example, by Sachs and Larraín (1993).

4. However, one should not exaggerate the inflexibility of fiscal policy. Most countries set the budget yearly, and this is an opportunity to alter the course of fiscal policy. Within the year, however, most budgets leave the excess of actual over budgeted fiscal revenues to the discretion of the finance minister. Moreover, a part of the budget is generally set aside for emergencies.

5. This idea runs along the lines of the hystereses argument.

6. The only exception was Mexico in the first half of 1994, but this appears to be a short-term movement, mainly related to political events.

7. Some discrete changes of the central rate have taken place also since 1983.

8. Due both to improved economic indicators and a smooth transition to democracy (Labán and Larraín, 1995).

9. Before, Central Bank intervention was triggered only when the exchange rate touched the limits of the band.

10. In fact, these three countries have had current account surpluses during some years of this decade, while Argentina and Mexico have had significant current account deficits in every year.

11 Currency Convertibility and External Reserves

Laurence Clarke

This is a topic of potential and growing importance to Africa as a whole, but especially to Southern Africa. The paper is intended to be both introspective (examining the current position in the region in these areas) and prospective (where the region should be going as the 21st century dawns). It looks, first, at the question of currency convertibility, making clear distinctions between this and other forms of convertibility; secondly, at the principles and objectives of external reserves; thirdly, at the interface between, and implications for, currency convertibility and the management of external reserves; and lastly, at specific proposals for the future of Southern Africa. Eight Southern Africa countries are examined: Botswana, Lesotho, Mauritius, Namibia, South Africa, Swaziland, Zambia and Zimbabwe.

CONVERTIBILITY

The broad consensus today is that *currency convertibility* is about the capacity for readily exchanging one's domestic currency at market rates for an external, usually 'harder', reserve currency within or outside one's domicile. Full convertibility, therefore, relates to the absence of restrictions on foreign exchange transactions. In many respects currency convertibility is typically accompanied by another form of convertibility, namely, current account or trade convertibility or even partial or full capital convertibility. It is accepted, however, that the presence of currency convertibility does not automatically imply current or capital account convertibility, though it is desirable to have these first. The existence of no or limited trade and investment restrictions typically guarantees free convertibility of a given currency.

Current account convertibility represents the absence of restrictions on transactions of goods and services. It is typically the first stage towards wider convertibility and, in terms of membership of the International Monetary Fund (IMF), represents a move, once formally acceded to, to Article VIII status in the Fund by member nations. However, accession to Article VIII status does not necessarily imply full current account convertibility, but rather an intent to move in this direction over a usually defined timeframe. Thus, it is possible that some countries which have not formally accepted Article VIII status could, as is currently the case in Botswana, have a more liberal regime of exchange controls on the current account than countries already in Article VIII status. South Africa, for example, still has a number of restrictions on payments for trade in goods and services even though it attained Article VIII status in 1973. According to the IMF, as at July 1994, Mauritius, South Africa and Swaziland had accepted Article VIII status with Botswana formally declaring its intention to move to this status. As Table 11.1 indicates, however, only Swaziland does not still have some restrictions on its current account. All eight of these countries still require some form of surrender/repatriation of export proceeds by domestic entrepreneurs.

Current account convertibility is desirable to the extent that it enhances a country's supply-side capacity, creates a more competitive environment and promotes production and investment decisions relative to a nation's comparative advantage. Yet, there are some costs and risks, including short-run adverse domestic employment effects, current account imbalances and possible considerable increases in consumption. On balance, though, this form of convertibility is widely accepted as a necessary prerequisite for wider liberalisation and reform efforts in emerging economies (Greene and Isard, 1991).

Capital account convertibility represents no or limited restrictions on the flow of capital or investment funds and is typically a more difficult status to be attained, even for more advanced countries. Indeed, it is well known that many West European countries, for example, France and Italy, did not attain final capital account convertibility until the late 1980s (Mathieson and Rojas-Suarez, 1993). As Table 11.1 also indicates, no Southern African country has removed all restrictions on investment flows. In terms of the degree of liberalisation, it would appear that Botswana is the most advanced, with remittances up to the equivalent of US$18 million being automatically permitted on capital transactions. Other countries are rapidly also dismantling these capital controls to underpin their wider move towards fuller currency convertibility.

It is widely accepted that capital account convertibility could, on balance, induce net foreign resource inflows and ultimately promote macroeconomic progress, though the risk of short-run capital flight and

Table 11.1 Status of Payments Convertibility – Selected Southern Africa
Countries (as at early 1994)[a]

	Article XIV[b]	*Article VIII status*[c]	*Restrictions on current account*	*Capital controls*
Botswana	X		X	X
Lesotho	X		X	X
Mauritius		X	X	X
Namibia	X		X	X
South Africa		X	X	X
Swaziland		X		X
Zambia[d]	X		X	X
Zimbabwe	X		X	X

Notes: a. X = yes.
   b. Status upon joining Fund.
   c. Formal Commitment to Removal of restrictions on current account.
   d. Exchange Control Act suspended on 23 January 1994.

Source: Exchange Arrangements and Exchange Restrictions – Annual Report
1994: IMF.

greater exchange rate variability, especially in regimes of flexible exchange rates, are often cited as real possibilities. In practice, however, capital flight takes place, even with the presence of stringent exchange controls (Clarke, 1993).

Currency convertibility itself, however, does not have to be only external in the sense that domestic funds would be converted into foreign currency for export abroad, or vice versa. There could also be 'internal convertibility', involving the availability of foreign currency-denominated accounts (FCAs), domiciled in a given economy, side by side with its own currency. As is already the case in several Southern African countries (Zimbabwe, Mozambique and Zambia included), it is then possible both for residents and non-residents to maintain local currency accounts and FCAs in their domestic banks without necessarily being able to make payments abroad. The growing tendency towards this system on the part of developing countries arises out of a desire progressively to integrate with global economies and relax exchange restrictions while offering alternative investment opportunities for residents without the 'permanent loss' of the use of these funds from the domestic economy. As will be seen below, a number of issues of a policy and operational nature could emerge from such scenarios.

The ideal, therefore, is for currency convertibility to be underpinned by full current and capital account convertibility which, as a general rule, would in turn need to be underpinned, if they are to be sustainable and effective, by adequate volumes of external reserves, especially in a fixed exchange rate regime. Further, it is emerging common cause that attempts at serious current or capital account as well as full currency convertibility before an appropriate exchange rate, sound macroeconomic policies and a market-based environment are in place, are likely to be less than effective (Mathieson and Rojas-Suarez, 1993).

EXTERNAL RESERVES: PRINCIPLES AND PRACTICE

The external reserves of a nation are in some respects its buffer or cushion against future changes in economic circumstances affecting its external sector. They represent a nation's savings held outside its domestic economy and in foreign currency-denominated assets, to meet expected and unexpected national balance of payments (consumption and investment) requirements. External reserves often consist of two elements: (1) working balances to meet and settle normal external transactions, emphasising a liquidity factor; and (2) investment balances to meet future national capital contingencies or to permit a form of store of wealth. Reserves could include gold, foreign currency instruments, reserve tranches in the IMF, Special Drawing Rights, and so on. To the extent that external reserves are in effect national financial assets externalised, among other things, they are represented by domestic counterparts in the form of private and/or public sector savings/liabilities, in the hands typically of the monetary authorities. While external reserves themselves are most widely used for balance of payments transaction-hedging purposes, implicit in their existence are issues of national confidence; the degree of a nation's creditworthiness, strength of its currency, collateral for external borrowing or simply a partial store of national welfare or wealth over time. The availability of external reserves has come to be closely viewed, in developed foreign exchange markets in particular, as a barometer of a nation's capacity to defend the strength of its currency through appropriate intervention in support of a given policy position.

In determining what constitutes an adequate level of international reserves, a country needs to recognise that, to the extent that external reserves are prudently meant to be maintained in as liquid a form as possible in satisfaction of usually short-term balance of payments needs, there potentially exists a real opportunity cost from the holding of a stock of reserves in this form. The potential for realising higher social and financial rates of return in domestic or international markets than those attainable from the maintenance of such reserves in typically liquid instruments, is possibly forgone. The significance of this cost reflects the extent to which preservation of national savings in a liquid form precludes their alternative use in the domestic economy for perhaps more welfare-enhancing objectives, for example, public sector investments or private productive capital formation.

Often, it becomes necessary for a country to build up significant balances of reserves, say, in excess of the internationally accepted norm of 12–15 weeks of cover for its average imports of goods and services. In these circumstances, it is particularly important for such 'excesses' to be adequately tranched and managed to assure a balance between sustaining the intertemporal purchasing power to the nation and enhancing the yields of those stocks, thus reducing the opportunity cost to the economy of these holdings.

For African countries as a group, growth in gross external reserves has been well below the average yearly level for both the world as a whole and developing countries as a group, representing as little as only a third of the latter. In the case of Southern Africa, IMF data show that total gross reserves increased from 4280 million to 6731 million SDRs between 1983 and 1993, fuelled largely by an almost ten-fold increase for Botswana on the back of diamond exports. The picture changes dramatically, however, if net as opposed to gross reserves are examined, reflecting a growing external debt profile in the region, influenced to a large extent by the poor economic performance of South Africa. In fact, South Africa's net foreign assets were actually negative in early 1994. A deterioration in Zambia's and Zimbabwe's balance of payments also contributed substantially to the worsening net reserves position for the region as a whole between 1983 and 1993. With the exception of Botswana (78 weeks) and Mauritius (19 weeks), all countries on average over the period 1983–93 had fewer gross reserves, in terms of weeks of import coverage, than the typical industrial country norm. Further, aggregate reserves for Southern Africa have for the past decade been consistently less than 1 per cent of global reserves, though very significant in wider Africa terms.

Given the well-known foreign exchange constraint in most developing countries, it is essential that countries manage their stock of foreign reserves efficiently and effectively at all times. In this regard, a number of factors must be kept uppermost in the minds of national reserve portfolio managers, *inter alia*: (1) the preservation of the purchasing power over time of such reserves for the nation (safety factor); (2) timely availability of resources for settlements of transactions (liquidity factor); and (3) because of the risk of significant opportunity costs, assurance of as adequate a yield as possible (return factor). In many respects the first two of these factors are fundamental to the question of currency convertibility. The extent to which the foreign reserves of nations are invested within or outside the region, how liquidly and in what readily convertible currencies, is an issue that cannot be ignored by national portfolio managers. Similarly, ensuring that the effective value of these reserves does not erode over time is also central.

ISSUES AND IMPLICATIONS FOR SOUTHERN AFRICA

Aspects of currency convertibility and reserve management in general raise a number of issues in their individual as well as conjunctive rights, especially when applied to the Southern African situation. These include fundamental ones in respect of regional and national (1) trade patterns and policy, (2) capital/investment flows, (3) monetisation and monetary management, (4) exchange rate policy, and (5) broad reserve management strategy.

Trade Patterns

IMF data show that South Africa enjoys a very favourable balance of trade with the rest of Southern Africa, the ratio averaging about 5:1. A couple of points arise from this situation.

(1) The tendency to asymmetry in trade patterns whereby imports tend to be overwhelmingly obtained from South Africa and exports move largely overseas, especially in Botswana's and to a lesser extent Namibia's case, raises interesting questions with respect to payment settlements, exchange risk management and, by implication, reserve management. More fundamentally, it also begs the question as to the desirability, or not, of full intra-regional currency convertibility, having regard to the fact that there are still substantial offsetting payment flows which could reduce transaction costs resulting from the need for conversion in and out of foreign exchange, that is, the potential for accommodating some form of local currency payment arrangements within the region itself. Such an approach should in fact be only a

short-term solution as it is likely that the new GATT arrangements and renegotiation of the SACU itself may well significantly alter trading patterns within the region over time, with the result that divergences from the existing flows of goods and payments could emerge. This would, therefore, imply the need for greater currency convertibility within the region to smooth out such flows. Whilst in general the experience of multilateral clearing facilities in Africa, the Caribbean and other regions has not been great, perhaps a variant of this whereby regional currencies are over time convertible relative to themselves, may be an adjunct to intraregional trade development.

(2) The question as to whether exchange control barriers could not be removed or capital convertibility enhanced for transactions becomes fundamental. Whilst this may initially be a radical step that could ultimately lead to greater monetary and trade integration, it is likely to raise other issues such as the position of regional currencies – assuming that initially these are not unified – relative to non-regional ones, and the extent to which exchange leakages could be facilitated from any regional country to the rest of the world. At best, it suggests the need for progressively dismantling such controls at the earliest possible opportunity throughout the region and against the rest of the world – a clear longer-term objective, having regard to the differential stages of development in the region.

Capital/Investment Flows

As has already been noted, there is little question that full capital account convertibility virtually presupposes or facilitates full currency convertibility. One principal concern of monetary authorities in developing countries in their agony over the decision to dismantle exchange controls, or not, is their capacity adequately to defend/support their currency in the event of full exchange liberalisation. The presence of adequate external reserves apparently makes a fundamental difference in this policy choice. In fact, it is precisely this kind of situation with which South Africa is largely faced in contemplating abolition of exchange controls. Yet, there is a school of thought that suggests that the best time fully to abolish exchange controls is when there are no foreign reserves – nothing to flow out or with which to defend the currency!

The reality, though, is that an environment of full or partial currency convertibility backed by adequate reserves, as in Botswana, Mauritius and South Africa in particular, is likely to have most of the necessary, though not totally sufficient, ingredients for attracting foreign capital. In turn, where the situation is currently only one of partial capital or current account convertibility, full currency convertibility is likely to follow in time, assuming other macroeconomic structural issues are addressed.

One central concern in this regard is the kind of external flows that may be induced, for example, direct versus portfolio or debt versus equity. The general feeling among policy-makers is that portfolio rather than direct inflows could be more destabilising, while debt capital is less helpful than equity capital. But the fact is that portfolio flows, however disequilibrating and disruptive they may be in the short run, typically are basic forerunners to more substantive direct investment flows if they are actively encouraged and properly managed. Equity flows, while more desirable, impose greater exchange risks on external investors, requiring higher rates of return for their benefit. Perhaps, however, the real issues in respect of capital convertibility and its impact and relationship to currency convertibility and reserve management, are the policy and operational implications raised for monetary and exchange rate management. These are discussed sequentially below.

Monetisation/Monetary Management

A couple of features stand out from an examination of IMF data on the evolution of broad money and reserve money in key Southern African economies between 1983 and 1993.

1. The more developed economies – South Africa and Zimbabwe – have had markedly lower reserve money/GDP ratios than the rest. This could suggest either greater economic activity on their part (and thus larger expansions and levels of their GDPs) or less reliance by them on reserve requirements and greater emphasis on other intermediate tools such as interest rates for the conduct of monetary policy, hence lower ratios.
2. It is not coincidental that Zambia, possibly the weakest economy of the eight, has tended to have the greatest average expansion in both M3 and reserve money over the period, reflecting in large measure its very high rates of inflation. In this context, though, relatively high rates of growth in both indicators for Botswana was in large measure a function of very high levels of capital inflows resulting in chronic 'excess liquidity' system-wide rather than budgetary deficit-driven forms of inflation, fuelling public sector borrowing and monetary expansions.

3. Some proxy measure of 'excess liquidity' in the form of expansions in levels of reserve money may be indicated, certainly in the cases of Botswana, Zambia and Zimbabwe in recent years. This would reflect itself presumably in higher balances by commercial banks with the central banks (hence increases in reserve money), especially if interest is payable on such funds, or to some extent if they are 'sterilised' through open market operations, or simply through higher liquid asset ratios in general.

One upshot of 1–3 above is that policies of internal convertibility of currencies, in particular, must clearly consider the likely implications for future expansion of the money supply and probably, by implication, reserve money and the money multiplier. This is of specific relevance at a time when virtually all the principal economies in the region have signalled an intention to introduce, or have actually already introduced, FCAs. Whilst this trend may be desirable and should be encouraged, the treatment of such accounts, and their capacity to facilitate internal currency convertibility (switching in and out of the domestic currency), will have significant implications for money supply and reserve money behaviour, depending on how these are addressed in each economy.

More important, expansions in net reserves through additional exports or investment flows are likely to enhance monetisation if not quickly sterilised through conventional means or diverted to FCAs. It is by implication, therefore, important that FCAs are as far as possible kept outside of the money supply stream. The future experience of Zimbabwe, which has introduced FCAs recently but held reserve requirements against them, will be very interesting to observe in this context.

Exchange Rate Management

The principal issue here is the extent to which movement to full currency convertibility, with overall balance of payments convertibility, could affect management of the external value of an economy's currency. The principal currencies in Southern Africa outside the CMA are pegged to a basket of currencies, the rand playing a major trade weighted part in the Botswana composite. South Africa's currency, by contrast, is independently floating (the other CMA currencies are at present linked to the rand at par, so this also applies to them), while Zimbabwe's is also effectively floating with its increased foreign exchange market liberalisation activities recently. Zambia is already also moving in this direction by virtue of the emergence of bureaux de change.

In the case of Botswana, with the largest volumes of reserves in the region, any move to float the very strong pula would present a real question for the authorities. The government's policy is to maintain a constant real effective exchange rate vis-à-vis its major international trading partners as far as possible, with the result that there is a desire to reduce the variability in the rand/pula rate as much as possible, as the rand's external value to the SDR currencies changes. This has also meant a gradual nominal depreciation of the pula vis-à-vis most SDR currencies, especially the dollar, a strategy that simultaneously supports the effort for non-traditional export development by Botswana to the region in particular. The general view of the Botswana authorities is that this policy stance could be dangerous if things fall apart in South Africa and massive importation of the expected hikes in South African inflation to Botswana occurs. Alternative views, therefore, are emerging that some kind of a float of the pula should follow full liberalisation of exchange controls which, it is common cause, would, even in the absence of massive inflows, induce the real effective rate of the pula to rapidly appreciate. This could in turn present major problems of monetary management and stabilisation for Botswana, and further raise questions as to whether the capital account should be made fully convertible at once, phased in, or left as is, wiping out all forms of emerging non-traditional exports on which employment generation continues to be so heavily dependent.

Full foreign exchange liberalisation could, therefore, present major policy challenges for most Southern Africa economies, which would at that time be faced with the choice of continued pegs or a freer or free float. The experiences of Switzerland in the 1970s, and of Chile and Argentina more recently, present ample evidence of the risks involved (BOCCIM, 1994; Mathieson and Rojas-Suarez, 1993).

Reserve Management

The above risks become all the more complicated when the issue of management of gross and net reserves is considered. While at the moment this is probably not a problem for most Southern African economies, it is already a problem for Botswana and to a lesser extent Mauritius and South Africa. As Zimbabwe and other regional economies restructure themselves, they will all need to confront this question of the optimal management of such reserves. The fundamental problem lies

in the investment of these reserves and the major risks such investments face, especially currency risks. Whilst for Botswana, which has
already tranched its reserves into longer-term and shorter-term liquidity components with differing performance standards, guidelines and
benchmarks, there would be other types of risks (such as duration/
interest rate risks) about which to be preoccupied for the near and
medium term, it is likely that most reserve portfolios for countries in
the region would have shorter durations, staying as liquid as possible,
to meet transaction needs and flows. For Botswana, however, and for
other strongly emerging economies in the future, the challenge is and
will be how to preserve the capital value and effective purchasing power
of the nation's precious reserve assets, having regard to existing or
future trading patterns and their payment liabilities. More specifically,
the preponderance of imports emanates from, and therefore payment
liabilities for most regional economies are owed to, South Africa. Conventional currency risk management would, therefore, dictate corre-
spondingly large weights of reserve asset holdings in rands to insulate
adverse changes in the future value of such assets. But the realities of
an emerging South Africa are already with us, and at best, the long-
run prognosis for economic and political success for South Africa is
mixed. An investment posture with heavy rand rates, therefore, is always
a source of major concern.

The question, then, is whether regional investment portfolios of reserve assets should be fully currency-weighted by trade patterns or
whether their rand components should be arbitrarily underweighted,
thus exposing the portfolios to the risk of major losses in value especially if the rand appreciates vis-à-vis SDR currencies. While this is
already a trade-specific problem for Botswana, it may already also be
a problem for other countries in terms of their larger foreign debt service liabilities, in which repayment streams may be required in stronger
foreign currencies over long durations. The appropriate balance of
portfolios, therefore, is an issue that cannot be treated lightly, as is the
extent to which attempts to require asset cover for known liabilities
within the region itself are practical and workable, given the thinness
and relatively illiquid states of regional bond and equity markets. The
fact that most regional economies do not have fully convertible currencies does not simplify but rather compounds the problem, nor does
the fact that exchange rate adjustment policies throughout the region
are largely influenced by the rand, help matters in any way.

IMPLICATIONS AND CONCLUSIONS FOR THE REGION

What, therefore, are some necessary conclusions and inferences for the region in the area of monetary management and cooperation, against the background of present and future strategies for currency convertibility and management of external reserves? A few clearly stand out.

For individual national economies, these include:

1. Continued steady progress towards current account convertibility and formal access to Article VIII status is essential. There are no longer defensible arguments for continued payment restrictions and other restraints on trade transactions. This is particularly important for intra-regional trade, multilateral or bilateral.
2. The growing tendency towards internal convertibility in regional economies must be encouraged, with the liberalisation of current accounts and the steady movement to capital account convertibility. This encourages domestic foreign exchange market development and management, fosters integration of domestic with external economies, induces reverse flows of leaked or externalised foreign currency by citizens and non-citizens, and encourages diversification of portfolio holdings by residents and non-residents. Care, however, has to be taken to reduce the potentially adverse effects on the money supply if uncontrolled switching in and out of such currencies is permitted, and such foreign balances are included as part of the money supply, which is probably not a good idea. Further, the implications for multiple exchange rate practices should not be ignored if the inter-bank foreign exchange markets created through FCAs exist, in addition to separate markets for 'official' transactions.
3. More balanced intra-regional trade must be initiated domestically and encouraged at national levels, especially in terms of the heavy trade dependence on South Africa for most regional economies. This would not only enhance currency convertibility sooner rather than later, but would reduce problems arising from efforts to retain and manage larger volumes of reserve assets while simultaneously attempting to deepen debt and equity markets.
4. Capital account convertibility at the national level should be carefully introduced, having due regard to issues of excess monetisation and possible exchange rate upheavals. Fiscal policy would also need to be more responsible and responsive in such unconstrained environments, especially as the short-term effects of possible balance of payments stresses and increased interest rates begin to bite in

the early post-liberalisation phases. Tax environments also need to be appropriate to capture global as opposed to domestic incomes from investments by citizens.

At a regional level, conclusions are:

1. Southern Africa should be aiming at full convertibility of regional currencies as soon as possible, thus setting the basis for possible currency unification.
2. Some form of pooling of reserves, or at least greater intra-regional investment of larger shares of individual country reserves, should facilitate this sooner rather than later, having regard to existing trade patterns.
3. The full liberalisation of current accounts and gradual abolition of capital controls by individual economies should set the basis for enhanced monetary cooperation in the longer term.
4. The desire for early convertibility of regional currencies and of trade/investment accounts should not necessarily imply evolution of flexible exchange rates either at the level of regional economies vis-à-vis external ones or among themselves. In fact, whilst domestic liberalisation proceeds respectively, it may be more appropriate as wider economic convergence progresses within the region, to fix exchange rates in relation to regional currencies themselves with comfortable operating bands, or at a later stage against a central rate for a truly regional currency (a composite), or with an unquestionably strong regional one as anchor.
5. Finally, this raises the perennial but still very elusive question as to the ultimate form of monetary integration for Southern Africa. That it should be encouraged there is virtually no doubt, but how is another matter? One obvious way is, of course, to build on and expand the existing Common Monetary Area, initially allowing independent national currencies to coexist with the rand and ultimately moving to a more unified currency arrangement. This, however, implies a strong rand which at this point could not be taken as a given; in fact, the pula is unquestionably in a stronger position to do so than the rand. It also implies continuation of existing trade patterns which with the emergence of GATT, for instance, is not necessarily assured, and would probably also be influenced by the outcome of the SACU negotiations. Alternatively, a gradual but planned movement to regional and financial convergence along the lines of the evolution of the European Monetary System and an

ERM structure could be encouraged, with the ultimate goal of a full regional monetary union. While this is probably the longer way to proceed, if eventually successful it is likely to be the more enduring and workable option, given the clear emerging commitment region-wide to enhanced fiscal and monetary discipline and the externally imposed realities of an increasingly competitive non-regional environment.

12 Internationalisation of Capital Markets

S. Ghon Rhee

The opening of a market is easy, but the process of 'real' internationalisation is slow and painful. It becomes even slower and more painful when government regulators fail to recognise that it is market-driven. Very often, they are reluctant to solve the principal problem causing disorder in the financial system because they fear losing their authority over the market. Rather, only minor problems are addressed, creating unnecessary rules and regulations. Asian experiences in internationalising capital markets indicate that numerous problems are caused by government regulators: countries frequently experience a painful transition because government authorities fail to adapt to the dynamic environments of the capital markets or take the necessary actions after the fact. This paper reflects upon past Asian experiences and identifies some lessons which may be applied to the development of capital markets in the Southern African region.[1]

STAGES OF INTERNATIONALISATION

Internationalisation is part of capital market development and, therefore, depends on the degree of market integration. As illustrated in Table 12.1, capital markets undergo four stages of internationalisation: (1) closed market; (2) partially open market with unilateral capital flows; (3) partially open market with multilateral capital flows; and (4) open market.

Closed Markets

A closed market is common in the early stages of economic development. It is characterised by government-dictated resource and credit allocation among different sectors of the economy. The financial system is considered by economic planners as a vehicle for economic development, resulting in control and management of financial institutions by the government. To support the industrial and export sectors of the

Table 12.1 Stages of Internationalisation

Stages	Closed market	Partially open market with unilateral capital flows	Partially open market with multilateral capital flows	Open market
Policies	Foreign exchange control Interest rate control Government-dictated resource allocation	Partial deregulation of foreign exchange and interest rate control Foreign direct investment and foreign portfolio investment	Foreign exchange and interest rate control phased out Investment abroad by local investors Improvement of the securities industry infrastructures Investor protection and market transparency	No entry barrier No restriction on capital flows
Capital market	No secondary market for fixed income securities Undeveloped short-term money market Equity market shadowed by the banking sector	Short-term money market and fixed income securities market introduced GDRs and ADRs introduced Established offshore banking facilities	Money market and bond market further developed Financial derivative market introduced Broader participation by foreign investors in local corporate ownership	Money market, foreign currency, derivative market, fully developed
Development by country	Korea (1956–81)[a] Taiwan (1960–83)[a] Thailand (1975–85)[a] Japan (1949–55)[a]	Korea (1982–93) Taiwan (1984–7) Thailand (1986–present) Japan (1956–69)	Korea (1994–present) Taiwan (1988–present) Malaysia (1987–present)[b] Japan (1970–7)	HK (1973–present)[b] Japan (1978–present) Singapore (1978–present)[b]

Notes: a. Organised stock exchanges started trading at the beginning of this period.
b. Exchange control was eliminated at the beginning of this period.

economy, the financial system is designed and managed without regard to the optimal allocation of resources. Of the traditional monetary policy tools, open market operations cannot be employed since government-issued securities are not priced by market demand and supply. As a result, monetary authorities rely on reserve requirements and lending policies (including changes in official discount rates) to meet monetary targets. Both interest rates and exchange rates are controlled and capital flows are closely monitored.

Due to the government's control over interest rates, a secondary market of fixed income securities is virtually non-existent at this stage of market development. Primary market activities exist in government-issued securities, but they are limited to such organisations as commercial banks, specialised banks, government-owned non-bank financial institutions (NBFIs) and pension funds which serve as captive demanders of government-issued securities. The short-term money market is not developed other than for overnight or short-term borrowing arrangements among financial institutions and central banks. Most lending to the private sector takes the form of short-term credit provided by the banking sector. Credit volume and interest rates are dictated by the monetary authority or the finance ministry which also involves itself in the daily management of financial institutions. The capital market's function of mobilising savings is overshadowed by the banking sector since credit allocation is largely undertaken by deposit money banks and NBFIs. This achieves the government's top priority of developing selected sectors of the economy. Domestic investors are allowed to invest only in local securities. Since there is no fully developed securities industry, individual investors are frequently victims of price manipulation as well as widespread clearing and settlement default. In general, the securities market is completely closed to foreign investors as witnessed in Korea (1956–81), Taiwan (1960–83) and Thailand (1975–85).[2]

Partially Open Market with Unilateral Capital Flows

At this stage of market integration, economic development remains the government's primary goal. Hence, protectionist policy dictates capital market-related activities. As a result, capital outflow is not allowed in order to protect local economies, whilst capital inflows are encouraged to promote economic development. Early in this stage, indirect access to the local securities market is made possible for foreign investors through open- and/or close-ended investment funds. A good example of this is the popular 'country' funds.

Government control over interest rates and foreign exchange is still in place, but partial deregulation is underway, further encouraging direct portfolio investment by foreigners in local securities and allowing domestic corporations to raise funds overseas. Typically, equity-linked securities such as convertible bonds, bonds with warrants and depository receipts are issued, but the finance ministry tends to exercise complete control over the selection of issuing firms, timing and terms and conditions of issue.

In the presence of controlled or administered interest rates, the fixed income securities market is not developed with the exception of that for short-term money market instruments. Since the equity and fixed income securities markets are not yet mature enough to recognise the need for developing a market for financial derivatives, this has to wait until the next stage of capital market development.

A partially open market can be conveniently illustrated in a three-stage internationalisation programme announced by the government of Taiwan in 1982. This envisaged only unilateral rather than multilateral capital flows. In the first stage, foreign investors had indirect access to the Taiwanese capital market through investment trusts and/or country funds. The second stage involved giving foreign institutional investors direct access to Taiwanese securities. The third stage, which is yet to be implemented, will provide foreign investors with complete access to Taiwanese securities. Major capital market activities which are common at this stage of market development include: (1) international investment trust funds; (2) overseas issue of equity-linked bonds; (3) fund-raising by domestic companies through global depository receipts (GDR) and American depository receipts (ADR); (4) direct foreign portfolio investment; (5) establishment of offshore banking facilities; and (6) internationalisation of securities business.

At present, Korea, Malaysia and Taiwan have graduated from this stage of market development, while the Thai capital market is still allowing only unilateral capital flows.

Partially Open Market with Multilateral Capital Flows

Several significant developments characterise this stage of market integration. They include: (1) portfolio investment abroad by local investors; (2) further deregulation of interest rates and foreign exchange control; (3) gradual opening of the financial services industry; (4) development of the financial derivative market; and (5) reinforcing the securities industry infrastructures for investor protection and market transparency.

Foreign exchange and interest rate control are phased out so that the open-market operations become the primary tool for monetary policy with the help of reserve requirements. As a result, government-issued securities are priced by market forces and the short-term money market is fully developed. To facilitate risk-hedging for local and foreign investors, the derivative market is also developed at this stage especially for stock index futures/options, short-term interest rate futures/options and long-term government bond futures/options. Foreign securities companies are allowed to compete with local counterparts. Local brokerage houses engage in full-fledged brokerage, dealing and underwriting businesses abroad.

As the capital markets become mature, the primary task of government regulators is to build investor confidence and market transparency. This is achieved through better defined securities industry infrastructures in preparing for the opening of the capital markets. A wide range of policy measures is introduced to liberalise and open the capital markets. A substantial improvement is noted in the introduction of an automated trading system, clearing and settlement systems, financial disclosure requirements, capital adequacy of securities companies, listing rules, initial public offering processes, and so on. Korea, Malaysia and Taiwan are beginning this stage of development.

Open Market

Hong Kong and Singapore positioned themselves as open economies and have been developing their capital markets as regional financial centres. As a result, their capital markets are open with only slight barriers to entry into the local securities industry or market. No significant restrictions are imposed on capital flows.

LESSONS FROM THE ASIAN CAPITAL MARKETS

Sequence of Policy Measures

The major consequence of capital market internationalisation is that it means more competition among financial intermediaries. Although this competition comes in many different forms, nothing is more important than price competition which deregulates the fixed commission system. Negotiable commissions were introduced in the US market in 1975, followed by Canada (1983), Australia and New Zealand (1984), the United Kingdom (1986), France (1988), Switzerland (1990) and Spain

(1992). Japan is one exception among the world's advanced markets which still maintains a fixed commission system. Although Japanese authorities have been successful in using this system as an entry barrier to foreign brokerage firms with Tokyo Stock Exchange membership attempting to enter the domestic retail market, problems occurred elsewhere, specifically the index futures arbitrage between Tokyo's cash market and Osaka's index futures market.

Japan's finance ministry was unhappy that foreign brokerages were making large profits from index futures arbitrage while Tokyo's cash market had experienced a significant downturn since January 1990. Recently, the finance ministry imposed stricter controls on stock index futures trading. In addition to introducing American-style circuit-breakers, increased disclosure requirements of trading activities and increased margin requirements in the futures market, the ministry bans arbitrage and proprietary trading whenever the futures market is overheated or is in danger of overheating (Sato, 1993).

A direct result of these reforms is that the Osaka futures market has become a more costly place in which to trade. Index futures arbitrage in Japan is not motivated by price differentials between the cash and the futures market, but rather is transaction cost-driven given the substantial differences in transaction costs between the cash and the futures market (Miller, 1994: 95–6). What Japan really needs is a less. expensive cash market rather than a more costly futures market. Unfortunately, Japan's finance ministry is doing exactly the opposite.

This is a good example of market regulators failing to recognise the real problem which they face as well as not considering the necessary policy measures. As part of Japan's internationalisation programme, the fixed commission system in the cash market should have been deregulated before foreign brokerage houses were admitted to Tokyo Stock Exchange membership. Instead, Japanese authorities effectively caused the Osaka Securities Exchange to lose a large portion of its index futures trading volume to the Singapore International Monetary Exchange. The identical Nikkei Stock Average (NSA) futures contracts are traded there with less stringent trading rules (Rhee, 1993a: 27–33).

Government Intervention in the Securities Market

In late 1994, the Korean government announced plans to boost the flagging popularity of preferred stocks in the local market. The Securities and Exchange Commission (SEC) asked all listed companies that have more than 25 per cent of their total shares in preferred stock to buy back at least 2 per cent of the outstanding preferred shares before the first quarter of 1995. Securities companies were also requested to buy back at least 3 per cent of preferred shares. At the same time, the SEC banned listed companies and securities companies from reselling newly purchased preferred stocks for one year. Two reasons were cited by the SEC: first, preferred stock price was depressed; and second, preferred holders deserve higher returns for not having voting rights. This is but one example of the government's proclivity to meddle in the Asian securities markets.[3]

In the past, the Korean and Thai governments have occasionally turned to indirect intervention in the stock market to shore up price levels, hoping to slow the rapid decline in stock prices. Japan used similar methods in the early 1960s to support the Tokyo market price level. The most recent example is that of two stabilisation funds established in Thailand in November 1992. The last Korean stock market stabilisation fund was established in May 1990 with a contributed fund of approximately 4 per cent of Korea's total market capitalisation at that time (Rhee, 1992: 34–5).

The establishment of these funds was not initiated voluntarily by financial institutions, but imposed by the finance ministries of Korea and Thailand. Stock market rescue funds represent an example of misdirected policy measures. Their long-term effectiveness is questionable in coping with falling stock prices. A lasting solution would have been the introduction of stock index futures and options which investors can use for hedging.

Real Commitment

The Korean finance ministry recently announced that: (1) foreign investors may now buy convertible bonds issued by small and medium-sized Korean companies; (2) foreign securities companies may now underwrite Korean government bonds; and (3) foreign investors may invest in Korean bonds through mutual funds, while international financial institutions will be permitted to issue Korean currency-denominated bonds by 1995.

This announcement was unexpected considering that Korea is one of the few countries in Asia where interest rates are still controlled or administered by the finance ministry. Without complete deregulation of interest rates, one wonders how effective the specific measures outlined above will be. The Asian Development Bank or the International Finance Corporation might go to Korea to issue long-term bonds denominated in the US dollar or Korean currency, but it is doubtful whether such issues would promote the Korean bond market considering the small contribution made by so-called 'dragon bonds' which were issued by the same institutions in Hong Kong, Singapore and Taiwan. Without the establishment of a competitive auction system to issue Korean government bonds, it is doubtful how many foreign securities firms will be eager to engage in the underwriting of Korean government bonds, while with very little liquidity in the secondary market for fixed income securities, it is questionable whether foreign investors will invest in Korean bond funds.

Common sense will tell us the type of adverse impact which regulated interest rates will have on bond market development. Effective yields on government bonds are kept at low levels in the primary market without reflecting current credit market conditions. As a result, the Korean government has relied on financial institutions as captive demanders of government bonds at their initial issue. For example, Korea's monetary stabilisation bonds are not popular among subscribing financial institutions because their primary market yields are comparable to the savings and time deposit rates of 4–8 per cent, while their prices in the secondary market are adjusted downward to reflect current interest rates of over 12 per cent. Because of the large difference between the primary and secondary market yield, subscribing financial institutions cannot sell the monetary stabilisation bonds without incurring large capital losses. These securities are naturally held until maturity and are used to meet the reserve and liquidity requirements of the Bank of Korea. As a result, the secondary market cannot function owing to a lack of supply of government bonds. Although the size of the primary long-term bond market in Korea is approximately 30 per cent of GDP, which is about the same size as its equity market, turnover ratios of government and corporate bonds are extremely low (less than 10 per cent), once transaction volume related to bond repurchase has been excluded. This is essentially a short-term financing vehicle for business corporations for daily operation rather than for long-term investment.

To make the situation worse, the banking sector still dominates the securities industry in Korea (as it does in other Asian countries). For example, no more than 3 per cent of individual investors' investments are held in debt securities, whilst approximately 65 per cent are with banking institutions in the form of deposits and cash. By contrast, the amount of individual holdings in long-term, fixed income securities is about 25 per cent in the United States and 30 per cent in Germany, and bank assets are approximately three times greater than equity market capitalisation in Korea. Firms usually rely on short-term borrowing from various financial institutions as their primary source of financing. In fact, commercial banks encourage private corporations to borrow on a short-term basis rather than losing them to the securities markets.

In the majority of Asian countries including Korea, corporate debt issues are usually required to be collateralised or guaranteed by a third-party financial institution. For example, about 90 per cent of corporate bonds in Korea are secured. In all Asian countries, the banking sector lobbies very hard to maintain the collateralisation requirement. For instance, in Japan, commercial banks strongly resisted the issue of unsecured debt by business corporations as late as 1979. As long as the bond rating system is in place and the pricing mechanism is functioning, the choice between secured and unsecured debt should be left to the discretion of issuing companies and underwriting merchant banks (Rhee, 1993b: 88).

Given its current status, is the Korean bond market really ready to open to foreign investors? The first issue to be addressed is the deregulation of interest rates. On the surface, it is easy to open the market, but often this cannot easily be done because of the unwillingness of government officials to reform existing regulations and controls.

Fragmented Regulatory Environment

A fragmented regulatory environment poses a serious problem for any country's capital market. Although the US market survived the October 1987 market break, a lack of coordination among various regulatory agencies was revealed as the major weakness of the US financial system.[4] The Hong Kong market crash in 1987 serves as a classic example in which clearing and settlement systems failed both in the cash and futures markets. This failure is attributed to Hong Kong's fragmented regulatory structure which existed prior to 1987. At that time, no central clearing and depository functions were in place in the Hong Kong cash market while the risk management system in the futures market suffered from several structural flaws (Rhee, 1992: 46–8).

Coordination Among Government Agencies

A serious lack of coordination between the Securities and Exchange Commission (SEC) and the Central Bank of China (CBC) is noted in Taiwan's internationalisation programme. In January 1991, foreign institutional investors (banks, securities companies, insurance companies and fund managers) were allowed to invest directly in Taiwanese securities. At present, each individual foreign institution is permitted to invest no more than US$200 million. All foreign investors, however, must observe the maximum of not holding more than 10 per cent of a listed firm's capital, and individual institution holdings shall not exceed 5 per cent. As of mid-October 1994, the Taiwanese authorities approved investment quotas for 76 foreign institutions totalling US$6.44 billion, while the ceiling was US$7.5 billion (less than 4 per cent of the Taiwan Stock Exchange's (TSE) market capitalisation). Of this amount, only US$4.88 billion was remitted to Taiwan for stock investment.

Semkow (1994) identifies the CBC's implementation policy as the primary reason for the less than overwhelming response of foreign institutional investors to this direct investment programme. The CBC has been reluctant to allow large amounts of capital inflow in fear of currency appreciation and high inflation. The CBC had initially limited the inward remittance to US$5 million weekly, and allowed outward remittance of principal and capital gains only once a year. This caused a great deal of frustration among foreign institutional investors. In early 1992, they went so far as to ban the inward remittance. By contrast, the SEC wants to raise the ceiling of direct foreign equity investment to US$20 billion.

Another example of the lack of coordination among government agencies is found in convertible bonds and global depository receipts issued by Taiwanese companies. In 1989, the first convertible bonds were issued in the Eurobond market. Although several firms followed suit, foreign investors outside Taiwan have been unable to convert them into stocks owing to the absence of necessary rules and regulations. Conversion must first be approved by the Ministry of Economic Affairs, and the remittance of proceeds from convertible bonds needs to be approved by the CBC, while bond issue approval is provided by the SEC. The issue of global depository receipts (GDR) by TSE-listed firms was delayed until April 1992 when the relevant guidelines were issued by the SEC. In 1992 alone, four firms, including China Steel, took advantage of the GDR programme for offshore funds, but the proceeds had to be used for overseas investment and purchase of raw materials because of CBC-imposed guidelines. In October 1993, the CBC permitted the proceeds from GDR issues to be converted into local currency for the purpose of financing plant expansion only, making overseas financing for Taiwan companies extremely difficult.

CONCLUSION

Although capital market development has been dictated by different philosophies among the Asian countries, they have now converged to a point where internationalisation and regional integration are aggressively pursued. Kane (1991) emphasises that internationalisation of capital markets is a process in which increasing international competition imposes *market discipline* on government regulators, restricting their freedoms. From the Asian experience, it is obvious that government regulators play a significant role in promoting internationalisation. They can impede this process through: (1) the incorrect sequence of policy measures; (2) intervention in the market; (3) the lack of real commitment; (4) a fragmented regulatory structure; and (5) the lack of coordination among government agencies. These are points which Southern African governments would do well to recognise.

Notes

1. For an overview of the Asian capital markets, see Rhee and Chang (1992).
2. Although portfolio investment by foreign investors in the Thai securities was possible before 1985 from the legal standpoint, exchange control, withholding taxes on dividend and capital gains and complicated paperwork made it an impossible task in practice.
3. It is a well-known fact that even today Japanese institutional investors, especially insurance companies, pension funds and brokerage house, buy securities at the urging of the finance ministry whenever the NSA goes down below an acceptable level. See 'The Invisible Hand', *Financial Times* (10 October 1994).
4. See the *Report of the Presidential Task Force on Market Mechanisms* (1988).

13 Macroeconomic Policy Lessons from Africa[1]

Anselm London

The early tradition in economics made little distinction between economic growth and economic development. Accordingly, a country's advancement was, as a matter of practice, almost invariably measured by the level of real per capita income, and it was only subsequently that clear distinctions began to be made between growth and development. Indeed, it was Seers (1972) who stressed that among the key questions to be asked about a country's development should be: what has been happening to poverty, unemployment and inequality? Indeed, he went on to caution that if one or two of these central problems grew worse, and especially if all three did, it would be strange to call the result 'development' even if real per capita income had soared. In today's circumstances, Seers would probably have added at least three other questions to his list, namely, what has been happening to the environment, to sex equality and to human freedom?

Attention is drawn to these considerations, given their centrality to any discussion of future economic policy in South Africa and, indeed, in all Africa. For not only have already low real per capita income levels declined significantly in various parts of the continent over the past decade, but development, as measured by the above criteria, has lagged considerably in spite of important policy initiatives undertaken. This paper is based on two premises: first, that despite its unique economic and political characteristics, South Africa's challenges of policy formation and implementation are not too dissimilar from those in the rest of Africa; and secondly, there is much that South Africa can learn from the rest of Africa, in the sense both of policy pitfalls that should be avoided and of pro-active measures that need to be undertaken if the challenge of sustainable development is to be successfully met.

ECONOMIC OVERVIEW AND POLICY PERSPECTIVES

Africa as a whole is today in the throes of serious economic and social difficulties. Some of the symptoms are manifested in a persistent decline in real per capita income; large fiscal and external imbalances; and rapid population growth. Indeed, it would now require almost a decade of continuous annual real per capita income growth of 1 per cent simply to return to the output level of 1980. The continuing economic crisis has also increased the incidence of poverty; accelerated environmental degradation; ruptured the social and political fabric of many nations; and, in the process, threatened their very survival. Although important distinctions can be made among individual countries, the overall picture is not satisfactory and is, in some instances, worse than a decade and a half ago. In the case of South Africa, important parallels can be drawn with this experience of the rest of Africa. Recent years have also witnessed a decline in real per capita income, aggravating an already skewed distribution of income; inflation, even though lower than in the rest of Africa, has remained a matter of concern; and there has been a deterioration in the rate of overall investment and domestic savings.

However, there are also important differences between the performance of South Africa and the rest of Africa over the past several years. For instance, the persistent current account deficits of the rest of Africa have not been observed in South Africa and, related to this, the problems of external indebtedness have been markedly different. Indeed, whilst the rest of Africa saw the ratio of its external debt to GDP more than triple between 1980 and 1993, rising to close to 60 per cent, in South Africa in 1993 this ratio stood at less than 15 per cent. Although the political factors underlying these trends in South Africa are no longer at work and the situation can change abruptly, the fact is that, in significant contrast to the rest of Africa, these key economic indicators point to greater degrees of freedom for South Africa's macroeconomic policy in the years ahead.

One easy conclusion that could be drawn from an assessment of Africa's recent economic record is that its policies have been misconceived and inappropriate, and thus are incapable of providing any positive clues as to the directions of future policy in South Africa. However, taking as fundamental the view that the analytical logic underlying the broad elements of recent policy in the rest of Africa are not really a matter of dispute, few would question the need, in the normal conduct of macroeconomic policy, to avoid monetary and fiscal excesses; to correct overvalued exchange rates; to contain inflation; to eliminate price distortions; to enhance tax administration; or to ensure that parastatal enterprises do not represent a burden on the public treasury – all of which are (admittedly, with varying intensities) important elements of current policy in Africa. But few also would challenge the fact that, in spite of efforts in these and other similar directions, Africa today remains the poorest region of the world and that its current development prospects are, for the main part, not measurably different from that which obtained in the early 1980s when major shifts in policy were introduced.

Clearly, any assessment of recent macroeconomic policy in the rest of Africa – with a view to drawing lessons for the new South Africa – must pay special attention to its impact on poverty reduction and on accelerated growth with equity, since sustainable development requires that growth be achieved with equity and that it results in broad-based improvements in standards of living and in large-scale employment generation. It is evident that these goals have not been achieved within the present policy context, and efforts towards mid-course corrections, as reflected in programmes aimed at addressing the so-called social dimensions of adjustment, have (at least initially) been largely policy add-ons or programming afterthoughts which have not fundamentally altered the circumstances of the poor. It is, thus, a legitimate policy concern that, even in countries such as Ghana where reform and adjustment programmes have been steadfastly pursued over a considerable period of time, and in spite of some advances made, standards of living on the whole remain unacceptably low, and sustainable growth and development are yet to be attained.

This raises several important questions. For instance, why have current policies not led to more positive changes in welfare, even as measured by increases in real per capita GDP? Do the results obtained to date reflect fundamental deficiencies in the underlying theoretical constructs or a lack of understanding of how these constructs are to be applied, in practice, in different African environments? Or is their limited success rate due to some other yet unknown economic and 'non-economic' factors? In this context, it is instructive to note the recent conclusion of the World Bank (1994: 2) that:

> Adjustment alone will not put countries on a sustained, poverty-reducing growth path. That is the challenge of long-term development, which requires better economic policies and more investment in human capital, infrastructure, and institution-building, along with better governance.

However, while this prescription of the World Bank may be interpreted as a call for more of the same, the case must also be made that, beyond the question of policy dosages, current policies, notwithstanding their theoretical rigour, must be made to work with greater developmental impact and effectiveness.

LINKAGES AND TRANSMISSION MECHANISMS

Given that the theoretical constructs underlying current macroeconomic policies in the rest of Africa are broadly valid, the limited success rate to date may well lie in the insufficient attention that seems to have been paid to linkages and transmission mechanisms inherent in current policy – issues which would need to be addressed more forcefully if, in fact, policies are to have greater development impact and effectiveness. This question is explored below in respect of three key elements of current policy: exchange rate management and the balance of payments, financial liberalisation and regional economic integration.

Exchange Rate Management and the Balance of Payments

Current policy in Africa includes various balance of payments enhancement measures, a major element of which has been exchange rate devaluation. However, whilst the need to correct obviously overvalued exchange rates cannot be disputed, the results, particularly in terms of the impact on the balance of payments, have fallen far short of expectations. If exchange rate overvaluation has been corrected, as is now largely the case in many African countries, why has this not been reflected, as theory would predict, in a more favourable and substantial turnaround in the current account? Is it simply that the trade elasticities are much smaller or the lags are much longer (and perhaps unknown) in Africa? But even so, should the actual impact of exchange rate adjustments on Africa's trade performance not also be evaluated in the light of the external environment – structural terms of trade difficulties; protectionism; GATT rules; and the macroeconomic policy-setting of the industrialised countries? Is it that, because of internal and external constraints, including those related to distribution and marketing, the hypothesised transmission mechanisms from an exchange rate devaluation to an improvement in the balance of trade have been unable to work more effectively? Or is it that expectations regarding the impact of exchange rate adjustments have been exaggerated, or even ill-founded, given the narrow production structures of the majority of African countries and the virtual non-existence of the necessary transmission mechanisms on which the underlying theoretical constructs and their predictions depend? (Lahouel, 1994).

In considering the experience of the rest of Africa, the case can broadly be made that the devaluation of the exchange rate and its supporting demand management policies which are emphasised as central for increasing export supply, growth and employment, are quite ineffective in the absence of various non-price factors whose importance looms especially large in Africa. Indeed, the production effect of a devaluation may be quite negligible if inputs necessary for production are not available; if there is inadequate transport that frustrates or impedes the timely delivery of both inputs and outputs; or if appropriate technologies and products that call for additional labour absorption are scare or do not exist altogether. In short, actions on the price front (such as changing the price of foreign currency) might be sufficient only in those cases where the necessary non-price factors are in place.

However, even then, a devaluation will yield positive results in terms of increased foreign exchange earnings only if there are adequate markets to absorb the forthcoming supply of exports – and at prices which are not so low as to offset the potential income gains accruing from the increase in quantity supplied. Indeed, the well-documented deterioration in the terms of trade of producers and exporters of primary commodities, as a result of events in international markets, has more often than not meant that some African countries have had to supply increasingly larger amounts of exports just to keep their already meagre foreign exchange earnings intact.

Thus, it is clear that previously pursued policies resulting in real exchange rate appreciation, such as in the CFA Zone countries, are fundamentally inimical to the growth and development objectives of these countries. However, it should also be clear that exchange rate adjustments will have significantly less impact in an environment in which the necessary supporting economic and non-economic infrastructure is deficient. In South Africa, the recent experience has included some appreciation of the real exchange rate since 1990. Whether or not policy should be directed at reversing this appreciation should not be a matter of debate. What would be especially important for South Africa, however, would be not to delay this process as so many African countries have done and to use its superior economic and non-economic structures to exploit the trade and growth opportunities which an exchange rate adjustment can offer. Indeed, South Africa seems much better positioned to exploit such opportunities than are the majority of countries in Africa.

Financial Liberalisation

Recent policy in Africa has also correctly stressed the importance of financial liberalisation (ADB, 1994a). Movements towards increases in real interest rates have been central to this policy, but it is notable that such increases have so far failed to raise the level of overall savings and have not led to measurable improvements in the allocation of credit or in the volume or productivity of investment. This, however, should not, *a priori*, be interpreted as an indictment of received theory on domestic resource mobilisation, but as a reflection of the fact that there are Africa-specific considerations which policies of financial liberalisation, as currently applied, have not adequately addressed.

The theory of financial liberalisation argues that if interest rates are allowed to find their market levels, this will raise both the level of saving and investment and improve the allocation of investment resources by eliminating credit rationing and investment in low-risk, low-yield projects. The theory is appealing in its simplicity but, by itself, is open to a number of objections and subject to a number of qualifications. Positive and high real interest rates may encourage financial saving but not necessarily total saving. Investment in a credit money economy is not constrained by prior saving, and may be discouraged by high real interest rates which raise costs and may lead to stagflation. The informal money market, or curb market, may also be adversely affected. Finally, a free market in loans does not eliminate credit rationing since asymmetric information and the problem of adverse selection make profit-maximising banks risk-averse.

This is not to deny the importance of financial liberalisation in Africa's, and indeed South Africa's, development efforts, but to raise questions about the degree and pace of such liberalisation, and the institutional background against which it takes place. Indeed, the transmission mechanisms from interest rates to savings need to be examined at the practical African level, as would the structure of financial systems (both formal and informal) and institutional issues related to the role of the State, the transformation of informal institutions to formal ones, the spread of institutions to the rural sector and the availability of appropriate financial instruments.

Liberalising interest rates and eliminating credit rationing are, of course, only aspects of financial liberalisation. There are also the issues of restructuring financial institutions and the relief of financial distress; improving the regulation and supervision of the financial system; and coping with the consequences of financial liberalisation. Liberalisation also needs to be considered within the broader context of macroeconomic adjustment and other structural reforms. This raises the question of the sequencing of financial liberalisation and how it interrelates with other aspects of liberalisation, particularly of the foreign sector. Financial liberalisation against a background of large budget deficits, rising inflation and the abolition of capital controls may cause as many problems as it solves. Beyond this, not all government intervention in financial markets should be regarded as misguided, because financial markets, like other markets, suffer from a wide variety of market failures, including imperfect information and divergences between social and private costs and benefits associated with externalities and economies of scale and scope. Government intervention, directly or through taxes and subsidies, may be necessary to capture externalities; to provide for special needs; and to ensure that banks are of an adequate size to reap the benefits of specialisation and diversification simultaneously. All this is in addition to the regulatory functions of government to avoid financial distress.

The results of financial liberalisation in Africa have been mixed. There have been some benefits, but also some costs. In Egypt, for instance, the programme can be judged as successful with reference to the de-dollarisation of the economy, the virtual eradication of the parallel market for foreign exchange and the reduction in the size of the underground economy. However, interest rate liberalisation has attracted large capital inflows and increased the cost of monetary sterilisation, worsening the budget deficit (Hussain, 1994). In Ghana, new financial instruments and higher interest rates led to a switch from private lending into treasury bills (Jebuni, 1994). In Nigeria, there has been a massive growth in banking, but increased competition has brought financial distress through a deterioration in the quality of assets and the inadequate capital base of some banks (Oshikoya, 1994). In Tanzania, where interest rates were liberalised in 1988 and the banking system was decontrolled in 1991, the cost of budget deficits has increased and the ability to fund government expenditure by non-inflationary means has been reduced (Kimei, 1994).

Experiences in the rest of Africa suggest that policy in South Africa should be guided by the fundamental premise that the ultimate objective of financial reforms is to raise the level of saving and investment as well as the rate of economic growth. The evidence for Africa shows that financial saving responds positively to real interest rates but that the relation between total saving and interest rates is insignificant. Investment, if anything, is negatively related to interest rates, responding positively to the supply of credit but negatively to the cost of credit, and the latter outweighs the former as interest rates rise. There is no discernible relation between interest rates and economic growth. This would seem to suggest that financial liberalisation, in certain country-specific circumstances, may fail to raise the level of saving and investment as well as the productivity of investment by improving the allocation of resources.

However, the case for liberalisation must remain strong provided due attention is paid to the institutional background against which it takes place, and also to the macroeconomic environment and the costs involved. Financial liberalisation in the context of well-sequenced macroeconomic reforms would tend to increase financial saving, even though total saving is stagnant, by encouraging the return of flight capital. Successful liberalisation requires not only a strong regulatory and legal framework with proper standards of accounting and auditing but also macro-stability in terms of fiscal discipline and low inflation, and it must have due regard to the exchange rate and capital flows.

Regional Economic Integration

A third unique characteristic of current macroeconomic policy in Africa is the pursuit of economic adjustment and reform measures with little practical linkage to the broader concerns of economic integration. It is evident that conscious efforts need to be made to ensure that SAPs and economic integration become more mutually reinforcing. If this is to be achieved, there should be full exchange of information among countries about national SAPs and the programmes of relevant integration groupings, at the design as well as at subsequent stages. Furthermore, it should be possible for regional economic groupings to assess the regional impact of national SAPs as well as the national impact of regional programmes on the implementation of SAPs, and the idea of a regional structural adjustment programme must be strongly encouraged.

However, it should be noted that controversy has already surfaced as to whether an aggressive approach to integrated macroeconomic policy, based on the principle of flexible membership in various sub-regional organisations – which is contrary to that implied by the Abuja Treaty – should not be attempted as a way of making faster progress. But care must be taken not to exaggerate this concern. Within ECOWAS, for instance, should Benin, Togo, Ghana and Côte d'Ivoire fail to harmonise tariff policy simply because Nigeria is not ready to go along at the same pace? Similarly, can the exchange rate arrangements of the CMA be profitably expanded to some SADC or COMESA members, and not to others, if this will accelerate the integrative process?

Whilst answers to these and related questions may seem obvious, attention should also be drawn to some important risks that need to be taken into account in recommending a multi-speed approach to integration in Africa. If the more advanced member states of an economic community proceed with decisions in which the remaining members have not taken part, the multi-speed strategy can become disintegrative, splitting the community in two, as the remaining members have only two options: implementing the decisions taken by the 'core group' or taking a direction more consistent with their joint interests. A multi-speed strategy can become an especially important concern when the pace of progress of the core countries depends on the impetus carried into the community from outside the region. Indeed, an integrative strategy is unlikely to succeed if the steam for the locomotive is not generated by the member states forming the very community. The critical questions relate to the practicality of the arrangements and their positive implications for growth and development, without violating the principle of community action espoused by the Abuja Treaty.

It is this spirit of pragmatism that has guided the main recommendations of a recent study (ADB, 1994b) on Southern Africa. The study identified certain activities where sectoral cooperation can be established, and at the macroeconomic level made proposals were made for stimulating trade, restructuring the financial sector and facilitating payments and cross-border investments. For the countries of Southern Africa, this implies concerted actions to reduce tariff and non-tariff barriers to intra-regional trade, investments and payments; and greater convergence and stability in fiscal policy, monetary policy, exchange rates and currency convertibility systems. The study notes that: (1) each country stands to gain from the economic integration process and that there can be no losers; and (2) a multi-speed approach could be adopted to allow some countries to advance faster than others in meeting the integration schedule. This approach to macroeconomic policy and regional economic integration which the rest of Africa has so far not pursued with any measurable intensity could provide an important building-block for future policy in the sub-region – led, perhaps, by South Africa.

Policy Design and Implementation Issues

Regardless of the particulars of any policy instrument, effective design and implementation are essential to the acceleration of growth and development in South Africa as well as in the rest of Africa. However, there is hardly universal agreement on the precise practical mechanisms required for a country or a group of countries to grow and develop. What may be readily agreed upon, though, is the notion that the management of development is a multi-dimensional process within which there is a complicated web of interrelationships, interdependence and trade-offs. In this respect, the interdependence between the choice of a strategy, policy design and the question of effective implementation needs to be specially recognised. These three aspects, though theoretically distinct, are practically inseparable. It follows that even the best-designed macroeconomic policy cannot be implemented successfully if the overall development strategy is flawed. Similarly, the best-designed projects at the micro level are virtually doomed to failure if the macroeconomic environment is hostile. And, by the same token, a policy which may be properly designed and implemented at the technical level is likely to fail because of deficiencies in the overall economic and human resource infrastructure.

The strategy of import-substitution is an important case in point. Experience has shown that reliance on this approach to development would lead, after some time, to slow economic growth and, in a number of cases, to the very breakdown of the growth process itself. Because of the high import content of import-substitution, the approach becomes increasingly import-using and not import-replacing, as is intended. And as the demand for imports increases and eventually hits the foreign exchange constraint, idle and unutilised physical capacity are the normal consequences. These are compounded by the smallness of markets, shortages of skilled labour and managerial talents, that is, structural issues that would need to be addressed if the strategy of import substitution is to mature towards export-led growth.

Similarly, there is no quarrel that 'getting prices right' is essential to any development policy. Yet the successful implementation of policy requires 'getting right' many other things in addition to prices. This raises important issues of timing, phasing and sequencing in relation to policy design and effective implementation, and there are at least five non-price factors (inputs, institutions, infrastructure, innovations and information) that ought to be in place before actions on the price front can be implemented successfully. In the majority of African countries which have implemented major macroeconomic reforms, actions on price incentives have not proved sufficient to accelerate growth and development, essentially because these five elements were either lacking or inadequate. For South Africa, important questions are whether it is capable of undertaking actions on all these fronts simultaneously, whether this would result in overloading the system, and what role should be assigned to the state vis-à-vis the individual given the drift of current policy in the rest of Africa towards what may be described as the minimalist state.

CONCLUSION

This paper has highlighted a concern not with the underlying theoretical constructs that form the basis of current policy in Africa, but with issues particularly related to transmission mechanisms and policy implementation. These are issues which South Africa must aggressively address if its policies are to be suitably tailored to its particular circumstances. In a sense, the key lesson for South Africa is the need for 'domestication' of policy, in design and implementation.

Notes

1. This paper has benefited from some earlier work by Dr M. Hussain of the Development Policy and Research Department of the African Development Bank. However, the views expressed are solely those of the author, and no responsibility for them should be attributed to the African Development Bank or its shareholders.

14 Macroeconomics and Marginalisation: The Triumph of Hope over Experience

Tony Hawkins

The search for appropriate macroeconomic policies to entrench recovery and restore growth to sub-Saharan Africa is increasingly bedevilled by disputes over the trade-off between economic efficiency and equity. In the two decades prior to Africa's widespread adoption of structural adjustment, macroeconomic policy 'unmarginalised' a number of economies – Angola, Nigeria, Zambia, Zaire – for limited periods, while marginalising the poor. Resource-intensive development of plantation agriculture, energy or mining achieved growth of an enclave economy nature with very little, if any, trickledown to the poor, especially the rural poor.

In some Southern African countries well-intentioned, if poorly targeted and implemented, policies designed to unmarginalise the poor also achieved temporary success, albeit at the cost of eventually marginalising the economy. Tanzania and Zambia in the 1970s and 1980s, and Zimbabwe in the 1980s, fit this pattern. Ultimately, such populist strategies collapsed because marginalisation of the economy undermined the fiscal, infrastructural and institutional capacity needed to improve the lot of the poor.

Throughout the region, the shortcomings of both approaches, combined with increased dependence on foreign capital, usually aid, resulted in the reluctant adoption of generic structural adjustment programmes (SAPs). These were designed to restore macroeconomic stability while restructuring the pattern of incentives, thereby creating a platform for self-sustaining economic growth.

After more than a decade of such programmes across the region, there has been a partial change of focus in response to the disappointing results achieved thus far. Not only have adjustment policies failed to restore sustainable growth, but they have contributed to the further marginalisation of those in society benefiting from food and transport subsidies or from free education and health, whilst creating unemployment amongst retrenched civil servants and parastatal employees as well as in manufacturing industries forced to close by the loss of protection.

The emphasis in the early 1980s on getting macro-policies right was based on the confident expectation that this would automatically restore economic growth whilst simultaneously reducing poverty, that is, achieving growth with equity. Today that confidence has dissipated as the World Bank, the International Monetary Fund and bilateral donors have come under increasing attack, especially from the NGOs, who blame structural adjustment for deepening poverty in many African countries.

Unable to convince either its critics or its shareholders that structural reform is helping reduce poverty, the Bank now accepts the need for an explicit poverty reduction component in SAPs. According to the World Bank's Chief Economist for Africa, 'protecting the poor in the transitional stages of the reform process should be an explicit objective of adjustment programmes' (Husain, 1994: 19).

Despite this, tensions remain as NGOs continue to accuse the Bank and the IMF of giving precedence to market reform over poverty reduction. Implicit in this debate is their strongly held conviction that efficiency-creating macroeconomic policies do not reduce poverty. In their opinion, more aid, debt forgiveness, the use of targeted subsidies, a partial rejection of privatisation, the abolition of user charges for social services and more rather than less state intervention in directing credit and investment are needed to protect, if not enhance, the position of the poor. Such advocacy has sparked a sharp rejoinder from the World Bank, with Husain (1994: 20) rightly noting that 'the misery and failure this strategy has caused during the last twenty-five years does not seem to have sunk in'.

The combination of deteriorating institutional capacity, the blurred distinction between 'party' and 'government', and an already overstretched state under pressure to restore fiscal balance suggests that such NGO advice is precisely wrong. Africa needs smaller, more efficient and more effective government.

THE LIMITS OF MACRO-POLICY

The contribution of macroeconomic policy to reversing marginalisation is inextricably entwined with structural adjustment. Whilst there is more to structural adjustment than macroeconomic policy, successful adjustment depends crucially on the restoration of macroeconomic stability, without which structural and micro-level components – deregulation, liberalisation and privatisation – are unlikely to pay off.

Adjustment takes two forms, and it is important to distinguish between them. The external environment is constantly changing – commodity price fluctuations, aggressive export expansion by Russian mineral producers, new technologies and different business strategies – resulting either in automatic adjustment on the part of economies and firms adversely (or positively) affected, or in explicit government intervention designed to offset such influences. Perhaps the best recent example of this kind of 'automatic adjustment' is the global response to the oil price rises of the 1970s.

Adjustment also takes the form of deliberate policy measures designed to improve efficiency and restructure the economy. Over the past 15 years, both effects have been felt in sub-Saharan Africa. The frequency and strength of adverse exogenous shocks – drought, sluggish world economic growth, deteriorating terms of trade, civil war and rapid technological change – have been such as to force African economies into a combination of both automatic and policy adjustment (White and Luttik, 1994).

At the same time, adjustment *policies* are a necessary, not a sufficient, prerequisite for self-sustaining economic growth. On its own, macroeconomic policy is inadequate to the task of creating an enabling environment, let alone setting an economy on the road to self-sustaining economic growth. Yet, typically, new administrations take up the reins of political power convinced that macroeconomic policy is an effective instrument to achieve the desired supply response – increased investment, output, exports and employment, coupled with improved patterns of income and wealth distribution.

In their study of economic policies for the 1990s, two senior OECD officials conclude: 'While bad policy almost always results in bad performance – witness the performance of central planning in the eastern European economies – good policy can generally only *permit*, or at most *encourage*, good performance' (Llewellyn and Potter, 1991).

Here it is worth recalling that when the OECD's first *Economic Outlook* was published in July 1967, there was 'widespread confidence among both academic economists and policymakers' that the 1960s record of 5 per cent annual growth and stable inflation (3.5 per cent annually) could be sustained along with unemployment of no more than 3–3.5 per cent (OECD, 1991). But, in the 20 years since the first oil price shock, industrial country growth has averaged 2.6 per cent annually, unemployment almost 7 per cent and inflation 5.75 per cent (IMF, 1994b). Llewellyn and Potter (1991) argue that supply-side shocks are now the rule rather than the exception – that policy-makers and business managers cannot expect a return to the golden age of rapid growth combined with low inflation and unemployment.

In the post-1975 global business environment, macro-policy is no cure-all, if indeed it ever was. Furthermore, if sophisticated administrations in OECD countries, richly endowed with technical and managerial skills and a strong database, underpinned by an innovative, competitive private sector, have been unable to solve the growth with equity problem, then what can be expected in sub-Saharan Africa, including South Africa? Not only has fine-tuning failed in OECD countries but African administrations lack the capacity to implement such policies. Furthermore, in Africa the policy agenda is not restricted to economic goals since state intervention is inseparable from political patronage.

Reconstruction and Development in South Africa

South Africa's Reconstruction and Development Programme (RDP) is the mirror image of some more recent SAPs – a statement of social and development goals and intentions within a very loose, non-specific, macroeconomic framework. In the RDP, macroeconomic policy is treated as an add-on in the same way that poverty reduction and social dimension programmes have been added on to generic SAPs in the hope, rather than the expectation, that this will insulate the poor from the adverse effects of adjustment.

The absence of hard macroeconomic numbers from the RDP suggests that its authors have no illusions over the limits to the trickle-down effects of macro-policies, and have opted for a direct, interventionist approach. At the same time, however, the design of the RDP has potentially far-reaching implications, not just for structural adjustment in South Africa itself, but also for the country's potential as the economy most likely to kickstart regional development.

Conscious of sub-Saharan Africa's record of economic failure, foreign investors, multinational companies and South African business are understandably concerned at the prospect of the new South Africa contracting the Africa disease – the marginalisation of both the poor and of the economy at large. Such fears are readily understandable given: (1) the ANC's ideological roots; (2) the magnitude of the challenges of social uplifting and black economic empowerment; and (3) structural weaknesses in the economy, specifically low labour productivity, high levels of import dependence, the debt-trap, the necessity to shift resources from consumption into savings and investment, and the certainty of increasing dependence on foreign capital.

Given South Africa's economic domination of the region, accounting for some 80 per cent of SADC GDP, the implications of its marginalisation are daunting. It will be a devastating setback to regional hopes of rapid development if the regional locomotive were to degenerate into a regional millstone.

The Sub-Saharan Experience

Recent sub-Saharan experience is a case study of the inadequacy of macroeconomic policy-making. Five years after the World Bank's (1989) Long-term Perspective Study (LTPS) proclaimed a new order of sustainable growth, even the minimalist goals of African and international policy-makers have not been met. Per capita incomes have fallen a further 10 per cent since 1989 despite repeated claims by the World Bank, IMF and others that structural adjustment is at last beginning to pay off.

Such claims, couched in terms of the resumption of growth, include extraordinarily specious interpretations of country experiences. Thus, Nigeria, which abandoned structural adjustment in 1988/9 and which has since reversed much of its original reforms, is listed as one of six countries to achieve a 'large improvement' in macroeconomic policies between 1981 and 1991. Zimbabwe, whose Economic Structural Adjustment Programme only took off in 1991, is also included in the 'large improver' category (World Bank, 1994). The reality is that while some African countries are experiencing recovery as distinct from 'growth',[1] nowhere in sub-Saharan Africa, with the exception of Mauritius, has the transition yet been made from aid-funded, donor-dependent, artificially-driven recovery to self-sustaining development.

Furthermore, if these findings of the Africa Adjustment Study are taken at face value, the 'success' of a handful of African countries suggests that getting macro-policies right is not enough. Even where governments have managed to get the policy framework broadly right – Ghana is perhaps the best example, but Kenya, Uganda, Tanzania,

Zambia and Zimbabwe are all progressing in that direction – recovery rather than growth continues to depend heavily on aid inflows and positive exogenous shocks. Concluding that the 'overall results of adjustment achieved so far have been modest relative to original expectations', Husain concedes that 'adjustment has not yet succeeded in raising the rate of growth to levels needed to make major inroads into poverty. It is equally clear that adjustment policies, even when they are put in place after reaching internal consensus will not be able, by themselves, to lift African countries out of poverty' (1994: 22).

Explanations of this state of affairs raise four questions:

1. Are the policies themselves wrong, that is, is the generic structural adjustment 'model' fatally flawed?
2. To what extent is implementation – the conduct of macro-policy – to blame?
3. Can macro-policy on its own create an enabling environment?
4. Once that environment is in place, will self-sustaining, poverty-reducing growth necessarily follow?

Invariably, the answers to the questions tell us more about the viewpoint of the participants than the issues. There is, however, broad agreement that while adjustment programmes have been found wanting in Africa, failure is explained more by the combination of limp political commitment and weak administrative and institutional capacity than by faulty programme design. The answers to (3) and (4) are both negative since efficiently administered, sound macro-policies do not guarantee either the creation of an enabling environment or subsequent self-sustaining economic growth. The recent Bank report notes that even in the most successful countries, investment has failed to reach the 25 per cent of GDP target specified in the LTPS.

Nor can sustainable growth ensure improved patterns of income and wealth distribution. The UN's Human Development Index (HDI) shows wide disparities between the income per head and HDI rankings of many countries, though rapid economic growth of the kind achieved in East Asia is clearly correlated with reduced marginalisation. But Botswana, sub-Saharan Africa's most successful economy in terms of conventionally measured growth, has experienced a highly inequitable pattern of growth. The ratio between the income share of the bottom 20 per cent of the population and the top 20 per cent is 1:47 while in less 'successful' Kenya it is 1:23 and in Uganda 1:5. Similar points can be made about the marginalisation of women or of regions within a country. The trade-offs are difficult to assess; thus, although Malawi with its very different natural resource endowment and its dependence on small-scale agriculture, has achieved a more equitable pattern of income distribution than Botswana, 82 per cent of its population lives in 'absolute poverty' compared with only 43 per cent in Botswana (UNDP, 1994).

Two conclusions are drawn from the HDI. First, economic growth is a necessary, though not a sufficient, condition for reversing marginalisation of the poor. Contrast Botswana's 224 per cent increase in HDI between 1960 and 1992 with Malawi's 80 per cent, Zimbabwe's 67 per cent, Zambia's 36 per cent, and 64 per cent in the structural adjustment 'success story', Ghana. Growth matters; but so also does the pattern of that growth. Secondly, trickledown effects from stronger economic growth do not overcome regional and sex disparities or guarantee equitable patterns of income distribution.

In an ideal world, macroeconomic policy should influence the nature and pattern, as well as the rate, of growth. No economy operates in a vacuum; all are buffeted by exogenous shocks, whilst macroeconomic policy is constrained by trade-offs with political and social imperatives. African empowerment and indigenisation in Zimbabwe and South Africa is not a positive-sum game – there will be a price to pay in terms of foreign, and possibly also domestic, investment. The use of the reserved list in Zimbabwe to restrict foreign investment in certain sectors will – indeed has – meant the loss of some projects to other countries. It can be argued, too, that while land redistribution will give rise to more acceptable patterns of income and wealth distribution, there will be a cost in the form of lower rates of both investment and growth than might otherwise have been achieved.

In a world of narrowing options, donors, lenders and policy-makers see East Asia's success in achieving growth with equity as the optimal development path for sub-Saharan Africa. According to the World Bank, the rapid growth of the eight High-performing Asian Economies had two core complementary components: (1) getting the fundamentals right – high levels of domestic savings and investment, broadly-based human capital, good macroeconomic management and limited price distortions; and (2) careful policy interventions, though these were subsidiary to the 'overriding importance ascribed to macroeconomic stability' (1993a: 24). The Bank's assessment is that the intervention most likely to accelerate development and reduce inequality in developing countries is an export-push strategy.

Successful African imitation of the East Asian miracle is unlikely, certainly during the 1990s, given the enormous backlog in infrastructure, skills, savings levels, attitudes and institutional capacity. The challenge to African policy-makers goes beyond the *sine qua non* of getting the fundamentals right, since the creation of an enabling environment is no more than first base. Phase two involves tackling the twin challenges of raising investment levels and investment efficiency, whilst securing rapid growth of non-traditional exports, including services.

INVESTMENT

Private *domestic* investment and rapidly growing human capital were 'the principal engines of growth' (World Bank 1993a: 5) in East Asia. In Africa, however, uncritical acceptance of the centrality of investment's role in the development process has resulted in a preoccupation with physical, rather than human, capital. This, allied with project selection often influenced by political and social rather than economic criteria, and low levels of both private and domestic investment relative to foreign and public sector activity, explains at least some of the disappointing growth response to investment. High levels of public sector investment in economies with weak institutional capacity and where spending on human capital accumulation as well as maintenance and repair were neglected, as in Nigeria, failed to generate a commensurate growth response.

African policy-makers have been force-fed on capital fundamentalism – the conviction that investment is the best, if not the only, way to secure future economic growth. Yet some recent research suggests that, contrary to the findings of the World Bank's (1993a) East Asian study, the role of investment in the growth process may have been exaggerated. King and Levine (1994: 27), citing a study of 105 countries, conclude that 'growth in capital per person typically accounts for less than 40 per cent of output per person'; while high investment ratios are strongly associated with economic growth, they find 'little reason to believe that this constitutes evidence that increasing investment will cause faster growth'. Echoing Kaldor, they conclude that capital accumulation is a *feature* rather than a *cause* of growth. Indeed, market growth invariably precedes capital accumulation rather than the other way around. Business does not invest in a vacuum but rather in response to market opportunity and in anticipation of profits.

Given the International Finance Corporation's (1993) common-sense conclusion that market demand is the prime determinant of private sector investment, there is limited scope for domestically driven growth and investment in Africa's tiny markets, South Africa and Nigeria excluded. Thus, in addition to getting the fundamentals right, the role of macro-policy is to create the conditions for export-led growth since this will have to be the main stimulus for investment.

It is not surprising that the short-term investment response to a changed set of structural adjustment-driven economic incentives has been weak. In most African countries, such policy changes lack credibility, and in Nigeria, Kenya and Zambia they have been seen to be reversible, albeit temporarily. Serven and Solimano (1993) argue that the stability and predictability of the incentive structure is at least as important as the level of any investment incentives: private investors may wait for at least three years before committing themselves, while investment will not respond where continued macroeconomic instability results in high inflation as well as high nominal and real interest rates.

The Regional Dimension

In Southern Africa, regional uncertainties have become a major obstacle to new investment beyond the traditional resource-intensive fields of mining and agriculture and the new growth area of tourism. Pending development of a new regional order, investors are either staying on the sidelines or taking the plunge in South Africa where justified by the $120 billion per annum domestic market.

This regional factor highlights a pervasive weakness in the design of SAPs. It is ironic that so many in government, business and the donor community see great potential in regional trade and cooperation while simultaneously advocating programmes and strategies that lack any sort of regional dimension. The regional issue is ignored in structural adjustment programmes in Kenya, Tanzania, Uganda, Malawi, Zambia and Zimbabwe.

A regional perspective is necessary *not* simply as a vehicle for entry to 'soft' COMESA export markets or preferential entry to the South African market, but because, increasingly, regional considerations are affecting investment decisions. Firms are restructuring and relocating, choosing South Africa as the gateway to, the launchpad for, the regional market. Today no major multinational makes a significant investment decision in Zimbabwe, Zambia, Botswana or Malawi without explicitly considering the regional dimension.

In part, this is Southern African-style downsizing, but it also marks the first steps towards the globalisation of African business. In Southern

Africa, the arrival of the worldwide shift towards enhanced geographical and organisational integration of production was delayed by political instability, sanctions against South Africa and pervasive trade and exchange controls which precluded cross-border vertical integration. The new regional political order, combined with liberalisation and deregulation of exchange controls and foreign payments systems, is changing the rules of the game. Outside, investment decisions in agriculture and mining as well as in low-value, high-bulk manufacturing (cement, beverages, construction materials) and some location-specific services (tourism, retail banking, distribution) are being regionalised.

Competitive Advantage Versus Comparative Advantage

Ironically, this development coincided with the liberalisation of investment regimes and the establishment in several countries in the region of 'one-stop' investment promotion centres. Whilst these are improving the investment climate, their impact is largely confined to traditional location-specific activities rather than broadening and diversifying the economy. In the 1990s, multinational business is adopting complex integration strategies designed to improve efficiency and cut costs. Increasingly, location decisions are influenced by global efficiency criteria rather than by country-specific macroeconomic considerations such as taxes, tariffs and the cost of capital.

Unlike East Asia, comparative advantage in Africa is largely a function of physical resource endowments – gas, oil and mineral deposits, arable land and plentiful unskilled labour. The value of such 'lower-order' advantages has been eroded by the march of technology and supplanted by 'higher-order' advantages that are more mobile across national boundaries (Porter, 1990). In several East Asian countries, firms have managed to create higher-order competitive advantage where lower-order comparative advantage did not exist, with the result that poorly endowed economies significantly outperformed their resource-rich neighbours. Contrast 4.1 per cent average annual growth in per capita income in resource-rich South-East Asia (Indonesia, Malaysia and Thailand) between 1965 and 1988 with 6.8 per cent in resource-poor East Asia (Korea, Hong Kong and Singapore) (Larraín and Vergara, 1993).

When it comes to manufacturing, Africa's comparative advantage is largely confined to low-cost labour and linkages with primary sector activities – agro-processing and minerals beneficiation – and the supply of inputs to service activities like tourism. With the increased mobility of both capital and technology, differences in the cost and quality of immobile factors of production (labour, energy and low-value, high-bulk inputs) influence location decisions only where such costs are a significant proportion of total costs. In many industries the labour-cost component has fallen to 10 per cent and below as a result of techno-logical advance, thereby reducing, if not eliminating, the basis for re-gional comparative advantage in many activities (ILO, 1992).

Taken together, these considerations suggest that investment decisions are likely to be determined more by corporate strategy considerations than macroeconomic fundamentals. Macro-policy continues to play a key role in terms of establishing price, exchange rate and interest rate stability, but in tiny sub-Saharan markets (Nigeria and South Africa excluded) macroeconomic influences are likely to be swamped by strategic considerations.

Linkages

In the 1990s investment and export-led growth are different sides of the same coin, with the emphasis in investment having switched from physical capital to human capital and technology. The links run both ways – export growth depends on up-front investment in technology, human capital and product and market development. In turn, given the domestic market constraint, private investment is a function of export expansion, the more so because of the central role of foreign inves-tors. As a recent report states:

> Much of the new investment required to compete internationally is in capital intensive technologies, requires large research-and-devel-opment expenditures and involves the simultaneous penetration of many markets to combat shortening product cycles. New investments are also required to modernise the organizational structure and skills profile of firms and industries. All this requires access to sizeable funds and a stable investment climate. (UNCTAD, 1994: 152)

Few sub-Saharan economies, with the partial exception of South Africa, have the private sector capacity to fund and implement such invest-ments. The new emphasis on quality (African exporters without ISO 9000 status are finding it increasingly difficult to secure First World orders) and on skilled labour also militate against the 'sweatshop' model of labour-intensive, export-led growth deemed appropriate for the region in numerous structural adjustment programmes. Yet plentiful unskilled labour is often an obstacle rather than a stimulus to modern industrial investment (World Bank, 1992).

Firms, not governments, make production and investment decisions and win export orders. The competitive advantage of a firm depends on the creation of an enabling environment, and the role of macro-economic policy is to establish the fundamentals on which firms can build such advantage. If the fundamentals are absent, so too will be the multinational enterprise whose participation is crucial both to investment and export-led growth.

CONCLUSION

Globalisation means that investment decisions of firms will be determined primarily by corporate strategy considerations rather than comparative advantage alone. Until comparatively recently, sub-Saharan governments have seen foreign direct investment by multinational enterprise as part of the problem of marginalisation rather than a major contribution to its solution. As a result, the region's share of the global stock of inward FDI has fallen from 6.5 per cent in 1980 to 2 per cent in 1992 (UNCTAD, 1994). Unfortunately, changed attitudes and policies on their own will not reverse this marginalisation trend, given the region's geographical distance from the triad clusters of North America, the European Union and East Asia, and its comparative disadvantage in terms of capital, skills and technology.

A vital component, too, in the East Asian miracle has been the supportive, constructive relationship between government and private enterprise. This is seldom found in Africa. Moreover, East Asia has increasingly courted foreign direct investment with a commitment that African governments find difficult to match, especially given vocal demands for the indigenisation of business.

In the light of the phenomenon of capital-intensive 'jobless growth' and increasingly intense competition for both foreign investment and export markets, NGO criticisms of economic policies designed to create competitiveness in Africa are misplaced. Above all, as global economic integration proceeds, national policies are increasingly circumscribed, either by international agreements such as the GATT or by the transfer of power from governments, especially weak African administrations, to global businesses. International linkages and cross-border economic and business ties are reducing the autonomy of national governments.

Policy-making is becoming both more complex and less effective.[2]

Accordingly, macroeconomic policy's potential contribution towards unmarginalising the poor should not be exaggerated: 'sound macroeconomic policy is a necessary but not a sufficient condition for sustained growth with poverty reduction' (World Bank, 1994: 36).

The best the macroeconomic policy-maker can do is to create an enabling environment by establishing macroeconomic stability, getting prices right, 'levelling the playing field' and eliminating obstacles to exports and to investment inflows. This, complemented by targeted interventions to tilt the incentive structure (taxes and tariffs) in favour of exports and investment in human capital and technology, while eradicating obstacles to, and investing in, small enterprise development programmes, offers the greatest promise for unmarginalising the poor within a framework of sustainable growth.

Notes

1. A World Bank 1994/5 report, *Africa's Development Strategy Revisited* (mimeo), states that between 1988 and 1993, 21 African countries achieved per capita growth, noting that this list includes Tanzania, Ghana and Uganda, all of which 'overturned a negative performance in 1981–87' (p. 7). IMF statistics show that per capita incomes in sub-Saharan Africa have fallen in all but three of the last 15 years.
2. See UNCTAD's *World Investment Report* for 1992, 1993 and 1994 where this theme is developed.

15 Effective Investment and Competitiveness

Michael Unger

The importance of sub-Saharan Africa's competitiveness, and of the effectiveness of investment, for donors, governments and investors is evident as one looks at the disappointing results of development strategies pursued to date. Africa's disappointing economic performance has not been for want of donor assistance: net ODA nearly doubled between 1985 and 1992 from US$9.5 to US$18.3 billion, increasing from 5.1 to 11.3 per cent as a share of GDP. This assistance has failed to promote rapid and sustained economic growth, and donors must therefore rethink their strategies. Governments in Africa are showing increasing interest in the concept of competitiveness and realise that this is critical in attracting the private investment which is necessary for generating the new employment required by a growing population. Many investors and corporations do not perceive Africa to be an enticing investment location. Yet, on closer observation, it is evident that money is being generated in Africa and that opportunities are indeed emerging in various sectors.

DEFINING AND QUANTIFYING COMPETITIVENESS AND EFFECTIVENESS

For the purposes of this paper, competitiveness is defined as 'the ability of business or government to mobilise investment, labour, technology, information and other resources to gain markets at home and abroad on the basis of cost, quality, uniqueness or other differentiating factors'. Competitiveness, in its most simple formulation, is the ability to compete, and is a motivating factor imperative for success. Its basic components are efficiency and productivity. There are firms which seek to compete solely on the basis of the low cost of their product, and countries which compete on the low cost of their raw materials or labour. But these strategies have become less and less effective over time, and competitiveness is now more closely related to the notion of

172

quality. Today, the successful company is one that presents a high level of quality at a competitive price. The combination of efficiency and quality is referred to as 'value'. Competitiveness also requires an environment that requires being a competitor. In many parts of Africa, however, considerable energy is expended in limiting competition: State-owned monopolies and protected private industry exist for the benefit of the few and to the detriment of the many, yet without competitors there can be little competitiveness. Other essential elements of competitiveness are service (or responsiveness or customer-orientation); the ability to identify and strive for world-class standards in the particular industry; access to markets and the ability to tap technology and investment capital; and a constant ability to improve and adapt.

'Effectiveness' of investment can be defined as 'that investment which generates the highest level of sustained growth and capital formation per dollar invested'. When USAID-Nairobi was developing a strategy of assistance to Kenya in the late 1980s, it assumed that the primary need was for higher levels of 'investment'. However, a study found that the absolute level of investment, as a percentage of GDP, was not particularly low and was above average for most African countries. The problem was that the investment was not generating sustained economic growth commensurate with the level of investment, and this was due to the quality and not the quantity of investment. The 'quality' of investment can be as important or more important than the quantity: it is the effective use of investment that matters, that is, generating sustained economic growth, sustainable jobs and sustainable increases in the capital base of a company or a country. Effective investment is that investment which leads to greater competitiveness.

It is important not only to define but also to quantify competitiveness, but this is difficult owing to the lack of a universal gauge: companies and countries use different scales by which they measure competitiveness and effectiveness of investment. Thus, companies look at sales and profits whilst countries look at GDP. The most important indicator for companies is their net income, expressed as a percentage of sales, assets or profits. The equivalent indicator for countries and governments is income per capita, and the most fundamental test of a country's economic strategy is the extent to which its people have a higher standard of living. Whilst income per capita is not all-inclusive, it remains as the basic monetary indicator measuring economic success.

Achieving growth in income for companies or populations requires investment. Private investors calculate price:earnings ratios and profit momentum while governments do the same with GDP growth rates.

Private companies defer to their rates of return on plant, equipment and other capital investment whilst governments analyse the levels of GDP growth obtained for given levels of gross fixed domestic investment. Too much emphasis is often placed on mobilising higher levels of investment without looking at the levels of growth obtained with such investment. The conversion ratio of investment to GDP growth must also be taken into account.

Private firms look at the productivity of labour and at market share while countries and governments measure output per capita and their share of world markets. Financial analysts in the private sector study different ratios and indicators to assess the appropriate debt capacity of a company while governments examine their debt burden, debt: service ratios and credit ratings. Just as private enterprises develop their own business strategies, it has now also become common for countries to determine their own strategies to achieve and maintain competitiveness.

ASSESSING OVERALL COMPETITIVE PERFORMANCE

What profits are to a company, income per capita is to a country. Whilst far from being a perfect indicator, this gives a rough measure of the level of prosperity or poverty of a people. The indicator for Southern Africa does not give rise to optimism at first glance: the region (excluding Angola for which good statistics are unavailable) has an income per capita which is about one quarter the world average. It has about 2 per cent of world population yet produces only 0.5 per cent of world GDP, and whereas the average worker in the world produces over $10 000 of GDP per annum, in Southern Africa the figure is only $2600 (or about 25 per cent of the world per capita mean production).

Not only is the region below the world average, but it has been growing at much lower per capita rates than other developing countries. As a result, GNP per capita has declined in real terms from US$589 in 1984 to US$483 in 1993. Such figures are an indictment of the economic policies of the past and demonstrate an urgent need to formulate new strategies, implement new reforms and reshape the environment for investment, employment and economic growth. The performance has been poor not only when compared with Asia but even compared to South America. Africa in the 1970s had about 33 per cent of the per capita GDP of South America, but by 1988 this figure had dropped to about 22 per cent. And this was prior to the strong growth registered in South America in the early 1990s. Part of this disparity can be explained by Africa's higher average annual population growth rate of 3.1 per cent as against South America's 2 per cent. But even in absolute terms, GDP growth over the last ten years in Africa has been extremely disappointing. In the 1990s, it has averaged less than 1 per cent per annum.

One of the causes of this disappointing growth is the modest and declining level of investment, which has fallen from around 18 per cent of GDP in the late 1980s to around 16 per cent in the 1990s. However, there has also been some difficulty with the quality of investment. By normal standards, even investment levels of 15 per cent of GDP should be generating a GDP growth rate of between 3 and 5 per cent per annum, but this has not been the case for Africa. This means that investment is not as effective as it is in other countries. For example, the high-performing Asian economies achieved approximately 1 percentage point of GDP growth for every 3 percentage points of GDP dedicated to investment. Part of the problem in Africa is that public sector investment is not being put to effective use while private sector investment is not as productive as it could be since it is hindered by an ineffective enabling environment. Investment enters the economy, but the expected burst of growth and jobs does not occur to the extent that it does in other countries given similar levels of investment.

If Africa is to maintain higher absolute levels of private sector investment, changes in the enabling environment must be made so that such investment can generate greater economic growth. Investment in manufacturing in Kenya, for example, has been made in a highly protective environment; the result is that the sector is often inefficient, and the decision is made to invest even when overcapacity may result. Another example of regulations obstructing efficient investment is a private sector assessment in Ghana a few years ago, which revealed that parts of the investment code were observed as having the tone of a penal code.

Southern African countries are failing to attract a share of international investment capital commensurate with their 2 per cent share of world population, despite the fact that foreign direct investors and mutual funds are again showing interest in South Africa and the Johannesburg Stock Exchange. However, there have been a number of export successes in the region and the rest of SSA in recent years which give rise to optimism. These have occurred in manufacturing (notably in the penetration of the US Afrocentric market niche for clothing and household products); agribusiness (in which Southern Africa offers excellent potential for biotechnology and seed companies which need southern hemisphere locations for counter-seasonal grow-out periods: the region will continue to play for Europe the role that South American locations play for the United States in terms of counter-seasonal production, and the end of war in Mozambique and Angola could bring vast new tracts of land back into production); and the service sector (especially the export of financial and business services from South Africa to the rest of the region). There is considerable potential for further expansion in all these sectors as well as in mining and tourism-related services.

OBSTACLES TO COMPETITIVENESS

Although manufacturing, mining, agriculture and services offer great opportunity, many obstacles to competitiveness remain. To understand these obstacles, one must first look at them from the point of view of the investors. Many surveys have shown that investors do not place a particularly high priority on tax concessions or favourable treatment and deals from the host government. Chief among the obstacles mentioned by these decision-makers are 'unreliable rules of the games'. Even difficult situations, if stable, can be managed, but uncertainty and constant change are not tolerated.

Overvalued exchange rates have also acted as a drag on investment while state-owned enterprises are obstacles to competitiveness. This is not only because they tend to drain away country finances: these enterprises often control sectors which are critical to the overall competitiveness of a country. They control land, electricity, banks and other critical services which can stifle growth across the board. Despite the lessons from the 1970s and 1980s, parastatals played an inordinate role in many African countries in 1990.

State marketing boards in Africa do much to stifle the productivity of farmers or to protect them from the realities of the marketplace, thus hurting the overall competitiveness of the country in the long run. Inadequate finance for investment and exports also poses a problem while import and export regulations make it difficult to do business in a competitive way. The lack of adequate infrastructure and local skills also plays a role.

These obstacles combine with other larger obstacles to create a climate of Afro-pessimism. Political instability in recent years, ethnic conflicts and outright civil wars have discouraged investment. The heavy hand of the government is all too visible to those who would otherwise like to emulate the principles of Adam Smith. Natural disasters and disease take their toll and limit the appeal of investing. This contrasts with the great strides being made in Asia and Latin America where growth is rapid and investment from developed countries has inundated the economies.

Obstacles to competitiveness are created even by well-meaning governments which are trying to cooperate with the private sector. Here, a case study on the South African textile and apparel sector is revealing: whilst it demonstrated the competitiveness of South African apparel manufacture, it also clearly showed the lack of competitiveness of the textile fabric industry. The clothing production system goes through four major stages from cotton production to yarn to fabric to cut-and-sew. The textile fabric operation is the most capital intensive requiring investment in expensive finishing equipment, dyeing operations, and other plant and equipment. The apparel manufacturing stage is far more labour-intensive. Whilst some South African textile operations are competitive, most are not. In its final offer to the GATT, however, the government of South Africa, for very understandable political reasons provides up to eight years of continued protection for the textile operations in order to preserve unionised jobs and companies in that sector. Unfortunately, many more potential jobs will not be created which could have met the needs of the unemployed. Tens and perhaps hundreds of thousands of jobs will go uncreated as a result.

IMPLICATIONS FOR GOVERNMENT, BUSINESS, NGOs AND DONORS

Many of these obstacles can only be addressed by the local governments. Still, there is much to be done by private companies, NGOs and donor agencies.

Government

African governments generally have been slow to discard their devotion to failed policies, import substitution and state control. There is a reluctance, because of painful legacies of colonialism, to appreciate the benefits of foreign investment in today's global village. But governments will be forced to rid themselves of the shackles of state-owned enterprises, onerous regulations, marketing boards and other instruments that hamper the sources of employment and economic growth.

The implications for governments include the need to: allow competition, enforce a fair legal structure, ensure a well-functioning financial sector, let markets determine the exchange rate, commit themselves to macroeconomic reforms, adopt an export orientation and create an environment conducive to raising the levels of private savings and investment. Government priorities must include investment in education and infrastructure which can make their people more productive. These are among the lessons learned from the high-performing Asian economies.

One common misperception in Africa is that investors primarily want access to cheap labour, tax holidays and special concessions. Survey after survey has revealed that these are not the first priorities of international companies. Rather, international companies are concerned with predictability, that is, a stable legal and regulatory regime; protection of their property (including intellectual property); minimal governmental intervention; free movement of capital to and from a country; and convertibility of currency. International investors prefer to be treated equally to national investors.

International business leaders must continue to look at and evaluate the investment and competitive prospects of Africa if they are to be faithful to their shareholders and active in their search to add value. The problem is that when they look at the business climate in Africa, they often come away with the same impression as the local investor. Governments must recognise that today's world is a thriving open economy and that foreign investors bring capital, technology, know-how, training, access to markets and other critical ingredients for growth. The problem is that many national environments are conducive neither to local nor international investors. Governments must commit themselves to allowing the investment climate to be attractive to investment.

Business

African businesses which currently enjoy protection would do well to learn from the experience of large Mexican companies. These companies vigorously opposed the government's plans to open up the country to international competition, fearing for their survival. However, they comfortably survived the dropping of tariff barriers: although their gross margins fell from 38 per cent to only 17 per cent, their volumes doubled. Many African companies are well positioned to enter into joint ventures with international companies to become competitive, but the bulk of investment will come from the local, not the international, investor. If the investment climate does not draw local savings and investment, it will not attract international investment either.

The implications for local businesses are that they must model them-selves after the world's best practices and make those their standard. Companies that wish to grab the golden ring of competitiveness must focus on the '5 Rs':

1. *Re-acquaint yourself with the customer*: In the world of today, com-panies that listen carefully to the consumer and put the customer first are the ones that are surviving. This is step number 1 for achieving competitiveness.

2. *Re-engineer the company organisation*: The word 're-engineering' is more than just a euphemism for job-shedding. In the information age it is necessary to re-examine processes and procedures, get rid of useless ones and adopt processes which serve the strategic needs of the company.

3. *Re-tool with competitive technology*: World-class technologies are now more small-scale and more available than in any time in re-cent memory. In almost every industry and sector the technologies are changing, for example, in agriculture, biotechnology is begin-ning to cause a profound transformation; medicine is changing at a revolutionary pace; finance has become increasingly automated; the computer-aided design and modelling technologies are changing manufacturing and allowing smaller-scale and more flexible pro-duction; and the information revolution is changing commerce and retailing. Every business must re-tool at a faster pace to keep up. Companies which are the first to introduce these new technologies in their markets have the advantage.

4. *Re-finance with lowest-cost sources of capital*: To be competitive also means getting access to competitive sources of capital. Port-folio investment is increasingly being made available in less-devel-oped countries, but the prerequisite is a well-functioning local stock market. Local sources of capital may or may not be cheaper now-adays than international sources. The important point, however, is to limit risk while also reducing the overall cost of capital.

5. *Research 'best practices' and adopt or adapt them*: One key factor for competitive success is the ability to scout out the best practices in the world for each kind of company and then adopt or adapt them to the local environment. This can often be done under fran-chise or under licence, but it is also often done independently by local entrepreneurs who read, interact extensively with others and/ or travel. Those who make the 'best practices' in the world their

own standard have the right reference point. The Japanese, not formerly known as world travellers prior to the 1860s, made it a point to travel to learn about best practices in the world.

Non-governmental Organisations

Business associations, educational institutions and NGOs have a role to play in identifying needs and coming up with solutions. Educational institutions can do more to relate the education being provided to the real job requirements of employers. Private firms can be involved in the design and execution of training programmes. Successful competitive regions in the United States, such as the Silicon Valley in California, Route 128 in Massachusetts and the Research Triangle in North Carolina have seen the economic benefits of this cooperation pay off handsomely.

Business associations must decide whether they will represent the narrow and short-term interests of their members or become leaders in advocating policies which will lead to rapid, sustained and broad-based growth. NGOs also have a role as incubators and promoters of micro-enterprise. There are few advocates for very small businesses, and there is often a need for NGOs to fill this role.

Donors

The implications for donors are to continue supporting economic liberalisation reforms and privatisation, while helping to finance business support infrastructure and the conditions conducive to fostering private sector investment. However, there is a role to play beyond encouraging reform and liberalisation, for example, the IFC has played a catalytic role in helping to open the way for larger than expected resource transfers via the private capital market. Donors can learn from this experience by choosing to devote scarce resources to areas where enormous leverage can be obtained. This is done by identifying and focusing on the key bottlenecks. In South Africa, a recent private sector assessment revealed multiple artificial barriers to entry and restraint-of-trade mechanisms. In still other cases the barriers may be market access, or financial, or technological. In almost all cases in Africa, education and training are important obstacles to private sector development and competitiveness.

Africa also has a shortage of what might be called business infrastructure. For example, Africa suffers from a deficit of adequate communication equipment. With only 1.4 per cent of the world's telephone lines, it trails all other major regions. As new technology comes on line which makes cellular and cellular-like communications more feasible, the region will enjoy greater flexibility to expand with minimum investment. South Africa is currently installing a system to cover wide swaths of territory not previously serviced by landlines through cellular installation. Prices are not yet competitive, but short-term subsidisation by urban users may give loss-making rural users easier access to communication.

Donors can show the way by linking local governments and businesses to successful examples, models and case studies worldwide. More must be done by the development agencies to help the local business community to take advantage of new opportunities and to ensure that there is life after liberalisation. While supporting such reforms, bilateral agencies have a role to play in linking the host country to the specific sources of capital and technology in their own countries and by helping to provide a forum for business contacts. Donor agencies have shown leadership in the area of lending programmes to small enterprise, which is a way of fostering not only private sector-led growth but a broad-based participation in the benefits of growth. Donor agencies can also help in the areas of infrastructure development, legal, judicial and financial reform and institution-building.

CONCLUSION

If Africa makes the transition to rapid and sustained economic growth, it will probably happen first in the Southern Africa region. Here one finds a technologically advanced First World economy coexisting with a low-cost developing economy. This provides an array of potential opportunities of combining know-how with low-cost labour. Where these kinds of First World–Third World borders are found, one finds rapidly rising standards of living, productivity and economic growth. The sophisticated Chinese of Hong Kong and Taiwan combine their finance and technology with the labour force of mainland China, and the world witnesses breathtaking economic growth. One can also look to the swath of northern Mexico where the *maquila* or assembly industries have transformed impoverished border towns into humming hives of activity. Eastern Europe is now becoming such a centre. There is great hope for Africa as a whole, and excellent prospects for Southern Africa in particular, to lead the way.

16 Improving the Business Environment[1]

Paul Holden

An important question for South Africa is whether the business environment is sufficiently conducive to private sector activity to promote investment at levels which will result in growth rates high enough to eradicate the poverty in which a large section of the population lives. If it is not, then the consequences are serious because there is substantial experience that the state cannot replace the private sector in bringing prosperity to its citizens. State ownership of resources or of productive units has invariably been associated with low productivity and high cost which has harmed rather than helped economic activity. Furthermore, the possibility of aiding the less fortunate through wholesale redistribution of wealth is not a sustainable option: there is ample evidence that, while the state can confiscate wealth, it cannot redistribute it. Therefore, the private sector, which is made up of firms and markets, has to be the engine for growth. This paper examines the business environment in South Africa through the perspective of the experience of Latin America over the past 30 years.

ECONOMIC GROWTH AND THE CONTRACTING ENVIRONMENT

The process of economic development, which in a broad sense is usually synonymous with industrialisation, involves a massive increase in the number and complexity of transactions, whether these occur within or among firms. As development proceeds, the number of transactions rises more than proportionately to the rate of growth of the economy, and the cost per transaction declines. The increasing division of labour means breaking down tasks and increasing specialisation to the benefit of all: 'The division of labour, however, so far as it can be introduced, occasions, in every art, a proportionate increase in the productive powers of labour ... what is the work of one man in a rude society being generally that of several in an improved one' (Smith, 1976: 9). In this

182

way, human capital becomes ever more important. Furthermore, the greater division of labour entails a far larger minimum efficient scale of production, which in turn demands geographically more widespread markets and increasingly complex and impersonal transactions. To attenuate the risks of such impersonality, property rights need to be clearly delineated and a framework for enforcement of contracts needs to be developed. Minimising the costs of transactions in this way will in turn further the division of labour.

The far greater capital intensity and larger scale of modern production in turn enlarge the gap in time between initiating production and selling the product. The capital that must be raised to cover this time-gap must be rewarded because the providers of capital forgo consumption and incur a risk. Since large amounts of capital are required, a financial mechanism for linking savings and investment then becomes a key factor in allowing the division of labour to be increased. In the least developed economies today (as was the case in medieval Western Europe), there is relatively little division of labour; markets tend to be local and productive units small. Transactions involve either barter or the exchange of simple goods for cash; any more complex transactions are most likely to happen through repeat transactions between people who know each other. Markets are few, simple and restricted across space and time.

To grow and develop, therefore, economies need an environment which allows for secure impersonal contracting and relatively low-cost transacting. To ensure that investment reflects scarcities, government policy should be neutral both between activities and between firms.

SOME BACKGROUND FROM LATIN AMERICA

A wave of economic and political reform which has spread across Latin America over the past few years has transformed the economic and political landscape from one which was characterised by repression in both areas to one which is democratic and increasingly based on market solutions to the problems of resource allocation and economic growth. The change, which has been nothing short of remarkable, was the result of the policy responses to the consequences of the debt crisis which began in the early 1980s. These events[2] forced a re-evaluation of the role of the state in economic life in Latin America. In the pre-reform era, numerous economic activities better performed by the private sector were in the domain of the public sector, either directly through ownership or indirectly through extensive regulation. At the same time, the state was not performing such essential functions as providing price stability, ensuring security and law enforcement, operating effective dispute resolution mechanisms, providing inexpensive and good quality school education systems and reliable, well-functioning infrastructure. By the time the second oil crisis occurred it was apparent that the widespread introduction of import-substitution policies and statist control had had the effect of drastically weakening most economies in the region – inefficiencies had mushroomed, growth rates had languished and income distribution had worsened. There was a growing realisation that the state was powerless to raise the prosperity of the vast bulk of Latin America's population.

Many aspects of Latin American economies in the pre-reform era were similar to South Africa, except perhaps for the greater macroeconomic instability that existed in most of Latin America. Both areas suffered from political repression and active industrial policies that attempted, through a system of taxes and subsidies, to direct economic activity into areas deemed to be strategic. There was strong promotion of import-substitution in the belief that self-sufficiency was important. Infrastructure was poor and the education of large portions of the population was neglected and inadequate. Powerful interest groups dominated economic life and, just as in South Africa, in spite of myriad controls on foreign exchange, Latin American citizens who could do so held their savings in the United States or Europe.

The crash came in Latin America with the default by Mexico on its external debt obligations. External finance dried up dramatically. With economic policies of dubious worth no longer feasible, many countries were forced into radical adjustment programmes. Over a period of little more than ten years, many countries abandoned the statist, import-substitution regimes of the earlier period for macroeconomic reform combined with outward-looking, market-oriented policies. While there were great differences in the extent to which these policies were applied, virtually every country in the region went through some type of reform episode. Although most of the reforms were of the so-called first generation type – fiscal discipline, trade reform, financial sector reform and privatisation – they were driven by the common philosophy that private sector activity had to be the source of economic growth. This in turn has prompted interest in factors that promote or hinder private business activity.

When the reforms were introduced there was hope that they would rapidly induce greater efficiency and investment, which in turn would result in higher growth. Many of the changes in policy required great political courage, not only in dealing with powerful government employees' unions and entrenched political interests, but also in pushing through market-oriented reforms which eliminated the substantial monopoly rents earned in many countries by sheltered industries. Having these taken away and being exposed to the harsh winds of international competition was not welcomed by many members of the private sector. Nevertheless, many countries in Latin America followed Deepak Lal's dictum, 'Get the prices right'.

The private sector response, however, has not been uniform. In some countries, particularly those where reform occurred early, growth rates have been high, approaching those achieved in the Asian 'miracle' economies. In others the response has been disappointing. The variance in private sector responses has led to the growing realisation that while macroeconomic reform is necessary to promote sustainable growth, it may not be sufficient if the response is to occur with the hoped-for speed. Other policy measures, the 'second generation' of reforms, may also be necessary to ensure that resources shift rapidly from inefficient activities into those with long-term growth potential. Clearly, there are other factors promoting private sector development that need to be better understood. Furthermore, the fact that many countries had gone through earlier reform episodes, most of which had been reversed either partially or fully, was not lost on potential investors, many of whom have reacted cautiously. The 'credible commitment' to the reforms by the reforming governments has assumed great importance.

FACTORS INFLUENCING THE ENVIRONMENT FOR DOING BUSINESS[3]

To try to gain greater understanding of what promotes economic growth, the World Bank has devoted significant resources to evaluating the private sector environments in Latin America. From the work done so far, a number of common themes have emerged, which both support the emphasis placed by international financial institutions on macroeconomic stability and trade reform and identify the importance of several factors which have not been accorded much weight in the past.

Macroeconomic Policies

Macroeconomic stability supports private sector development by reducing uncertainty from large fluctuations in relative prices and domestic demand. With greater certainty, savings and investment become more attractive than holding assets abroad or in domestic inflation hedges. Orthodox macroeconomic polices that do not distort relative prices have a better chance of success than heterodox polices to restore price stability and current account viability. However, restoration of stability by itself does not lead to GDP growth. When there have been long periods of uncertainty and lack of credibility of macroeconomic policy, the private sector needs more time to be convinced that the new policy regime will be maintained and that the government will not try to use inflation to appropriate resources.

Fiscal discipline is fundamental to winning the confidence of the private sector. Large, persistent public sector deficits carry with them expectations that they will eventually lead to inflation, which has an extremely damaging impact on private sector development. Furthermore, when more responsible policies are introduced, governments face a problem of credible commitment to reform, particularly if the country has a history of irresponsible macroeconomic policies. There is a time-lag before policy becomes credible.

In addition to the time-lag needed to win credibility, greater flexibility of relative prices aids macroeconomic adjustment. For a given use of a macroeconomic instrument such as monetary policy, the response is better when relative prices are flexible than otherwise. Flexibility of labour markets is also crucial for macroeconomic adjustment. The link between macroeconomic policies and incentive policies is closest here.

Incentive Policies

Trade, finance and the regulatory environment constitute the main incentive policies that determine the level and the structure of private sector activity.

Trade policy is a powerful determinant of private sector activity. In the past, the distorted trade regimes that prevailed in Latin America encouraged production for the domestic market just as they did in South Africa. Earlier attempts to liberalise trade regimes in the region and provide neutral incentives for domestic and international markets failed owing to macroeconomic uncertainty and the lack of strong commitment to liberal trade policies. The most recent round of reforms began in some countries as early as the mid-1970s but others undertook reforms in the mid- to late 1980s as a part of overall economic reform. As a result of changes in the incentive structures for private sector activity, production for the foreign market and the diversification of exports has been encouraged. With more stable macroeconomic policies and greater commitment to liberal trade, the reforms have changed the character and competitiveness of the private sector in many countries in Latin America.

The financial sector plays a vital role in promoting private sector development. Without effective intermediation between savers and investors, financing business growth is limited to existing businesses. This undoubtedly explains in part at least why there is such an unequal distribution of income in most countries in the region. Systems that are non-transparent and discretionary make entrepreneurial activity even more difficult than it already is.

Beyond the necessary phases of stabilisation and adjustment, governments must find an appropriate balance between financial liberalisation and sound regulation and supervision. There is a pressing need to develop money and capital markets. This implies deepening the financial market and enhancing its efficiency in mobilising and allocating domestic and foreign financial resources. These initiatives have to be complemented by legal reform and institutional development to ensure their success. Apart from sound macroeconomic management, the direction of the reform process should be in the development of the capital market, leading to a greater variety of financial activities and the lengthening of maturities in order to stimulate private sector activities.

The experience with *privatisation* in the region has been strongly positive in terms of realising the proceeds of assets sold, enhanced efficiency in the newly privatised industries and investment by the new owners. A World Bank (1992) study found that in all cases examined except one, privatisation had resulted in higher investment, higher productivity and an expansion of services.

Institutional Policies

While macroeconomic and incentive policies constitute the first generation of economic reform programmes, research by the World Bank into the determinants of private sector activity has identified a 'second generation' of issues which appear to influence strongly how the private sector will respond. These factors are consistent with the analysis of the so-called 'New Institutional Economics' developed by North (1990) and others. The most important are:

(1) *Property rights*: Insecurity of property rights is widespread in Latin America. It is costly and difficult to register rural and urban fixed property, with the result that property values are lower than they otherwise might be. In Peru, which is representative of most Latin American countries in this regard, less than 20 per cent of all land and dwellings have registered titles. As a result, property markets do not work efficiently, and this hampers the functioning of other markets, in particular for labour. Agricultural investment and output are also adversely affected. It is difficult or impossible to use moveable property as security for borrowing, with the result that financing business growth is restricted. Fortunately, methods of dealing with both these problems have been developed; unfortunately their implementation is proceeding slowly at best.

(2) *Legal systems*: There are many deficiencies in the legal systems in the countries studied. However, adequate enforcement of existing laws is an even greater problem. The saying in Brazil, 'To my enemies, I wish the law!' is apt for most countries in Latin America. The contracting environment is poor; dispute resolution mechanisms do not work well; the extrajudicial mechanisms for the settling of disagreements work badly, if at all; and the court mechanisms are so slow as to be considered useless by many in the business community. Thus, the already strong tendencies for the concentration of wealth are exacerbated because impersonal long-term and spatially separated contracts involve added risk, and it is better to deal with people who are known than with strangers.

(3) *Regulation*: As the state has withdrawn from many areas and activities for which it does not appear to be well suited, so the need for effective regulation has increased. However, many companies are still burdened with over-zealous regulation in areas where there appears to be no justification for governmental interference. Now, as in the past, the danger is much more in the direction of over-regulation and interference by the heavy hand of the state. This is exacerbated by the lack of coordination between different levels of government: state and municipal regulations are frequently in contradiction to federal rules. Significant reform is needed here, but it will not happen quickly because of the complexity and size of the task.

REFORM AND THE BUSINESS ENVIRONMENT IN SOUTH AFRICA

How, then, does the business environment in South Africa measure up in terms of the criteria outlined above? In some aspects, extremely well; in others, poorly. Where South Africa has a significant advantage over most of Latin America is that, in at least part of its economy, there is a stable and well-functioning set of institutions. The courts work well as a system of dispute resolution. Contracts can be drawn with confidence that the parties involved can test the limits of their positions in court. The financial system is sophisticated and effectively channels funds from savings to investors: the capitalisation of the Johannesburg Stock Exchange is larger than any in Latin America. Property rights in the developed sector of the economy are well defined and can be used as collateral to make loans.

That is not to say that all institutions are functioning as they should. In particular, the benefits of the existing institutional framework must be extended to the disadvantaged majority of the population who were systematically denied access in the past. The heritage of these actions could be that all formal institutions are viewed with suspicion, but at least South Africa does not have to develop or fundamentally reform the institutions of a market economy, as is required in many Latin American countries. From this perspective, South Africa starts with a huge advantage compared with most developing countries.

A few examples from Latin America will serve to illustrate just how large an advantage this is. Chile is currently the only country where loans for property purchases with a term of more than seven years are possible; in most countries mortgage finance is not available at all. Chile is also the only country where it is possible consistently to use business assets other than property as collateral to obtain loans. As a result, companies in Latin America are not able to leverage their assets to finance business growth. The civil law code governing business transactions and regulations has resulted in a plethora of laws relating to commercial activity; for example, on one count, Brazil produced over 50 000 laws, decrees and regulations relating to business activity over a two-year timespan at the federal, state and municipal levels of government. Many of these were contradictory and then had to be tested in court, which involves a wait of up to seven years to obtain a hearing. Hardly any countries have effective property registries where deeds can be recorded in a systematic way. Reforms in these areas are difficult because they involve habits and procedures that are deeply ingrained, and they are strongly opposed by entrenched interests which profit from the status quo.

In spite of this, investors clearly view Latin America as a far more promising environment that they do South Africa. There have been massive capital inflows both in the form of portfolio and direct investment into the reforming economies. Per capita capital inflows into Latin America were $180 in 1992 compared with $8 into Africa as a whole (and with capital outflows from South Africa). Why, then, is South Africa viewed with such disfavour as an environment for productive investment when it starts with so many advantages compared with Latin America? The obvious political uncertainty kept most investors away until the April 1994 elections. However, with the process of political change and reconciliation going far better than most observers could have hoped, capital still has not come into the country: South Africa has failed to take many of the steps that the reformed Latin American economies have taken. The budget deficit remains high; the trade regime, while better, still is distortionary; large sectors of the economy remain in the hands of the state; there are widespread controls on capital flows; and there are significant rigidities in the labour market. Each of these factors will be examined in turn.

Fiscal Restraint

Private sector activities are influenced by macroeconomic policies in many ways. The level and prices of firm outputs, the prices of the inputs they buy, the interest paid on debt, the wages they pay as well as the exchange rates at which they transact, are influenced by macroeconomic policies. Even more important from an economic growth perspective, the private sector's plans for saving and investment are heavily affected by macroeconomic conditions. When prices are stable and external payments are sustainable, the private sector can plan more easily future output levels and investment. It encourages saving and raises investment levels which has a positive impact on future growth. South Africa has made progress in reducing inflation, but a budget deficit that is close to 7 per cent of GDP inspires great caution among investors because it can easily re-ignite inflationary pressures.

Trade Reform

While trade reform has begun in South Africa, significant distortions in the trade regime remain. Furthermore, the average level of tariffs,

Table 16.1 Average Tariff and Non-Tariff Protection, 1985–92

Country	Average tariff protection (%)[a]		Average coverage of NTBs (%)[b]	
	1985	1991–2	1985–7	1991–2
Bolivia	20	8.0	25.0	0
Brazil	80	21.1	35.3	10
Chile	36	11.0	10.1	0
Colombia	83	6.7	73.2	1
Ecuador	50	18.0	59.3	N/A
Mexico	34	4.0	12.7	20
Peru	64	15.0	53.4	0
Uruguay	32	12.0	14.1	0
South Africa	46	27.5	22.0	5

Notes: a. Average total charges, unweighted.
    b. Unweighted.

Source: Edwards (1993: 59).

while not excessive by the standards of developing countries as a whole, is substantially above those of Latin America (Table 16.1).

The trade reforms of the 1980s and 1990s meant the opening of these economies through the reduction of tariff and non-tariff protection, the elimination of the traditional anti-export bias and the creation of new institutions, policies and programmes to support export activity. They were implemented rapidly and left little alternative to local producers other than to adjust to the new environment of international competition. Although this accelerated opening reduced the timespan for adjustment, fast implementation translated into fast access of the private sector to the benefits of a liberal trade regime. The depth of the trade reforms represents a guarantee to the private sector of their permanence and stability. It provides the regulatory framework firms need in order to carry out adjustments for increasing efficiency and participation in international trade activities.

An additional negative feature of trade policy in South Africa has been its variability and lack of transparency. Its complexity and lack of consistency has resulted in lobbying, with substantial rents being earned by those who are successful. Since it is the large producers who invariably have the most political influence, the result has been to distort incentives away from smaller operations and further skew income distribution.

Privatisation

The policy changes which were most successful in indicating that there was strong commitment to reform in Latin America concerned the wholesale privatisation of state-owned enterprises. Besides providing the strongest signals that there would be no turning back, the selling off of these assets improved efficiency, stimulated investment, led to large capital inflows and provided governments with funds to spend on alleviating poverty. Furthermore, the more extensive the process of privatisation initiated by the reforming government, the greater the credibility of the commitment to reform. Investors realise that a policy where most state-owned enterprises are sold off is far harder to reverse than one under which the state maintains control of companies that it owns. Extensive privatisation is possibly one of the strongest signals that governments can give of their long-term political will to continue with reform. No stronger indication of credible commitment to reform could be sent by South Africa than to sell off the entities providing power, telecommunications, transport, and so on. However, a further measure is necessary in order to obtain the full benefits.

Abolition of Exchange Controls

Exchange controls are an attempt by governments to protect foreign exchange reserves from the effect of their policies on investor expectations. As such, they are generally unsuccessful over the long run. Administrative controls may slow but cannot prevent capital outflows. Quite often, foreign borrowing by governments to bolster foreign exchange reserves and support the exchange rate finance capital outflows by private investors; this happened during the 1970s in Latin America (Edwards, 1993) and in South Africa in the mid-1980s (M. Holden, 1989). It is not difficult to make a case that if the capital account in South Africa had been more open, the government would not have been able to maintain its previous racial policies.

The usual case for exchange control is that it prevents a sustained decline in the real exchange rate. However, the experience of countries in Latin America which have abolished restrictions on foreign exchange in conjunction with a comprehensive reform programme has been the opposite. Capital inflows have put strong upward pressure on the real exchange rate to the point where producers of traded goods have been faced with severe competition from imports. For example, Argentina, Peru and Chile abolished all controls over foreign exchange, allowing anybody to open bank accounts in any currency they wished. The result was appreciation of over 20 per cent in the real exchange rate in each of the countries. Nevertheless, they also managed to increase exports strongly. A feature of capital inflows to Latin America has been the large amount that constitutes the repatriation of capital previously held abroad by residents. The citizens of many Latin American countries believe in the reforms of their governments. When South African citizens begin to repatriate their capital, the government will have a strong signal that its commitment to reform is credible.

Labour Markets

In South Africa, the most important question is how the economy can generate jobs for the huge mass of unemployed. It can only do so if there is investment in labour-intensive processes which in turn requires both a shift away from the bias in investment towards capital-intensive projects and greater flexibility in the labour market. Strong labour unions, cartelisation of employers, industrial councils which place restrictions on work and compensation practices, and widespread strike activity all contribute to labour market rigidities. The process of removing them is a complex political task. Perhaps the first step should be some sort of social compact between employers and trade unions, brokered by the government, which will provide some employment security in return for industrial peace and flexibility in work practices. Furthermore, there is an urgent need to change wage bargaining from an industry-wide to a firm-level system.

Security

In several Latin America countries, most notably Peru, inadequate public security hindered business growth. In Peru, some 20 per cent of GDP was devoted to security during the 1980s. The effects of this on the business environment are obvious. In South Africa lawlessness has to some extent replaced political violence, and its costs are rising rapidly. It is essential that this be dealt with, not only because of the deleterious effects on investment but also because violence of this sort inevitably has the most negative effects on the poorest section of the population. Furthermore, attempts by the poor to better their lot through establishing businesses will make them the most prominent target for criminals, thereby undermining incentives.

CONCLUSION

In one sense the environment for business in South Africa is the parallel of that in the Latin American countries which have undergone
radical reforms. In the latter, the first phase of reform is over; the
second and much harder task of improving inadequate institutions must
now begin. By contrast, South Africa starts out with the foundations
of an effectively functioning set of institutions but has failed to go far
enough with the traditional set of reforms. World Bank research in
Latin America shows that both elements are necessary for economies
to generate rapid growth. Macroeconomic stability must be maintained.
Rapid privatisation will generate funds for social investment, reduce
the budget deficit, improve efficiency and provide a strong signal of
policy intentions. Furthermore, if combined with liberalisation of the
foreign exchange market, it will attract much-needed savings from abroad
and perhaps will persuade South Africans to repatriate funds they are
holding overseas. Trade reform will stimulate efficiency and remove
the bias against exports that is inherent in the current trade regime.
Labour practices need to become more flexible and a social compact
would be desirable. Improving security will both reduce the amount of
resources currently being expended as well as improve the lot of the
poorer sections of the community. It is important also to note that
elements of reform programmes are not separable; to work well they
all have to be implemented.

Improving the business environment, however, cannot be done without
an understanding of the political economy of policy reform. Realistically, to improve the incomes of many of the poor in South Africa
substantially will require 10–15 years of rapid growth, not the four
years to the next election. How then can South African policy-makers
implement policies that are supported by the mass of the electorate?
Populist policies are not a viable option: they have a long history of
failure in Latin America, and attempts to redistribute wealth and income ultimately have always impoverished most recipients. Other options, by contrast, do have the potential to improve the quality of life
and provide hope for a better future. Spending on the social service
infrastructure has high visibility but, to maintain fiscal discipline, it
should be financed by part of the proceeds of privatisation. The current wave of lawlessness is harming the poorest sections of the population, and reducing the crime rate will quickly benefit large sections
of the community. Whereas private resources spent on security are a
deadweight loss to the economy, governments have a strong compara-

tive advantage in enforcing the law. Housing programmes and site development need accelerating, and secure title must be granted to the recipients. Land redistribution must proceed, but it is essential that there be a strong market-oriented base to such a programme. Finally, although the benefits accrue in the long term, investment in education is urgently required, not only at school levels but also for adults. It provides the hope for a better future that will enable all members of society to participate in the rich potential of the new South Africa.

Notes

1. The findings, interpretations and conclusions expressed are entirely those of the author and should not in any way be attributed to the World Bank, its affiliated organisations, or to members of its Board of Executive Directors or to the countries they represent.
2. See Edwards (1993) for a discussion of the background and consequences of the debt crisis.
3. See Holden and Rajapatirana (1994) for a more detailed discussion of these points.

17 Avoiding Corporate Marginalisation

Millard W. Arnold

The theme of this conference is a subject of great concern to the Clinton administration. The United States has traditionally focused its international economic and commercial policy on Europe and Japan but, while the industrial nations will continue to be its largest markets for decades to come, the US Department of Commerce has recognised that another category of country holds far more promise for large incremental gains in exports. It has designated these nations the 'Big Emerging Markets' (BEMs) and has identified them as China, Indonesia, South Korea, India, Turkey, Poland, Argentina, Brazil, Mexico and South Africa.

The Department estimates that nearly three-quarters of the growth in world trade in the next two decades is likely to take place in the developing countries, mostly in the BEMs which are likely to double their share of world GDP in that time to 20 per cent from today's 10 per cent. By 2010, their share of world imports is likely to exceed that of Japan and the European Union combined. Indeed, the US believes that the BEMs will be the competitive battleground of the future. These are competitive nations in which significant commercial opportunities exist, not marginal nations on the fringe, and they represent the cutting edge of a new global dynamic.

BIG EMERGING MARKET OR MARGINALISED REGION?

It is important to note that when the US refers to South Africa as a Big Emerging Market, it is in fact referring to all of Southern Africa. Clearly, the BEM concept is predicated on the strengths of South Africa and its potential impact on regional growth. Indeed, exceptional opportunities are opening up within the region either tied to, or related to business prospects emanating from, South Africa. In Botswana, Mozambique, Zimbabwe and Swaziland, American companies are actively exploring exciting business prospects which justify the description of Southern Africa as a 'Big Emerging Market'.

But, if that is true, then in a paradoxical way one returns full circle to the theme of the conference: 'Avoiding Marginalisation: Can South and Southern Africa Become Globally Competitive?' Of course, the paradox is: how can the US see this region as a Big Emerging Market while others wonder if Southern Africa is doomed to exist on the periphery of global competition?

In addressing that paradox, it is important, if only from a psychological perspective, to dismiss this notion of marginalisation. There is, it seems, a tendency to equate marginalisation with the notion of competitiveness, that is, the more competitive a nation the more globally significant it becomes. However, this only serves to obfuscate the fundamental purpose of a nation which is to provide for its people. To the extent that the citizenry of a country are comfortable with the existing standard of living, the nation or government has fulfilled its portion of the implicit bargain between the state and the governed. What South Africa and other nations want is to enjoy a standard of living that is rising and sustainable. Not achieving this objective does not make a nation marginal: just as countries don't go bankrupt, so too they are not marginalised. A nation may not have the influence of others, but that hardly makes it marginal. Every nation has something positive to contribute and that alone negates its marginalisation. But even if marginalisation is to be equated with competitiveness, a provocative thought suggests itself: is global competitiveness the only way to achieve a rising and sustainable standard of living? One of America's leading economists, Krugman (1994), thinks not. None the less, the notion is not uncommon that nations compete – that global economics is a zero-sum game in which there are winners and losers. In this context, Africa invariably is seen as a loser, as uncompetitive. But, as Porter (1990) is at pains to point out, it is not nations but industries within nations which compete. A nation is, therefore, competitive if the industries that constitute the commercial life of the country are viable and productive. If they are not, the country does not become uncompetitive, it simply does not provide for its citizens the way that other nations do. There is, of course, the possible consequence that the nation will become less influential globally, but that does not mean that it has become marginalised. It is economic strength or some other form of leverage that provides a nation with influence in the global arena. Iran, Iraq and Saudi Arabia have a degree of leverage not because they are competitive but rather because they have oil. The Soviet Union was not economically competitive, but it had enormous leverage and influence militarily. To the degree that Africa is marginalised, it is a reflection not only of its competitiveness but of its lack of influence in almost all areas of global intercourse.

Whilst the argument that attracting investment and maintaining a nation's talent can be seen as a form of competition, it is still important to stress that nations do not compete: they have interests which they pursue with various degrees of success. However, the notion of global competition remains. To the extent that one believes it critical that a country's economic fortunes are largely determined by its success on world markets, it is important to explore the significance of foreign direct investment as a potent means of avoiding the so-called 'corporate marginalisation'.

CAN AFRICAN PRODUCTS BE COMPETITIVE?

Perhaps the first issue that should be addressed is whether Africa is competitive or not. Can Africa produce items or products that can compete internationally? While most of the empirical evidence would seem overwhelmingly to say no, there are some interesting trend lines that are worth considering. For instance, Biggs et al. (1994) noted that there is a significant niche in the US market for Afrocentric products, and that producers of standardised garments in Africa have become competitive with Asian rivals in countries where structural adjustment programmes have improved the economic environment. They noted that in the US, the African-American population represented almost 30 million consumers with a market size of between $200 and $270 billion. More important, African-Americans have demonstrated that they are favourably disposed to purchasing products that address their ethnic heritage. Acutely aware of this trend, over the past year major retailers have been successful in marketing African products bearing African labels. With that in mind, the largest minority producer of ethnic dolls in the US visited South Africa in October and has developed plans to manufacture dolls for the US market that prominently display the fact that they are produced in South Africa.

The study also pointed out a little noted, but extremely important, phenomenon: with low labour costs, competitive task-level efficiencies and the quota-free status of nearly all African countries, the continent compares favourably with garment producers around the world, particularly when African factories are administered by knowledgeable, internationally experienced managers. Being competitive in garment production is largely a matter of unit labour costs. As Biggs et al. (1994: 2) note:

> While fabric is the most important input, it is easily and cheaply transportable, making it an insignificant factor in deciding where to produce. Furthermore, the industry does not depend upon sophisticated skills or technology. The mobility of the industry and the importance of low unit labour costs explains how countries like Bangladesh, Sri Lanka and Mauritius – all of which have no significant sources of fabric, are far from their principal markets, lack elaborate infrastructure but offer low-cost labour – have developed a substantial export garment industry.

Having reviewed data on labour costs and task-level efficiency, the study concluded that African labour is competitive with Asian labour in factories run by experienced managers. It also stressed that African workers could be made even more efficient if management practices were improved to provide better worker incentives.

Perhaps the most significant factor in determining Africa's competitiveness in the manufacture of standardised garments for the US market is that all but two African countries are quota-free. This advantage is critical since all important garment-producing countries in Asia face quotas for their exports to the US and Europe. Aware of this advantage, a major US jeans manufacturer is looking to establish an operation in the Western Cape, whilst other global manufacturers have located in Botswana to produce for the US market. The leading US retailers are now looking to Africa to identify and evaluate factories which might qualify as suppliers.

However encouraging their study may be, the important point made by Biggs et al. (1994) is that it is now time to disaggregate economic (and political) discussions of Africa. The continent is nearly as large as the former Soviet Union and China combined, so that to talk of economic development in Africa is to talk about the development of nearly a quarter of the world's land mass. Thus, whilst it can be fairly noted that garment manufacturing alone is not enough to make a country competitive or reverse the decline in Africa's economic development, it is worth pointing out that for Southern Africa, the clothing and textile industry is a step in the direction of greater economic fulfilment, but obviously more is needed.

It is commonly believed that international competitiveness is dependent on macroeconomic factors such as economic liberalisation, exchange rate manipulation or budgetary management. While these are important considerations in determining a nation's competitiveness, Porter (1994: 63) has pointed out that competitiveness is derived from a country's microeconomic foundation, that is, the actual behaviour, strengths and capabilities of firms and industries within the economy. Porter stresses that it is productivity, not the level of trade or the rate of investment in a country, which is central to competitiveness.

The challenge for Africa, therefore, is how to raise the productivity of its economies so that wages rise and sound, sustainable development can take place over a broader segment of society. At the same time it is important to note, as Porter stresses, that competitiveness does not occur in the economy as a whole. Success in all economies tends to be concentrated in a few industries where the nation has some attributes that permit it to become uniquely competitive. No country can become fully competitive in all areas. The goal is to establish selected areas where a country can create unique circumstances and a comparative advantage.

ATTRACTING FOREIGN INVESTMENT

For Southern Africa effectively to meet this challenge and avoid the drift towards marginalisation, FDI has a major role to play in upgrading the private sector throughout the region. More often than not, when the issue of FDI is raised, particularly in South Africa, the emphasis has been on why there has not been more American investment. There also tends to be a focus on inflows of capital and, to a lesser degree, technology. While this is understandable, this level of debate often misses the more fundamental issue which is the *quality* of the investment. An investment really represents an optimal combination of funds invested for the long term, augmented by sound management capabilities. Moreover, the corporate control of performance efficiency and other intangible assets linked to an investment, generates added value for the developing country.

In looking at the positive effects of FDI, the European Round Table of Industrialists (1993) noted that investments from abroad do four essential things. They (1) expand domestic production of goods and services, thus enhancing economic development and employment and, in some cases, generating exports; (2) mobilise resources and allocate them efficiently (through constant transfers of know-how); (3) enrich local technological developments by introducing internationally respected and competitive standards of quality and safety; and (4) stimulate entrepreneurship, and hence contribute to the international competitiveness of other sectors of the receiving country. However, perhaps the most significant contribution that FDI makes to a host country – a contribution that is appropriate to the issue of marginalisation – is in the area of increased productivity. As Summers (1991: 2) wrote:

> While [resource] flows are crucial, the reality is that improving efficiency ... will often make a greater contribution to growth. Consider, for example, the following comparison: a two-tenths of one per cent increase in total factor productivity in developing countries would contribute more to their GNP growth than an additional $100 billion of capital at historical rates of return.

The basic argument in support of FDI as a means of avoiding marginalisation is simple. Local industry benefits from the cross-fertilisation it receives from new technologies and skills supplied by foreign investors. Indeed, foreign investors establish relations with local supporting industries step by step or, if necessary, assisting in the developing of such industries. It has been noted in several instances that spin-offs initiated by a foreign investor improve quality in related and supporting local industries. At the same time, FDI creates and guarantees necessary links to global markets, both organisational and institutional.

The reasons for this are obvious. A foreign investment will never be sustainable if it is isolated from, or in confrontation with, the local private sector. What this means for the region is that partnerships are necessary if corporate marginalisation is to be avoided. Such partnerships can occur in two forms: competition according to market rules, or cooperation. For Southern Africa's industries to be internationally competitive, the local enterprises must be exposed to international competition. Moreover, the local economy must be linked to international networks of sourcing and finance, technical intelligence and marketing know-how for local markets and exports. Much of this kind of networking has been denied Southern Africa, particularly South Africa, largely as a consequence of sanctions and disinvestment.

If FDI is a fundamental and perhaps necessary way to avoid marginalisation, what needs to be done in Southern Africa to improve conditions for such investment? Drawing from reports and surveys of European industrialists and American investors, the following requirements are suggested:

1. *A clearly articulated national vision*: The public and private sectors need to reach a broadly based acceptance of a general strategy conducive to long-term development.
2. *A sound legal and institutional framework*: This requires a set of simple, clear, transparent and goal-oriented rules applied by an efficient and competent administration, a well-established system to strengthen and protect intellectual property and a framework for curbing public and private monopolistic practices.
3. *A competitive environment*: There should be an acceptance of the benefits of competition as a means of increasing efficiency and wealth; adherence to market principles including freedom to set prices, free entry and a framework that maintains competition; and tax reform to ensure an efficiently structured tax system with improved fiscal administration.
4. *A symbiotic link between the corporate and financial sectors:* Efficient finance is essential for manufacturing companies. There should be market-determined interest rates and the abolition of preferential interest rates for privileged borrowers. Access to credit is a prerequisite, as is a broader, deeper and more efficient capital market.
5. *A competitiveness-oriented education policy*: The educational system should address the needs of private industry. Government, academia and business need to forge a common understanding of the long-term human resource needs of the economy and devise programmes designed to provide the skill base that industry requires.
6. *A productive and motivated labour force*: Labour and management need to recognise the competitive nature of business today and develop a coordinated strategy for productivity improvement in a less confrontational, cooperative framework of industrial relations.
7. *Market size and structure*: As Southern Africa struggles with issues of regional integration, consideration should be given to trade and investment projects that complement or substitute North–South movements of goods with South–South exchanges and that provide benefits to several participating countries in a balanced manner.

These seven suggestions are by no means exhaustive. However, it has been pointed out that three elements determined the success of the NIEs: outward orientation (exports, exchange rates, imports); strong, long-lived governments which enacted conservative policies for macroeconomic stability and competitive wages; and investments in a broadly conceived infrastructure.

The Southern African region is slowly extricating itself from decades of debilitating civil strife and conflict. Turmoil and discriminatory policies of the past have prevented the region from fully conforming to the pattern of success realised by the NIEs. None the less, the broad framework for success is evident in the region. Foreign direct investment is simply a catalyst, a means to assist the nations of this region close the competitive gap between themselves and others competing in the international marketplace.

It is this notion of assisting the region through private sector development that is at the heart of current US policy towards Southern Africa. Although it is frequently argued that American investment is lagging, the reality is that it takes time for business to assess the marketplace, determine its competitive advantage, work out its sourcing requires, ascertain its human resource needs, establish its market strategy and create the organisational structures necessary to sustain a foreign operation. This process often takes as long as 18–24 months to complete.

In the case of South Africa, as it becomes clearer that the country is a trading market of some substance, the decision to invest there becomes all the more likely particularly if it can be demonstrated that an investment will reduce operating margins and thereby enhance profitability. For those who are sceptical of the return of American companies to the market, it is important to note that the companies which have declared their intention to set up an operation in South Africa are largely those which had previously divested. What this says, of course, is that those companies with prior experience in South Africa which know the market and understand how to do business there, are among the first to return. And that is an important signal to other US companies which constantly monitor what their competitors are doing.

What this suggests is that while South Africa will not see a flood of American investment, it will be the recipient of a strong, steady stream of new companies, which will have a measurable and positive impact on the country's economy. American investors are coming quietly but continually, and will continue to do so for the principal reason that the United States sees South Africa as a Big Emerging Market. Over the next few years the kind of investment South and Southern Africa are looking for will begin to take place at a level, depth and quality that will allay any misgivings that South Africans might currently hold.

18 Technology and Unmarginalising

Roger Riddell

In many respects, the relationship between technology, global competitiveness and marginalisation addresses some of the core issues of development. Past and current development problems of most African economies, not least the failure to resolve the problem of absolute poverty for so many people and to provide productive employment for the working population, are closely linked both to the manner in which technology has been used and to the way that recent changes in technology have *not* been taken up. Africa's development prospects will be determined no longer in terms of choosing *whether* to adopt new approaches to technology and production processes, but in choices focused increasingly on *how* to do so.

KEY POINTS FROM THE LITERATURE

One part of the literature on the links between technology, employment, income distribution and poverty focuses on national and macro-issues. A recent overview highlights the central role of education and training, and points to the necessity of coming to grips with new technological developments:

> Education and training have moved from being a complement to the growth process to becoming the most powerful tool at the core of development strategies. . . . No market position is safe without continuing upgrading of technological capabilities and monitoring of the market. (Perez, 1994: 66, 74)

Another part of the literature analyses the impact of the new technologies and organisational processes on employment. Perhaps surprisingly, there is little published evidence at the macro-level which provides conclusive results of the link between new technologies and employment levels. Thus, an ILO survey came to the following conclusion:

No studies at all exist to aid policy makers who are (one would think frequently) confronted with the related question of whether not adopting the new technologies will result, via a loss of export markets, in fewer jobs than would follow from the adoption of those same techniques. The most one finds is a discussion of the variables that are likely to affect the outcome and some informed guesses about the direction that this is going to take in particular cases. (James, 1992: 24)

A major reason for this uncertainty is shown from the results of studies carried out at the micro-level. Thus, even at the level of the firm and even with a labour-saving bias, new microelectronics technologies need not necessarily lead to an increase in unemployment, whilst, at the economy-wide level, rising exports resulting from increased competitiveness have led to an overall rise in demand for labour, the composition of labour required depending upon the type of goods exported. Rather than there being any simple (direct or inverse) relationship between the new technologies, employment levels and skill requirements, the relationship depends not merely on the embedded technologies but also on the social context in which the new technologies are applied. Indeed, the same ILO survey reports that, depending upon differences in markets, management and the way that production is organised, the very same technology may appear to raise or lower qualification requirements (ibid.: 22).

Yet the literature provides two more robust conclusions of relevance to the current discussion. First, a longer-term perspective suggests that the pace at which new technologies are introduced and dispersed is invariably far slower than initial research and evidence would have suggested. This conclusion appears to be as true for the automobile and more complex processes as it is for less complex ones like textiles. One possible explanation could be that knowledge about new technologies invariably comes from those (private sector) firms which have been involved in developing them: they have a (commercial) interest in trying to convince potential customers of the 'need' to buy their products – one often influential marketing technique involves pointing to the (real) loss of competitive advantage when (or if) everyone else adopts the new product/process.

A contemporary example of this first-fast-then-slow phenomenon would be the so-called information superhighway. Until recently, it was asserted that, quite soon, nations covered by the new electronic information highway would achieve very marked productivity gains across whole economies. The implication was that nations that failed to build their own superhighways quickly would 'forever' fall behind in the competitive race. Yet it is increasingly apparent that the information superhighway is going to be far slower in coming even to the most advanced economies, that it is unlikely to come in the form currently envisaged, and that its coverage is likely to be quite limited. A combination of very high costs of installation, considerable consumer resistance among those who might afford to purchase access and concern among governments about marginalising poorer potential users has pushed back the time period when any one OECD country might conceivably have such a network covering a majority of businesses and homes to 2005 at the very earliest, even though the potential gains in terms of higher productivity seem reasonably clear.[1]

Secondly, and relatedly, the literature suggests that it is quite common for the effect of new and changing technologies to be far more complex than was initially thought. Thus, early work on the textiles, garment and footwear industries suggested that the new competition theory, with its emphasis on product flexibility and links to consumers, would result in major changes in the place where production was located because of the overriding locational advantages of having industries near to final markets, especially when seen alongside the far lower share of basic wage costs in total production costs. In practice, major shifts have not occurred; indeed, transnational corporations involved in these industries have continued to invest in low-wage economies, and some have even set up R&D facilities there.

One reason for this growing complexity is that sometimes rigid production processes have been split, with products differentiated into more distinct sub-products (for instance, high fashion and more mass-produced goods) or with high and lower volume production runs leading to different investment and production process decisions. Likewise, against the prevailing early views, in some countries microelectronic technologies in the automobile industry have tended to reinforce rather than supersede Fordist work organisation patterns and routines.

AFRICA'S MARGINAL RELATIONSHIP TO THE NEW TECHNOLOGIES

Identifying the Problems

The ILO (1994) sums up sub-Saharan Africa's (SSA) relationship to the growing phenomenon of globalisation in two words: it 'remains untouched' by it. This suggests not merely that SSA has been marginal to the process of globalisation and recent technological changes but, more starkly, that it has been excluded from them.

To some extent, such a sweeping comment appears strongly at variance with much direct experience. Thus, new technologies, especially new information and computer processing equipment, are now visible in most of the main cities of Africa, in the mines and even on commercial farms. In South Africa, and increasingly across other Southern African countries, financial services and offices are dominated by new technologies; computers are being used in growing numbers of secondary, as well as primary, schools; while computer-aided design and other new technologies are increasingly common in factories. Traditional production processes are also changing; flexible production is taking place, total quality management techniques have been adopted and 'lean production' is sometimes in evidence.

So what is different in Africa, and in Africa's marginalisation, from the mainstream of global trends? Two clusters of factors seem to be important.

First, the use of new technologies is far from comprehensive. New technologies are particularly absent among poorer households, in agriculture (where most of the people derive their living), and in many linked government departments. They are almost exclusively being used within the confines of the modern sectors of the economy, and thus their influence is very narrowly focused. Furthermore, even in areas where new technologies have been used, their incidence and influence remains both partial and patchy. Not even whole sub-sectors of the economy tend to be covered, nor even whole government departments. The marked lack of extensive use of new production processes and the limited linkages within and across sectors and sub-sectors constitute major impediments to the penetration and influence of the new technologies.

Secondly, and linked to the first point, one of the most important attributes of the new technologies in modern expanding and dynamic economies is not so much their extensive use but the context in which they used. Where African countries have used new technologies they have tended to do so in a passive manner, thereby reducing significantly the potential economic gains, especially the longer-term ones. An active approach would be characterised not so much by utilising and extending the use of new technologies, but in the ability to choose whether and when to use them. This requires the nurturing of new approaches, attitudes and perspectives well beyond decisions made at the firm level. What is particularly absent is evidence of a wider capability to innovate, adapt and adopt a more flexible approach from the firm across to the national level. African countries remain steeped in the genre and mentalities of import-substituting industrialisation. Within such a framework, cooperation and networking among entrepreneurs, substantive discussion and adaptation of new organisational principles and processes, and cooperation between the private sector and different parts of government to nurture the new learning required, are largely absent in Africa.

It is these factors rather than the superficial visibility of new (often information-based) technologies which are critical. It is Africa's weaknesses in these areas which account for three sorts of evidence which point to the minimal influence of new technologies across economies: the growing lag in productivity increases compared with all other regions of the world, in both industry and agriculture; continuing structural rigidities, not least continued reliance on primary product exports rather than expanding manufacturing exports; and the failure to attract foreign productive investment on any substantial scale.

One result of SSA's technological marginalisation is that the influence and impact of new technologies have almost certainly *been far less important* to poverty, employment and marginalisation within and across African economies than many other factors. The following comment made in the context of South Asia applies, probably even more forcefully, to most of the Africa (Oshima, 1994: 253):

> technological forces may be too weak to have much impact on income distribution trends since the traditional technologies still dominate production in the rural and urban sectors. It is likely that institutional changes, such as agrarian reform in the agricultural sector, and policies to promote small industries and employment, will affect equity more than will technology.

Underlying Causes of SSA's Technological Marginalisation

What has inhibited and limited the use and spread of new technologies and organisational processes in SSA? One cluster of factors relates to the failure of macroeconomic policies: most African countries have pursued economic policies which have caused or exacerbated macroeconomic imbalance, frustrated the spread and deepening of markets, and restricted the movement of people and capital as well as the expansion of international trade.

Yet, SSA's failures have not only been economic. Crucially, they have included failures of institutional and political systems, rooted in widespread rigidity and inflexibility. What has caused and/or reinforced this inflexibility? In many countries, it can be attributed to the mix of an inflexible political system which has not sought to pursue policies for national betterment but which, to the contrary, has created or expanded a public sector permeated by patronage and corruption. This has exacerbated a system of weak and inappropriate institutions, reinforced by low levels of public accountability. In the words of Killick (1995: 182–3), the environment is one of governments

> seeking to compensate for a lack of popular legitimacy by using the resources of the state to bribe the support of key groups: the armed forces; the bureaucracy; the urban labour force; the trading and industrial elites; key ethnic groupings. The government is hemmed in by the alienation of its people from it, and it is in no position – except through desperation – to get tough with key interest groups whose support is contingent on a continuing flow of favours.

Reducing Technological Marginalisation

Clearly, one precondition for SSA countries to play a less marginal role in terms of evolving technologies is for them to address the range of problems associated with macroeconomic imbalance and structural rigidities. However, on their own, these will remain insufficient and inadequate to create the conditions necessary for the benefits of the new technologies to be maximised (Killick, 1995: 187).

Building on the experience of the East Asian NICs, Seddon and Belton-Jones (1995: 325, 360) focus on what are likely to stimulate the virtuous links between politics, institutions and flexibility. They point to the crucial importance of policy adaptability, which in turn requires a substantial degree of insulation of the government and the bureaucracy from immediate political pressures. The active role of government is similarly emphasised by Khan (1994: 85), who writes:

> The role of government must go far beyond the maintenance of law and order, and the efficient delivery of public administration. . . . a government must be sufficiently autonomous to the economic elite to be able to resist their pressures to let the state apparatus be used to set up a system of incentives and controls that benefits them at the cost of society's welfare.

But what should be on the government agenda? The experience of the East Asian NIEs suggests that four sets of policy measures, specifically linked to the expanded use of new technologies and the development of technological capabilities, would merit high priority:

1. policies to enhance the spread and deepening of information both across society as a whole and in relation to changes in the global economy and in terms of technological change;
2. policies that nurture the cementing of alliances between the public sector and the leading productive and supportive sectors, including the different segments of the entrepreneurial class;
3. policies that address the major gaps in the formal education system, notably by going beyond basic education for all to the provision of higher levels of across-the-board skills; and
4. policies which attempt to address the range of difficult but essential initiatives aimed at nurturing technological capabilities, and enhancing 'organising methods'.

The problems to be faced in each of these four policy sets should not be underestimated, education being a good example. In most African countries, including South Africa, the educational system is inadequately prepared in two main respects for the widespread penetration and deepening of new technologies: the low level of universal basic education and the even lower contribution made to secondary and tertiary education. Shortages of funds, caused or exacerbated by the need to trim public expenditures, mean that public funds for education and training will continue to be constrained when nations need to expand educational facilities in ways well beyond most current plans. African countries are faced with cruel choices. They are being encouraged to promote 'basic education for all' when this will be insufficient and inadequate for the widespread use and dissemination of new technologies for which more 'mass' higher education is a prerequisite. Added to that, increasing parental choice will ensure increasingly that it is not the children of the poor and marginalised who will gain access to the *quality* of education and training required. In other words, in relation to education and training, technological expansion is likely not merely to maintain present inequalities, but to expand them. As Singh comments (1994: 180):

to focus on early (primary) education as the World Bank does may not be the best way of enhancing the international industrial competitiveness of a developing economy. To compete in the world industrial economy, it is essential to have higher educational institutions, scientists, technologists and engineers. Universal primary and secondary education is a worthy goal in its own right, but alone it does not provide the wherewithal to compete in the international market.

It is in this context that one encounters the deepening belief that privatisation will help to resolve educational funding problems. But where schooling is inadequate and parents have unequal access to funds for school fees, the process of privatisation, if left relatively unchecked, tends to increase rather than decrease inequalities (Riddell and Cummings, 1994).

Without wishing to underplay the importance of implementing these sorts of policies, it is also necessary to place them in perspective. It is certain that a comprehensive and consistent set of national technology policies to promote the deepening and extension of new technologies are unlikely to be implemented in Africa. It is thus important to acknowledge that they have not been introduced in other parts of the world either, not even in Japan, South Korea and the United States.

What becomes particularly important is to assess where small gains can be made, not simply for their own sake, but in order to spread the influence and impact more widely and more deeply. While it is not possible to present a comprehensive array of all policies which might be considered in this regard in this short chapter, a few examples can be given.

1. *Transnational corporations*: There is a range of different ways in which transnational corporations might assist national technological policies. Thus, there is sometimes merit in providing special incentives to those considered particularly advantageous as a catalyst for skill dissemination, though this will require careful study of employment and other linkages across the economy. As emphasis is placed increasingly on innovation and on developing and enhancing technological capabilities, countries will need to focus less on importing fully packaged technologies and more on trying to unbundle these packages. Many TNCs may be resistant to such moves; developing skills in relation to licensing and patents become increasingly important areas that need to be developed or, minimally, purchased.

2. *Training levies*: Different countries have adopted different approaches to the role of the private sector in developing and providing training;

for example, Malaysia has used the public sector, Thailand a mix of public and private sector. Given the key importance of skilled labour, these experiences need to be the focus of particular urgent study.

3. *Utilising aid monies for pursuing technological gain*: Given the high levels of official aid coming into Africa, countries should review the extent to which financial aid as well as hardware and technical assistance is being used to maximum advantage in terms of encouraging the spread and development of local skills and the development of local industries (UNIDO, 1991).

4. *Building on niche markets*: African countries should focus on, and learn from, the experience of other countries in terms of trying to develop and expand niche markets, and to branch out from these narrow successes. One example of what can be achieved comes from India: it has one of the lowest telephone/population densities in the world and its transport system is totally inadequate for globalisation, yet Indian software exports have risen from $39 million in 1998 to $225 million in 1993 and are currently growing at 30–40 per cent a year. This is not general software, but a niche market of customised software for particular customers. What is more, success in software is beginning to encourage improvements in the quality of domestically produced hardware, potentially also a significant export in which again there has been the development of niche markets.

5. *Pursuing regional integration*: There is growing evidence that TNCs are locating in particular regions of the developing world not only to enjoy advantages in relation to production costs and production processes, but also in relation to final markets. If Southern Africa is to become more attractive to TNCs for these reasons, it will need to accelerate the process of reducing regional barriers in relation, minimally, to trade in goods and services as well as to financial flows. Additionally, particular attention needs to be focused on building and deepening regional networks, especially but not exclusively to enhance information exchange. Governments have a key role to play here both indirectly, through encouraging private sector networks, and directly, through sharing knowledge and different approaches (Mytelka, 1994).

6. *Building on advantages of small and medium-sized firms*: Without succumbing to the view that small- and medium-sized enterprises are 'the solution' to African development, there is scope for policies to focus on enhancing and nurturing the growth and expansion

of such industries, for instance, through stimulating access to finance capital. From the viewpoint of technological change, however, it is important to note at least two different groups of organisations which are likely to become increasingly polarised: those which can make use of the technologies, grow and become more dynamic, and those which are less likely to do so. Left to themselves, the gap between inferior and superior firms is likely to widen, and Navaretti (1994: 27) argues that 'interventions not specifically targeted to the lower end of the technology spectrum may push weaker firms out of business with serious employment implications'. To use Lall's (1995) terminology, entrepreneurs have to be taught to learn: they need to be informed and persuaded that traditional ways of training, production and management cannot cope with modern technologies.

NEW TECHNOLOGIES AND THE MARGINALISED WITHIN COUNTRIES

A report on science and technology in South Africa (IDRC, 1993) argued that it is necessary to address the problem of marginalisation *concurrently* with policies to extend and deepen the use of new technologies. This raises many questions. Is such an approach technically and politically possible? How can virtuous domestic alliances be created and nurtured, and destructive alliances have their power reduced? What room for domestic manoeuvre does an African country have when pursuing globalisation strategies which require less control and less intervention? Or, if trade-offs *have* to be made, where should they be made – in terms of enhancing or damaging growth or in terms of enhancing or damaging equity? Do African countries have governments and political processes which provide the necessary distance and linkage with different classes and interest groups both to ensure that technologically-relevant policies are enacted and that the gains will not accrue increasingly to the economic, social, cultural and racial elites?

To implement an effective technology programme requires not only a state, and state agencies, committed to the programme, but one that is competent to carry it out. Yet the tasks ahead for African countries are even more demanding. Faced with problems of widespread poverty, mass unemployment and marginalisation, they will need to focus on additional measures to try both to ensure that inequalities are minimised in the process of embarking upon a technologically focused strategy, and to compensate for adverse trends that cannot easily be corrected.

However, because African countries are poor, they will continue to be particularly ill-equipped to ensure that sufficient funds for the poor and marginalised are available from the economic benefits arising from the new technologies and which lead to gains for those who personally benefit. In the best of circumstances, African economies are *not* going to grow at the rates experienced by the East Asian NIEs, while they are burdened by widespread inequalities in wealth and income as well as by large rural, mostly agriculturally-dependent, populations relatively isolated from modern sector development. Resources available to fund those marginalised by new forms of development will be limited to non-existent. For their part, the OECD countries are currently going through their biggest crises in 50 years over the funding and purpose of welfare systems. The solution they are moving towards is to focus more on making people more employable than providing benefits for those without work – which creates yet further (financial) demands on educational systems already short of sufficient money to fund the 'normal' schooling period.

National Politics and Marginalisation

A central question for the poor and marginalised is the extent to which those who hold political power will in practice view the relationship between issues of equity and marginalisation and issues of growth, technology and the pursuit of global integration. In many ways, the important issue is not the question of sequencing, that is, whether technology policies should be aimed both at economic growth and at equity issues. What is of *more* importance is that equity issues are always in the focus of policy-makers. What are the prospects for this continuing to occur in South Africa?

Experience in other African countries suggests that *timing* is a crucial issue. In periods of transition in SSA, as elsewhere, it has been common for politicians to vocalise their concern with the poor and marginalised. It has been far less common for policies to be enacted which work to erode the potential power of the emerging political elites, and which have had a major impact in addressing the problems of poverty and marginalisation. In general, African experience suggests that the longer is the time that elapses before substantive policy issues are addressed, the less likely it will be either that prevailing economic elites will be challenged, or that the growing economic power of the new elites will be checked and halted. Thus, the less likely it will be for the new political and bureaucratic elites to take to themselves a decisive national role which maintains in central position the needs of the poor and marginalised. Recent Southern African experience suggests that as the language of solidarity with the poor continues well after the policies have effectively been discarded, there is an added danger that likely growing disparity between rhetoric and reality will not be widely noticed by the mass of the electorate.

How can the process described be checked (even if not halted)? It would appear that at least progress could be made by focusing on two types of linked approach. The first relates to promoting transparency in government and public life; the second focuses on efforts to strengthen the voice of the poor in civil society. Many African countries have been noted for their lack of transparency and openness. That there are some clear differences within and across contemporary South Africa thus provides grounds for some optimism. The substantial point to make is that increased transparency within and across government not only provides people with more information about what is going on, but the process of encouraging openness should itself provide a more rapid and wider realisation of when the system and the people governing are failing to deliver what has been expected. Thus, all policies which encourage the further opening up of government and society to public scrutiny are initiatives that will aid the process of keeping the poor and marginalised in focus.

Strengthening the Poor

Yet information-enhancing and information-deepening initiatives on their own are likely to lead to only limited gains for the poor and marginalised unless they are married to initiatives directly aimed at strengthening their voice and power. It was argued above that, for technology policies to have a chance of succeeding, they need to extend well beyond economic issues to institutional and political constraints and impediments. In discussing marginalisation and the marginalised, it is equally essential to focus on issues well beyond discussion and debate about the relative roles of the market and the state, to embrace the linked notions of civil society, empowerment and democratic processes.

Focusing solely on politics at the national level assumes (mostly wrongly in Africa) that a benign state will continue to act in favour of the poor who have no voice. Equally, focusing solely on trying to make markets work better will fail to incorporate those outside the market system unless specific action is taken to work for their inclusion. That means giving them voice, and that in turn means enabling them to increase their power within society, the polity and the economy. Discussion about civil society and empowerment is far from new: it has been going on in Latin American development debates for 20 years or more. What is comparatively new is for this type of discussion to be a focus for central areas of the development debate within much of Africa.

As in other countries of Africa, South Africa has recently witnessed a rapid growth in the numbers and influence of non-governmental organisations (NGOs). While NGOs can and do play a forceful role in helping to give voice to the poor and marginalised, and in strengthening their place within civil society, this by no means happens automatically. NGOs are particularly good at articulating both their concern for the poor and their ability to strengthen the voice, and relative and absolute power, of the poor. However, these claims need to be subject to far greater scrutiny (research) in order to assess their validity; analyse more carefully the strengths of particular NGOs and local organisations within the social, political and cultural context in which they operate; and analyse more carefully the conditions in which the voice and power of the poor and marginalised are most likely to be enhanced.

The rhetoric of NGOs needs to be weighed carefully against the reality of what they might realistically be able to achieve in different social, political and cultural contexts. Research which has been carried out (Riddell and Bebbington, 1995; Riddell, Bebbington and Peck, 1995) suggests that success will depend upon whether the NGO 'movement' will split into its different class/factional groupings and become merely a reflection of prevailing power relations in the wider society and, relatedly, whether the state will provide the political space for it to play a more effective enhancing role. Again, timing is likely to be a crucial factor here.

African countries are currently marginal to global technological change ultimately because the mix of economic and political forces have interacted to create such rigidities that they have been unable to respond to change. While they are being increasingly forced to expose themselves to global economic forces, their ability to harness change in a manner which will benefit their marginalised populations will itself also depend upon the mix of politics, power and institutions within different African countries from the national to the community level.

Notes

1. In October 1994, the results of a two-year, $1.4 million survey by SRI International concluded that the information superhighway was a myth created by commercial and media hype (*The Guardian* (London), 31 October 1994).
2. These are discussed more fully in other contributions to this volume, and thus will not be addressed further in this chapter.

Part 5

Some Southern African Issues

19 South Africa's Economic Reforms

Merle Holden

The fear of many policy-makers is that the sub-continent, by virtue of a combination of events, many of them in the form of external shocks and political upheavals, has been marginalised. The crisis in Africa has been characterised by stagnating or negative economic growth, balance-of-payments difficulties, fiscal problems, sluggish agricultural growth and rapid population growth. Many countries have undertaken structural adjustment programmes, often at the behest of the World Bank and IMF, and often in a climate of crisis but with the hope that these programmes could not worsen the economic situation. The verdict is still out on the efficacy of these programmes for Africa.

South Africa has recently emerged from decades of apartheid rule and state intervention in the economy which distorted the allocation of resources and bred severe inequality of wealth and income. The Government of National Unity has adopted the RDP in an attempt to tackle these problems.

This paper examines the major features of the RDP and its implications for the macroeconomic performance of the economy. Changes in the macroeconomy over the past two decades are analysed, identifying those periods when structural adjustment was undertaken in response to a variety of shocks which rocked the economy. In addition, it describes the evolution of trade and exchange-rate policy within this macroeconomic framework, paying particular attention to the role of the changing price of gold.

MACROECONOMIC PERFORMANCE

The macroeconomic performance of the economy in recent years can only be described as disappointing. Table 19.1 shows that average annual real GDP growth declined from a high of 7.4 per cent during the 1960s to a low of 0.8 per cent between 1986 and 1993.

As growth in GDP moderated, so the rate of inflation rose. During

Table 19.1 Macroeconomic Performance: Real GDP Growth and Inflation, 1960–93 (% p.a.)

	1960–9	1970–9	1980–5	1986–93
Real growth in GDP	7.4	3.3	1.2	0.8
Inflation	2.6	10.3	14.0	10.7

Source: South African Reserve Bank, *Quarterly Bulletin*.

Table 19.2 Structural Variables as Proportion of GDP, 1960–93 (% p.a.)

	1960–9	1970–9	1980–5	1986–93
Agriculture	11.2	8.2	6.1	5.5
Mining	12.4	12.5	15.3	10.8
Manufacturing	22.0	22.3	24.0	24.4
Exports	27.3	27.3	32.7	30.8
Imports	27.7	30.8	27.9	23.0
Govt revenue	13.7	19.7	25.9	29.6
Govt expenditure	15.2	19.0	25.0	31.9
Fiscal deficit	1.1	-0.7	-0.9	2.3
Investment	23.8	28.1	26.9	19.6
Foreign saving	-0.3	2.0	-2.4	-1.8

Source: South African Reserve Bank, *Quarterly Bulletin*.

the late 1980s, however, more conservative leadership at the Reserve Bank gave greater attention to the rate of inflation which was successfully reduced to 10.7 per cent.

Table 19.2 shows the changes which have occurred in the structural variables over the same time periods. This table shows the diminishing role played by the agricultural sector, which accounted for only 5.5 per cent of GDP between 1986 and 1993. Mining, by contrast, has fluctuated in importance according to the price of gold and other mineral resources. In the period 1980–5 it accounted for 15.3 per cent of GDP as compared with 10.8 per cent between 1986 and 1993 when commodity prices were lower. Manufacturing has increased in importance since 1960.

The decline in imports as a proportion of GDP should also be noted. This cannot be attributed to a reversal of trade liberalisation initiatives, but rather to the depressed state of the economy during the 1980s. Both central government revenue and expenditure have grown substantially in relation to GDP. The fiscal deficit, defined as the difference between the two, reached an all-time high of 2.3 per cent of GDP between 1986 and 1993.

Table 19.3 Gross Saving, Gross Domestic Investment and Foreign Saving, 1977–93

	Gross saving		Gross domestic investment		Foreign saving	
	Rm	*% GDP*	*Rm*	*% GDP*	*Rm*	*% GDP*
1977	9 540	27.8	9 128	26.6	-412	-1.2
1978	10 098	25.7	9 768	24.9	-330	-0.8
1979	15 355	32.9	12 385	26.5	-2970	-6.4
1980	21 658	34.9	18 840	30.4	-2818	-4.5
1981	19 944	28.1	24 033	33.8	4089	5.8
1982	17 401	21.8	20 746	26.0	3345	4.2
1983	23 128	25.7	23 206	25.8	78	0.1
1984	23 968	22.7	26 188	24.7	2220	2.1
1985	30 582	25.5	24 657	20.5	-5925	-4.9
1986	34 846	24.9	27 650	19.8	-7196	-5.2
1987	38 276	23.3	32 124	19.5	-6152	-3.7
1988	43 365	21.8	40 426	20.3	-2939	-1.5
1989	54 301	25.3	50 834	23.7	-3467	-1.6
1990	53 958	21.8	48 634	19.7	-5324	-2.1
1991	58 535	21.0	52 348	18.8	-6187	-2.2
1992	57 465	18.6	53 525	17.3	-3940	-1.3
1993	65 917	19.1	59 984	17.4	-5933	-1.7

Source: South African Reserve Bank, *Quarterly Bulletin*.

South Africa has been classified as a middle-income country with a per capita income of approximately US$2800. When expressed in terms of purchasing power parity, however, per capita income rises to US$3200. Although total household income inequality as measured by the Gini coefficient remained unchanged at 0.68 from 1975 to 1991 (Whiteford and McGrath, 1994), it remains amongst the highest in the world.

Table 19.3 shows the levels of gross savings, gross domestic investment and foreign saving for the period 1978–93. Whilst the price of gold rose in the late 1970s, South Africa continued to experience a capital outflow. In the aftermath of the gold boom, capital flows were reversed and the current account on the balance of payments swung into deficit. After the debt crisis of August 1985, the current account had to generate a substantial surplus amounting to 4.9 per cent of GDP to finance the ensuing capital outflow. Between 1985 and 1993, South Africa experienced sustained capital outflows as a result of international financial sanctions.

During the gold boom years, savings and investment remained high, but economic stagnation during the 1980s led to gross domestic investment as a proportion of GDP declining to 17 per cent by 1992.

Table 19.4 Debt Indicators, 1980–93

Year	Debt/GDP (%)	Debt/Export (%)
1980	20.3	56.7
1981	24.8	87.8
1982	29.7	111.2
1983	28.6	125.7
1984	32.2	170.7
1985	41.2	148.9
1986	35.4	198.4
1987	27.3	93.2
1988	24.2	82.0
1989	22.4	78.2
1990	18.2	69.4
1991	16.1	65.3
1992	14.4	61.1
1993	14.2	59.0

Source: South African Reserve Bank, *Quarterly Bulletin*.

The low savings rates of 1992 and 1993 are in part a reflection of dissaving on the part of government.

Table 19.4 shows the extensive build-up in foreign debt which occurred after the fall in the price of gold. The debt:GDP ratio rose as high as 41.2 per cent and the debt: exports ratio was 170.7 per cent in the mid-1980s. Prior to the debt standstill, the country also experienced extensive capital outflows, as indicated by the rise in the cumulative current account deficit for the same period. Since 1985 the foreign debt position has improved markedly to the point where, in international terms, South Africa is now considered to be under-borrowed.

Movements in nominal and real effective exchange rates are shown in Figure 19.1. Although the nominal rate has shown a downward trend since 1970, the real rate appreciated by 16 per cent during the gold boom and then depreciated by 6.5 per cent in 1982, followed by a significant 37.8 per cent depreciation in 1984 and 1985 prior to the debt crisis. Overall, the real rate has been remarkably constant, appreciating by a mere 17 per cent between 1985 and 1993.

As changes in the exchange rate have been shown to be influenced by the terms of trade and capital movements (Gerson and Kahn, 1988), Figures 19.2–19.4 show the terms of trade with and without gold, the current account balance, and the changes in net gold and foreign reserves, respectively. Excluding the price of gold, the terms of trade

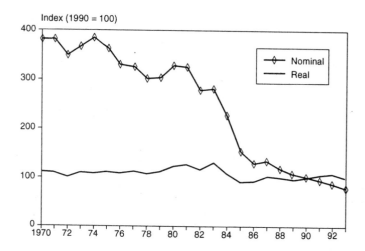

Figure 19.1 Nominal and Real Effective Exchange Rates, 1970–93

Source: South African Reserve Bank, *Quarterly Bulletin*.

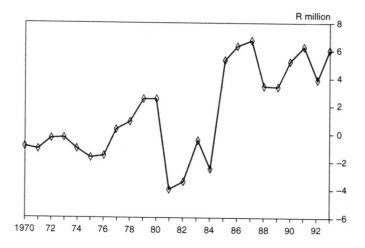

Figure 19.2 Current Account Balance, 1970–93

Source: South African Reserve Bank, *Quarterly Bulletin*.

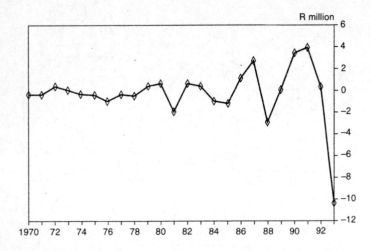

Figure 19.3 Change in Net Gold and Other Reserves, 1970–93

Source: South African Reserve Bank, *Quarterly Bulletin*.

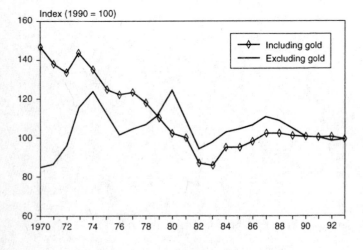

Figure 19.4 Terms of Trade, 1970–93

Source: South African Reserve Bank, *Quarterly Bulletin*.

Table 19.5   London Gold Price (US$), 1978–93

Year	US$ per ounce
1978	193.26
1979	306.99
1980	613.07
1981	459.68
1982	375.79
1983	424.31
1984	360.45
1985	317.29
1986	367.59
1987	446.60
1988	437.09
1989	381.54
1990	383.58
1991	362.19
1992	343.72
1993	359.70

declined from 1970 to 1983. This decline reflects the influence of rising oil prices over the decade. After 1983 there was a moderate recovery in the terms of trade which levelled off over the next six years. When the price of gold is included, the full extent of the external shocks which have buffeted the South African economy can be appreciated. Table 19.5 shows movements in the London gold price from 1978 to 1993, highlighting the gold boom years.

It has been estimated that between 1978 and 1980, the favourable terms of trade effect resulted in a 4.5 per cent gain in welfare. The subsequent decrease in the terms of trade resulted in a 4.1 per cent decline in welfare. It was also calculated that over the period 1980–5, international interest rate shocks reduced income by 10 per cent and the depreciation in the rand incurred a real foreign debt loss of 20.4 per cent (Holden, 1988).

After the debt standstill of 1985, the current account balance swung into surplus to finance the ensuing capital outflow (Figure 19.3). Disinvestment and the moratorium on any new lending by foreign banks and investors created a classical liquidity crisis.

STRUCTURAL ADJUSTMENT

The structural adjustment undertaken in South Africa was in response to the aftermath of the gold boom of 1979–81 and the sanctions and capital flight of the 1980s. During the boom, net reserves (Figure 19.4) as well as the real and nominal exchange rates rose and, although the windfall gain accrued to the private sector, government revenues and expenditures increased without an increase in the budget deficit. Initially, there was an increase in the rate of domestic saving, which then declined when growth fell.

In the meantime, trade liberalisation was proceeding with the replacement of import controls with equivalent tariffs and the reduction of the anti-export bias which existed (GATT, 1993).

Nevertheless, it has been shown that for the period 1974–87, 71 per cent of the protection granted to importables had been shifted in the form of an implicit tax on exportables (Holden, 1992). By 1983 the decline in the current account balance and the unification of the commercial and financial rand markets led policy-makers to suspend temporarily the process of trade liberalisation. Growth in the economy in many sectors, including construction, finally spilled over into increases in imports. This created a deficit on the current account despite the substantial nominal depreciation of the exchange rate. To protect the balance of payments, a 10 per cent import surcharge was introduced. This was subsequently increased to 60 per cent in 1988 on certain luxury goods. Since 1990 the import surcharge has been slowly lowered and by 1993 import controls were found to affect only 15 per cent of all tariff lines (GATT, 1993).

In April 1990, the General Export Incentive Scheme (GEIS) was introduced to replace the earlier, less transparent, export incentives. The GEIS goes part of the way in addressing anti-export bias in the economy. In recent research it has been estimated that, of the 67 subsectors in manufacturing, 27 would still have found it attractive to produce for the foreign market and 40 would have preferred production for the domestic market. Research has shown that exports have been very sensitive to changes in the real exchange rate and the degree of excess capacity in the economy, but the role of the GEIS in stimulating exports has not been firmly established (Holden, 1993).

During the early 1980s the Reserve Bank failed to apply restrictive monetary policy, and predictably the annual rate of inflation increased to above 25 per cent. Fears of an inflationary spiral led to stricter interest rate policy, which saw the prime interest rate rise to 24 per cent. Nevertheless, in general, the early 1980s were characterised by negative real rates of interest. It was only in 1989, when exchange rate policy was directed at curbing the rate of inflation and interest rates became positive, that the rate of inflation began to decline, reaching single digit figures by 1993.

Political unrest, capital outflows and the build-up of foreign debt led to the debt standstill of August 1985. When the stock and foreign exchange markets reopened, the financial rand was reintroduced in order to insulate the economy against capital flight. Soon afterwards, more general goods sanctions reinforced the financial sanctions, further isolating the economy.

Fiscal policy during the 1980s remained reasonably conservative with low deficit:GDP ratios. It has only been in the last four years that the deficit before borrowing has been a cause for concern, accounting for 6–7 per cent of GDP.

In summary, certain structural adjustments have been undertaken in the economy since the gold boom. The exchange rate depreciated in both nominal and real terms, fiscal and monetary policy was reasonably managed, and some attempts were made to ensure that the manufacturing sector in particular became more outwardly oriented. The economy remained under immense pressure from the outside world. It is not surprising, therefore, that economic performance remained poor given that the price of gold failed to recover to the heights of 1980 and the level of political violence and investor uncertainty remained high.

THE RECONSTRUCTION AND DEVELOPMENT PROGRAMME

Cognisant of the need for reform and reconstruction after decades of apartheid, the government introduced the RDP. The main thrust is the elimination of the legacy of poverty and degradation bequeathed by the apartheid regime, hence the provision of housing, health, education, employment and transport receives high priority. The intention is to reallocate the budget rather than increase taxes to meet these needs, and to maintain fiscal discipline even to the point of reducing the overall current deficit and containing growth in the money supply.

Experiments with a number of different scenarios have recently been published by the World Bank for their macroeconometric model of South Africa (Fallon and Pereira da Silva, 1994). The message which emerges is that, if South Africa wishes to increase government expenditures, the sustainability of such a path is dependent on economic growth. This in turn depends on investor confidence and certain supply-enhancing policies.

The success of the RDP is tied up with the need to reform trade policy. The RDP is committed to trade liberalisation and the goal of export growth as an income enhancer. The South African offer to the GATT included the reduction of import tariffs and the simplification of a tariff schedule, which has been described as being among the most complex in the world. The offer to the GATT includes an average cut in tariffs of 33 per cent on industrial products and 36 per cent on agricultural products over five years. Formula duties would be replaced with ad valorem duties, the intention being to reduce tariffs to a maximum of 30 per cent on consumer goods, 15 per cent on intermediate and capital goods, and 5 per cent on raw materials. As the GEIS contravenes the GATT, it will be phased out from 1995 and abolished by the end of 1997 at the latest.

It is hoped that this change in trade policy will elicit a supply response such as to stimulate exports by reducing the anti-export bias. At the same time the RDP envisages that the real exchange rate will remain constant. Michaely et al. (1991) have shown that the success of many trade liberalisations has depended on assistance from a real depreciation of the exchange rate as well as reductions in trade interventions. In many high-performing Asian economies, the effective exchange rate was used as a policy tool to promote non-traditional exports by undervaluing or devaluing to ensure competitiveness.

In the context of the RDP the message is clear to policy-makers. The programme will have to be implemented in a gradual manner so that capital inflows from foreign funding do not derail monetary and fiscal discipline, and real appreciations of the exchange rate are avoided. Although the consequences of macro-populism are well known to policy-makers in South Africa, the danger is that there may be short-run political reasons for pursuing such an unsustainable path, even though it is a path which over the longer run will marginalise the entire economy.

20 The South African Labour Market[1]

Julian Hofmeyr

The South African labour market has performed extremely badly in recent years in terms of creating employment. In the second half of the 1980s, for example, only 7 per cent of school-leavers could expect to find formal sector jobs. This has meant that increasing numbers have had to enter the informal sector in order to eke out some sort of a living. It has been estimated that average income in the informal sector was under R500 per month in 1989 as against R830 for Africans in the non-primary modern sector. Moreover, the distribution of income in the informal sector was highly skewed, with 27 per cent earning less than R150 and 44 per cent less than R250 per month. Taking into account also poor working conditions and insecurity, it is safe to assume that the majority would have preferred formal sector jobs. It should also be borne in mind that the informal sector includes criminal activities such as car theft and drug peddling, and that many of those drawn into these areas may be permanently lost to society as productive contributors to its net wealth. The poor performance of the labour market, therefore, has meant the economic marginalisation of an increasing proportion of the population. Dealing with this problem, and preventing its further growth, is perhaps the most serious challenge facing South Africa today. Without a solution, even Pacific Rim-type growth will at best provide the means to buy off the discontented and disillusioned masses with hand-outs of various types. Without such growth, the future is bleak indeed.

Yet the country's performance has not always been so poor: in the 1960s some 97 per cent of school-leavers could expect to find formal sector jobs, and even in the 1970s the figure was 72 per cent. It is, therefore, worthwhile examining past achievements to see whether any useful lessons can be learned.

POST-WAR GROWTH

Until 1975 the country experienced highly satisfactory growth: from 1946 to 1975 real GDP grew at 4.6 per cent per annum on average, and recessions were shallow and short. This may be compared to a population growth rate of 3 per cent per annum, meaning that, on average, the community was getting richer. However, after 1975 the economy performed considerably more poorly: average GDP growth dropped to 1.9 per cent per annum between 1975 and 1990 while population grew at 2.3 per cent per annum on average, meaning that the community was getting poorer on average. Moreover, recessions were of unprecedented depth and severity in post-depression experience. There were many reasons for this deterioration: the Soweto crisis of 1976, the oil crises, the severely contractionary policies of main trading partners in the early 1980s and the increasing weight of sanctions in the later 1980s, the country s lack of international competitiveness and the loss of momentum of the import-substitution policy, amongst others. The impact on the labour market was dramatic (Table 20.1).

Although overall formal sector growth was lower than population growth in the earlier period, once the low-wage (or residual) industrial sectors (these included mining before the mid-1970s) are excluded, the growth of the high-wage core is seen to be considerably greater, implying that this core was increasingly drawing in the population over a prolonged period and thereby substantially increasing their incomes. Thus, performance during the earlier period, while not stunning, was highly satisfactory. However, the same can certainly not be said of the subsequent period.

It is also of interest to examine the course of average wages (Table 20.2). Wages for Africans largely stagnated before 1960, thereafter picking up slightly in manufacturing and construction. The spectacular rises took place after 1972, however, particularly in mining. While wage growth slackened off after 1975, it continued at a substantial rate on the whole, the notable exception being construction. By contrast, White wages followed a very different course: having risen rapidly prior to 1972, they largely stagnated thereafter.

CAUSES OF WAGE MOVEMENTS

It is clear from Table 20.2 that the labour market underwent a substantial change between the late 1960s and the early 1970s. Prior to this,

Table 20.1 Population and Employment Growth (% p.a.)

Period	Population	Formal sector employment		
		(a)	(b)	(c)
1946–75	3.0	2.5	3.3	4.2
1975–90	2.3	1.0	0.7	0.5

Notes: a. Total formal sector.
  b. Excluding agriculture, trade and services.
  c. Excluding agriculture, trade and services, mining.

Sources: Population: J.L. van Tonder, Human Sciences Research Council; DBSA (1991).
Employment: RSA (1993).

Table 20.2 Growth Rates of Average Real Wages, 1945–89 (% p.a.)

Sector	Race	1945–60	1960–72	1972–5	1975–80	1980–5	1985–9
Manufacturing	Whites	3.05	3.35	0.88	1.18	-0.01	-0.98
	Africans	0.44	2.57	7.59	3.69	1.49	2.64
Construction	Whites	1.89	4.18	-1.67	1.17	-0.51	-2.89
	Africans	0.07	3.38	6.24	-0.15	2.65	-2.54
Mining[a]	Whites	2.35	2.48	4.35	-1.58	0.36	
	Africans	0.31	1.32	29.27	5.69	3.12	
	All races	1.57	1.51	15.48	2.64	1.89	1.94
Formal	Whites			0.76	-0.89	1.79	
sector[a]	Africans			10.33	3.83	2.88	
	All races			2.25	0.76	1.60	0.42
Non-primary	Whites				-0.86	0.87	-0.82
sectors	Africans				3.28	2.65	2.89
	All races				0.58	1.58	0.18

Note: a. The 1980–5 period is replaced by 1980–4 for the White and African groups as a racial breakdown was not provided after 1984.

Source: RSA (1964, 1976, 1992).

the growth in White wages was steady, stagnating thereafter, whereas African wages experienced exactly the opposite.

Early Period

Following demobilisation at the end of the Second World War and the ousting of the Smuts administration in 1948, a substantial number of

Africans lost their jobs and a surplus of labour developed. The result was that real wage levels for Africans in the modern sector, after having risen rapidly during the war years, stagnated. The steady rise in White wages over most of this period can be attributed at least partially to the apartheid policies which protected the White monopoly on skilled jobs. However, as noted above, the economy grew substantially faster than population in most years until 1976, as did employment in the high-wage core of the modern sector. Africans benefited through their rapid absorption into this core, thereby improving their earnings. It is likely that this rapid absorption owed much to the restraint of real wage growth over most of this period.

A shortage of skilled labour developed in the 1960s and forced the Nationalist government of the time to rethink its policies on immigration. Notwithstanding the greatly increased flow of skilled immigrants which resulted, and Verwoerd's statement that South Africa would rather be poor and White than rich and mixed, the shortages developed to such an extent that employers began defying the law, training and promoting Blacks to fill more skilled positions. This was done surreptitiously at first but became more and more open until the government itself acknowledged the need and began to expand education rapidly from the early 1970s. The processes of change were given an additional impetus by the Natal strikes of 1973–4, but it can be argued that even these were a product of the stresses and strains produced by economic growth and the possibilities which opened up as a result.

However, the shortage of labour which developed in the late 1960s was not confined to skilled workers but was also manifested at the unskilled level in wide areas of the country, at least as far as males were concerned. There are two key pieces of evidence which demonstrate this. First, farmers began experiencing shortages of labour and were forced to raise wages dramatically. While they had long complained of shortages of labour, this had not caused them to raise wages to compete with the pull of the cities until, even in areas where wages had remained constant in real terms for at least the previous 15 years, farmers were forced approximately to double real wages between the late 1960s and the late 1970s. Sugar farmers were also forced to raise wages substantially, particularly for cane-cutters. This happened despite the presence of influx control and a policy of discouraging the urbanisation of Africans.

The second piece of evidence relates to the gold mines. Forced by an internationally fixed gold price to contain costs, the mining industry managed to maintain African wages at much lower levels than other industrial employers through its access to foreign labour which was prepared to work at lower wages than local labour because of greater poverty and the lack of income-earning alternatives in the supplying countries. During the 1960s the mines found themselves less and less able to attract South African labour, and became increasingly dependent on foreign sources. It was plain to management that they would soon be entirely dependent on foreign labour if they continued to pursue their low-wage policy, and the rapid rise in the gold price from the early 1970s provided the means to revise this policy. Concurrently, the political risks attached to a dependence on foreign labour were becoming apparent, with Malawi cutting off recruiting following the crash of an aircraft carrying migrants, and a radical government coming to power in Mozambique. The mines thus took a policy decision to increase the proportion of local Africans, and the only way they could do this was by offering a more competitive wage. The result was that average wages trebled in real terms, and the proportion of local Africans in the mine labour force rose from 25 per cent to over 60 per cent between 1971 and 1977.

Thus, improving opportunities for urban employment meant that shortages of labour developed even in the rural areas, forcing traditionally low-wage employers to raise wages dramatically in order to compete. The shortages meant that wages of Africans in the main urban core rose at approximately 7 per cent per annum in real terms between 1972 and 1975, while those for Whites stagnated or fell, presumably because their monopoly on skilled occupations had been broken. Unfortunately, economic growth, and with it employment growth, collapsed after 1975, recovering only briefly at the end of the 1970s.

None the less, a process of beneficial change had been set in motion, which had acquired a momentum of its own, and legislated apartheid in the labour market had largely disappeared by the early 1980s with the advent of full trade union rights for Africans. In addition, African workers rapidly moved into more skilled positions from the early 1970s, and average African wages in the modern sector (excluding agriculture) rose from 15 to 25 per cent of White wages between 1970 and 1980. This was a result of many processes: the Natal strikes and general worker militancy, overseas pressure on multinationals, an increasing realisation by local employers that the situation had to change and the shift in government policies. However, it can be argued that all these pressures for change had their roots in the strains produced by the prolonged period of sustained growth. African trade unions made little or no contribution to this process as they did not become a serious factor in the wage equation until about 1984.

It had been one of the aims or effects of apartheid policy to segment the labour market into a number of watertight compartments: Blacks should not compete with Whites for jobs; rural Africans should not compete with urban Africans; Africans in one urban area should not compete with those in other urban areas; and no other employers should compete with White farmers for their labour. However, this pattern of segmentation started to break down in the late 1960s and the labour market became increasingly unified.

Later Period

The performance of the economy changed dramatically in the second half of the 1970s. Commercial agriculture continued to shed labour, the homeland populations grew while the homelands became less able to support even a constant population, and the mines found that they could recruit as much South African labour as they wished. Overall modern sector prime employment failed to keep pace with population. Without hypothesising a large and growing role for a highly success-ful informal sector, which is implausible, it is difficult to maintain that labour demand continued to press against supply. The performance of agricultural and domestic wages is largely consistent with this: after the mid-1970s they mostly stagnated, and the gap between them and industrial wages continued to grow.

Despite the poor performance of the economy after the mid-1970s and the disappearance of general labour market pressure, average wages for Africans in the modern sector (excluding agriculture) continued to increase, though at a slower pace, with a fall in 1984–6 in most of the formal sector. Detailed analysis, however, reveals that most occupa-tional wage rates for males fell in real terms between 1975 and 1985, particularly for the least skilled, and skill differentials grew. The major factors contributing to the increase in average wages were improving educational levels and upward movement through the occupational struc-ture, the closing of sectoral wage gaps and the increase in wages paid to women. This is consistent with the poor performance of the economy with less-skilled labour being in excess supply, but shortages none the less evident for certain types of skilled labour. The institutional re-forms which took place over this period obviously made a substantial contribution to the changes, but it has been argued that even these were the result of market pressures. It is, therefore, clear that such forces were responsible, directly or indirectly, for the broad movement in average wages which occurred.

However, it is also clear that the process underlying this increase in average wages underwent a fundamental change in the early to mid-1980s. Whereas prior to this, wage rates for African males in most sectors fell in real terms and occupational differentials grew, the reverse appears to have been the case thereafter, at least in manufacturing and mining, but probably in most urban sectors except construction.

Unfortunately, it has not been possible to analyse the period after 1985 in the same detail as the earlier one owing to a lack of adequate data.[2] The conclusions reached are therefore necessarily much more tentative. However, it is clear that after 1985, occupational wage rates for Africans in much of manufacturing began to rise; not only this, but they rose most for the least skilled. While wage rates for Africans in mining had been rising since the early 1970s, it is only from the early 1980s that those for the unskilled started rising faster than for the more skilled.[3] This suggests that trade unions, which have long had the stated aim of lessening the skilled–unskilled gap, started to have a significant influence on the wage-setting process from the early 1980s, the time at which mass-based unionism really took off. It is clear that institutional factors were more important than market forces in sectors where wage movements followed these patterns. By contrast, in the construction sector which is singularly subject to cyclical pressures, wage levels moved up and down broadly in line with market forces; there was no coherent relationship between the changes in unskilled and semi-skilled wages. In addition, as noted earlier, the gap between wages in industry and those in agriculture and domestic service continued to grow, indicating the absence of any shortage of labour which would force wages up.

BROADER IMPLICATIONS

The wage movements outlined above have had far-reaching implications for unemployment and labour market segmentation.

Unemployment

In examining the relationship between unemployment and the wage changes which took place, the post-war period can be divided into three phases. During the first, overall real wage increases were the result of a developing scarcity of African labour, even at the unskilled level for certain categories such as prime-age males. As such, labour market conditions were the cause rather than the consequence of the wage changes: it is clear that the wage increases would have had no adverse consequences for unemployment. Mechanisation, which resulted from the changing relative price of labour (leaving aside changes originating on the side of capital from government policy sources), would have been entirely appropriate, as the rising price represented a genuine increasing scarcity of labour. During this phase, then, the wage increases going to Africans can be seen as one of the natural consequences of a process of economic growth and, as such, would not have had any adverse consequences for the economy.

This phase came to an end in the mid-1970s with the onset of a severe recession. Labour market pressure for higher wages then fell away, and wage rates decreased for large parts of the labour force, particularly the less skilled. Formal employment hardly increased, and unemployment and underemployment grew. Once again, unemployment appears to have been more a cause than a consequence of the wage changes, which can be seen as the result mainly of a natural market process. In as far as this was the case, there would have been few adverse consequences for the economy as a whole.[4] Characteristic of this period was an apparent unification of the labour market where the formal and informal barriers to the mobility of Africans were increasingly broken down.

The third phase started in the early 1980s when patchy evidence suggests that wage rates began once again to rise for large parts of the labour force, and when the increases appear to be in inverse proportion to the level of skill. As noted above, it is clear that market pressures could not have been the underlying cause, which must therefore have been institutional in character. The most likely candidate is union pressure following the take-off of mass-based unionisation in the first half of the 1980s. It is clear that formal sector employment growth was totally inadequate to absorb the increment to the labour force. What precisely happened to unemployment is unclear as most of those without formal sector jobs would simply not have been able to be totally without some form of income-earning activity, given the absence of generalised unemployment support. Certainly, the sharp increase in criminal activity bears stark testimony to the shortage of legitimate economic opportunities. None the less, it can be safely concluded that there must have been some increase in unemployment and that many people would have been forced to take up grossly inadequate or illegal jobs in the informal sector.

The connection between union-driven wage increases and unemployment is complex, and it cannot simply be concluded that unemployment has been directly caused by them. What is clear, however, is that union action would have done nothing to help the problem and is likely to have exacerbated it indirectly. Such action would have resulted in significant wage differences between similar jobs in different sectors and regions, re-fragmenting the labour market but along different lines from the earlier apartheid-induced segmentation. Through decreasing the growth in unionised jobs, many more people than otherwise would have been forced to take up non-unionised jobs, further driving down wages for such jobs. This would have increased the incentive for job-queueing, which would probably have made some direct contribution to unemployment.

There is an alternative way of looking at the relationship between unions and unemployment. In terms of the approach adopted by Layard et al. (1991), the effect of unions is to move the supply curve of labour up, with unemployment (or the differential chances of employment in the unionised and non-unionised sectors) playing an equilibrating role. The extent of upward movement depends on how the union perceives the threat of job loss to its members if it pushes for too high a wage. The higher the general level of unemployment, or the greater the union/non-union wage differential, the less secure union members will feel, and the less likely they are to press for wage increases which can threaten their jobs. The institutional changes of the 1970s and early 1980s took the economy from a position of virtually no unionisation for African workers to one of substantial unionisation. One can, therefore, conceive of this change as effectively moving the supply curve(s) of labour for unionised jobs[5] upwards, with the equilibrium level of unemployment (or employment differentials) increasing. Clearly, the period concerned was one of testing newfound strengths and developing perceptions, and it is therefore likely that the curve(s) moved up sharply at first, settling down later. It is possible that the advent of the new government, which is perceived to be sympathetic to labour, has lessened the threat of job loss in the minds of workers notwithstanding the high level of unemployment, leading to a further upward shift in the curve since the April 1994 election.

Segmentation

More serious than the effect of unions on unemployment, however, is the segmentation of the labour market which results. Segmentation refers to the compartmentalisation of a market into non-competing segments, for example, the fact that workers in domestic service do not really compete with those in industry, with the result that differences in their wage levels bear no relation to skill differentials or differences in working conditions. Segmentation is a complex process which can take many forms, and there are likely to be multiple segments. However, it is sufficient here to concentrate on a simple bifurcation: a primary segment consisting of formal sector employment in large firms or under regulated conditions such as building workers, and a secondary segment comprising mainly the informal sector, but also farm labour, domestic service, and service-type jobs in small firms.[6]

What essentially distinguishes the two segments is the fact that conditions in the first segment are only loosely determined by market forces whereas, in the second, the connection is much more direct. This is particularly true of wage levels. In the prime segment, these are determined by considerations such as seniority, career scales, and the like, and are generally significantly above market-determined or market-clearing levels.[7] This is particularly true if working conditions, job security and promotional prospects are taken into account. This means that there is nearly always a queue of willing applicants for such jobs, who would prefer them to their current situation.[8] In other words, these jobs are rationed. In the secondary segment, however, wages (or equivalent earnings in self-employment) are much more directly related to market conditions, and will tend to be close to a market-clearing level, meaning that such jobs or opportunities are not rationed, but are fairly freely available. There will in general be little job security, prospects of promotion or opportunities for training. Thus, those who manage to obtain employment in the primary segment are in the position of privileged 'insiders', with the rest cast as 'outsiders' looking enviously in. Whilst this is obviously an oversimplification, it captures effectively the essential aspects of South Africa's present situation.

Segmentation arises for many reasons other than government intervention or union influence. However, unions can exacerbate segmentation, and one example will suffice to illustrate the point. An important factor leading to segmentation is the existence of one-off fixed costs which are associated with the hiring and firing of labour. These include search, screening, training and severance costs which must be incurred every time labour turns over. Any firm incurring such expenditure has an interest in minimising turnover and creating long-lasting employment relationships, and this interest will be shared by employees if they bear part of this cost through, for example, accepting a lower wage during training. The cost takes the form of an investment on the part of the firm and employee, and both can increase the return on this investment by maintaining the employment relationship as long as possible.[9] This creates a degree of bilateral monopoly, making room for bargaining over the exact size of the return each gets, and significantly loosens the direct link between conditions in the firm and in the labour market generally, since non-employees are only imperfect substitutes for those already in the firm. This type of situation is obviously fertile ground for unions to canvass support and exert their muscle. Whilst the existence of this type of segmentation cannot be attributed to union influence, unions can increase its degree by, for example, insisting on generous severance packages and increasing the costs of dismissal through strikes and so on. They are in a position to extract the maximum possible in wages, and thereby to maximise the wage differences which characterise segmentation of the labour market. The higher wages may justify further mechanisation, requiring the need for further training. Mechanisation will result in employment contracting (or growing more slowly than it otherwise would), meaning that an even greater proportion of the labour force is driven into the secondary segment of the labour market, further depressing earnings there and exacerbating segmentation still further. The degree to which this process can be taken will be enhanced still more if the firm has a high degree of monopoly power in the product market, and increased labour costs can simply be passed on to consumers through higher prices. This is obviously a significant factor in South Africa, with its high degree of protection against international competition.

Thus, segmentation leads directly back to the point made at the beginning of this paper, namely, that South Africa's major problem is the marginalisation of an increasing proportion of its population. The fact that unions, which represent part of the formally employed elite, have been able to exert such a decisive influence on the wage determination process, thereby presumably exacerbating segmentation, is a particular cause for concern.

Another cause for concern related to the institutionally determined nature of the wage-setting process over the last decade is the fact that many employers, particularly the larger ones in manufacturing, would have faced a distorted set of relative prices, and this would have

encouraged mechanisation, which in this case would have been inappropriate in that the price relativities would not have represented the underlying scarcities in the economy. This would, therefore, have damaged
its growth potential, and hence its ability to generate wealth and jobs.
There is some evidence that the number of formal sector jobs has been
significantly reduced through mechanisation induced by wage increases.

POLICY IMPLICATIONS

The lesson of the first 30 years of the post-war period is that rapid
economic growth with wage restraint enabled employment to expand
so rapidly that shortages of labour eventually appeared which forced
employers to raise wages rapidly, presumably at the same time improving productivity to justify these higher levels, while shortages of
skilled labour forced both them and the government to change their
attitudes to the question of Africans doing skilled work. At the same
time, the White monopoly on skilled occupations was broken and the
racial wage gap narrowed rapidly. Moreover, this process was spreading its beneficial effects right across the economy, forcing significant
change even in agriculture as well as in the institutional structure of
the labour market. In particular, it destroyed many of the structures
and attitudes created and perpetuated by the policy of apartheid. It is
likely that, had it continued, employers and workers even in the darkest
corners would have felt its effects in a way that institutional pressures
on their own will probably never be able to achieve, and even if they
could, would do this only at the expense of increasing unemployment
and segmentation.

Thus, economic growth was bringing about most of the changes which
are currently seen to be desirable, but which were certainly not at the
forefront of government policy at the time. The tragedy is that this
growth collapsed when it did, and the fact that the process has not
progressed much further should be blamed on the absence of adequate
growth rather than on the assumption that growth is unable to redress
at least some of the problems of the past.

It is clear that the problem of the marginalisation of an increasing
proportion of the labour force cannot be solved without adequate economic growth. However, this is not enough: it is essential that the economy
be put on a far more labour-intensive growth path. This is a complex
matter which cannot be dealt with in detail here, but it is clear that
such a process will not be helped by misplaced institutional pressures

for higher wages, however deserving the recipients might be.

It is clear, therefore, that what is required is rapid growth with wage restraint until the surplus of labour has been absorbed. The type of government intervention which is required to bring this about is the moderation or restraint of union demands, as well as less controversial measures such as improved education and training. Promotion and the acquisition of skills will then come about in a natural way without many of the problems inherent in a forced process. In addition, this would seem to be a vastly preferable route to pushing for ever higher wages in the formal sector while employing Band Aid-type measures such as a public works programme (PWP) to pick up those excluded through the increased mechanisation and automation which will inevitably result from a high-wage policy.

The suggestion that economic growth will lead to both the absorption of the unemployed and the promotion and training of Blacks in particular should not be taken to mean that employers can neglect forward-looking policies for the upgrading of the skills of the labour force generally, or should not strive to overcome the discriminatory legacy of the past, but rather that this is not an area requiring government intervention: it should be left to the market to sort out. Under a scenario of growth, market imperatives will soon dictate that the best possible use be made of all a company's resources, just as happened in the 1960s and 1970s. To look at the last 10–15 years and say that this will not happen without active intervention is inappropriate, as this was a period when growth was totally inadequate on any criterion.

It is clear that, even with the highest feasible growth and the most favourable labour market policies, it will take some considerable time for the surplus of labour to be absorbed. There consequently is a place for a PWP as a short- to medium-term measure while growth catches up; indeed, there would seem to be no other measure which can address the problem sufficiently rapidly. However, it is crucial that such a programme should be structured in such a way that it can be wound down rapidly once there is no longer a need for it. It should also facilitate the passage of workers through it and into conventional jobs, even if this is detrimental to efficiency in projects being carried out in terms of the PWP. In doing this, it should enable those who have become isolated from the labour market through loss of skills or confidence to obtain suitable training and re-enter the market. It is important, therefore, that it should not undermine existing markets through forcing wages up or attracting labour which is able to find conventional employment. The best way to ensure this is to offer a wage significantly below what is on offer in such jobs. By doing this, the applicants will select themselves in the appropriate fashion. There certainly is recognition of this in the proposals prepared by the National Manpower Commission for a PWP, but implementation may not meet these criteria if, as in the past, employers engaged in PWP-like projects have been forced by local unions to pay wages at union rates.

Notes

1. This paper draws extensively on Hofmeyr (1994a), which also contains full source referencing. For a simpler and more accessible treatment, see Hofmeyr (1994b).
2. The situation has recently improved dramatically with the availability of data from a number of surveys; however, there has not yet been time to incorporate these in the analyses.
3. The situation before 1976 is not clear owing to an absence of data.
4. This is not to belittle the effects on workers who found themselves in the unenviable position of being unable to find a job.
5. This is termed the bargained real wage curve.
6. Domestic service and farm labour are now coming under more stringent regulation, but have historically been part of the second segment and will be treated as such here.
7. This may not be the case at all times, e.g. at the height of the business cycle.
8. Again, this may not be true at particular junctures such as the height of the business cycle.
9. The investment may be an actual one, in the form of hiring costs, or a potential one in the form of severance costs.

21 Labour Legislation and the Zimbabwean Economy

Joe Foroma

Zimbabwe became independent in 1980 and, as in other post-colonial economies, there were many socio-economic disparities that needed to be redressed. The new government, with its stated socialist outlook, sought to do just this, and one field in which it took early action was that of labour legislation.

INDEPENDENCE AND LABOUR LEGISLATION

The new government was anxious to improve the economic position of the majority of the population. It is not disputed that the colonial employment and remuneration systems were inequitable and racially based, or that something needed to be done about them. What has become the subject of debate, however, is the approach adopted in attempting to redress pre-independence imbalances.

Minimum wages and related job security legislation were enacted with effect from 1 July 1980. The Employment Act 1980 introduced requirements for employers to seek government permission to terminate employment contracts. This legislation was a form of market intervention meant to protect workers and maintain jobs. It is not uncommon for governments generally to lay down formal procedures to be followed when workers are dismissed. Fallon and Lucas (1991) argue that 'in neither Zimbabwe (nor India) are these provisions particularly onerous by international standards. . . . the job security provisions in Zimbabwe (and India) differ from those of most other nations because of their permission requirement.' All undertakings generally, except the civil service, armed forces and some parastatals, were covered by job security legislation, as were temporary or casual employees. Stringent requirements had to be met, and delays in the processing of job termination formalities could sometimes take up to a year or more.

The minimum wages regulations were meant to ensure a minimum standard of livelihood for workers. Minimum wage pronouncements were made annually by the government until around 1990/1 when, with the introduction of the economic reform programme, the authorities progressively left wage and conditions of service negotiations to the market to determine.

It is difficult statistically to isolate the employment effect of minimum wage legislation in the case of Zimbabwe because the output perform-ance of the economy depended on a number of important variables. The availability of foreign exchange (which was allocated only twice every year), price controls and periodic droughts were key determi-nants of the sustainability of jobs. The unemployment rate in the economy is estimated to have been between 30–40 per cent during the 1980s, and no recorded statistics are available on informal sector employment: a 1993 study estimates that there are about 800 000 micro-enterprises in Zimbabwe. With only 1.3 million in formal employment, it is clear that the bulk of the population is engaged in informal sector activities.

EFFECTS OF MINIMUM WAGES AND JOB SECURITY LEGISLATION

Economists have long recognised the consequences of interfering with market forces in the determination of wages. Thus, for example, Hicks (1932) wrote that the 'raising of wages above the competitive level will contract the demand for labour, and make it impossible to absorb some of the new available'. More recently, Block (1982: 215) pointed out that 'the effect of intervention of minimum wages is to raise the wages of workers at the bottom of the ladder. The actual effect of such legislation has been to cut off the bottom few rungs, thus making it more difficult for less-skilled workers to obtain jobs for high or even middling pay.' Added to this,

> minimum wages, if set above the point at which the market will clear, would deprive the young of their opportunity to price them-selves into jobs. Moreover, when labour market conditions for the young worsen (if, for example, their numbers grow) minimum wages ensure that the maximum adverse effect is inflicted upon this vulnerable group. In a free market, an increased supply of teenagers would cause a fall in their price to enable extra numbers to be absorbed into employment. If the teenage wage remains fixed by legislation, however, no more teenagers can be employed and the extra numbers

of teenagers in the population will then simply be reflected in the longer employment queues. Minimum wages thus rob the labour market of flexibility to cope with exogenous changes. (Forest, 1982: 249)

Minimum wages and job security legislation have a number of effects on the labour market and the economy at large. High costs and obstacles to adjusting a firm's labour force, such as those imposed by job security legislation, tend to make a firm inflexible in its ability to adapt to changing market conditions. Thus, for example, when restrictive labour market legislation is in force, firms are reluctant to take on the necessary additional workers during a seasonal (or uncertain) upturn for fear of getting stuck with them during the downturn. Fallon and Lucas (1991: 396) wrote that 'restricting employers' ability to fire workers may actually reduce the size of the workforce employers wish to maintain'.

Also affected is the level of productivity. Fallon and Lucas (1991) suggest that

> the ability to fire workers may be an important aspect of maintaining worker productivity. It is common practice to apply on-the-job evaluations in the normal process of screening for more effective employees. . . . firms may be stuck with workers who prove to be poor matches with the specific demands of the job, thus reducing overall productivity.

In this way, job security legislation imposed on employers may reduce worker productivity.

Job security regulations tend to encourage the use of more capital-intensive techniques of production rather than labour-intensive ones, and so reduce the demand for labour. In Zimbabwe, a compounding factor was the general system of capital allowances applicable for tax purposes during the post-1980 period. This system encouraged the use of capital relative to labour even though labour was available in increasing abundance. Since independence some 180 000–220 000 school-leavers (aged 16–20 years) have joined the ranks of the unemployed each year, the formal sector being able to absorb only about 20 000 new employees annually. All in all, therefore, job security regulations result in a reduced ability to adjust by firms, an altered demand for labour, and higher costs per employee.

Because of the costs associated with getting rid of unwanted employees

when job security rules are in force, firms tend to struggle for as long
as they can, with the same employees, before recruiting additional staff.
This was noticeable in Zimbabwe during the period of job security
legislation.

By far the most important lesson to be learnt from the application
of minimum wages and job security legislation in Zimbabwe is that
the legislation protects only those already in employment and does not
do anything to assist the larger numbers who are without jobs. Where
possibly three people could have been employed, perhaps only two are
engaged, with adverse implications for the dependency ratios that the
African extended family concept entails. It is clearly more important
to allow the economy to grow so that many more legitimate jobs can
be created rather than to coerce firms to retain redundant or semi-
redundant employees.

Minimum wage legislation played a key role in Zimbabwe after independence, the minimum wage relative to the consumer price index
being raised by 27 per cent in industry and mining and by 43 per cent
in agriculture in the first 18 months (Fallon and Lucas, 1991: 397).
Although employment has expanded since independence, much of this
has been in public administration and teaching. Manufacturing and
agricultural employment has shown no appreciable growth, but population growth has averaged 3 per cent per annum. Moreover, only in
1994 did total employment exceed the previous peak which was attained in 1974 – 20 years earlier!

In the agricultural, construction, mining, manufacturing and private
household sectors, job losses as a result of minimum wages were particularly severe during the mid-1980s. The likelihood of job losses also
increases in direct proportion to the severity of an economic downturn
or drought, whilst the rate of recovery from a downturn is relatively
more difficult the more stringent the job security legislation in force
because of the additional costs per employee.

Minimum wage legislation has not been abolished since the advent
of economic reforms in 1990, but there are no legal minima except for
domestic workers and gardeners. Rather, the collective bargaining process
has now effectively allowed wages to increase above what a decreed
level may have achieved. At the factory floor wages are generally negotiated bilaterally between industrial employer representatives and industrial unions and, in other cases, directly between management and
employees. These negotiations arrive at agreed minima for each industry, but many workers are already clear of these minima.

The labour legislation had an adverse impact on investor confidence when it was applicable. This was because it involved the philosophy of control and it appeared to be deliberately tilted against the employer. Moreover, very restrictive provisions related to the employment of expatriates, and these were enforced by the immigration authorities. Fortunately, all these have been considerably relaxed and labour legislation is no longer a major issue when consideration is being given to investment, both by domestic and foreign sources.

The controls on the labour market were always cited by both existing and potential investors (local and foreign) as a major disincentive to investment in Zimbabwe. However, it is difficult to quantify the impact that job security legislation and minimum wages had on investment in Zimbabwe because other strong factors (such as foreign exchange shortages and price and exchange controls) were also at play. Qualitative indications from interviews carried out in the past with potential investors and from business opinion surveys of the Confederation of Zimbabwe Industries during the period 1987–91 indicate that minimum wages did result in increases in real wages, although the rate of inflation began to rise rather sharply from 1985 onwards. Those lucky enough to have jobs benefited from the regulations. This proportion, however, was small given the fact that only about 1.3 million people in a population of 10 million held formal sector jobs in 1990.

Strict job security measures tend to encourage firms to shift to the hiring of temporary employees for whom overheads are thought to be lower than for permanent staff. In Zimbabwe, the government legislated wage rates for casual employees that were twice those of permanent staff. The reality, of course, is that in a situation of excess labour such as obtained in Zimbabwe, the regulations can to some extent be subverted in favour of those wielding market power (the employer). In terms of poverty reduction, job security legislation improves the lot of those who retain jobs but substantially worsens the plight of those made redundant.

CONCLUSION

The serious, racially-based economic disparities in the Zimbabwean economy needed some form of intervention in markets to improve the lot of the African workforce. The above discussion, however, indicates the need for caution and rationality in looking at wage policy: stringently enforced wage and job security legislation produces counterproductive effects. It would have been preferable for the government to have set broad wage parameters during the early years with labour and employers agreeing final rates amongst themselves, and the authorities then progressively leaving collective bargaining to the market as both employees and employers acquired negotiating skills and gained confidence.

22 Helping Small and Medium Business

Marlene Hesketh

It is well documented that small and medium enterprises (SMEs) play a critical role in a successful economy. In Southern Africa, where countries are typically capital-poor and labour-rich, the emergence of the small, medium and micro-enterprise (SMME) sector provides opportunities for investment in industries with higher labour absorption at a lower cost of capital. The role of the SMME sector is also essential for technical and other innovation, which is so vital for the challenges facing the sub-continent. This paper addresses the contribution made by SMMEs to the South African economy, and the policy constraints facing the sector.

SMALL AND MEDIUM BUSINESS IN THE ECONOMY

There are many statistical definitions of a small enterprise in South Africa, based on one or more of such measures as the number of employees, turnover, value of assets, and even the amount of electricity consumed. While there is no general agreement on any one definition, employment seems to be the preferred dimension with firms of less than 20–30 employees being regarded as small. With more than this number of employees, owners usually have to raise more capital and delegate significant authority to at least one subordinate. This stage in the firm's lifecycle would bring it into the 'medium' category where the business is established and formal as opposed to emerging. The upper limit on this category usually varies across industries, and ranges from 200 to 500 employees.

A micro-enterprise is generally considered to be a business run by a single self-employed person or which employs only family members (often at no pay). The important policy consideration here is: when does this become a business? Research has indicated that some participants at this level become self-employed as a survival strategy and will revert to formal employment if it is offered.

These quantitative criteria are usually combined with qualitative definitions such as independence, owner-management and simple organisational structures. Although such definitions are inherently subjective, they highlight an essential difference between small and large firms: small firms are usually run by their owners. Whereas larger firms have separation of ownership and management through their access to capital markets, and derive efficiency through economies of scale, small business is less bureaucratic, more focused on core competences and relatively less capital-intensive. With lower fixed costs, small firms should be more flexible and more innovative.

Formal small and medium businesses are found in virtually all sectors of the South African economy, even in mining (Ruiters, 1994: 15). Micro-enterprise is not confined to hawking, taxis, shebeens and panel-beating (Thomas, 1989: 5), but extends to catering, home-based manufacturing, building, child-minding, informal schools, goods transport, accommodation, music and more sophisticated activities such as consulting, broking and commodity trading (CSS, 1991: 5). Most successful African-owned businesses are in retailing, wholesaling and consumer goods manufacturing (BMR, 1992: 26). There is only limited participation by African owners in 'hard' manufacturing such as in chemicals, plastics, metal products and mineral processing (World Bank, 1993b: 12). Whereas the micro-enterprise sector is typical of the pattern found in other parts of Africa, the percentage of African-owned manufacturing activities in South Africa is considered to be smaller than that found in other African countries (Ruiters, 1994: 21).

SMMEs, both formal and informal, employ some 7 million people, or about a half of the economically active population of 14.3 million. It is further estimated that the contribution of SMMEs to GDP is at least 45 per cent (Vosloo, 1993: 21). This pattern of small business accounting for about one half of GDP seems to hold for most countries in the West and in Africa.

Definitive research has not been done in South Africa, but it seems clear that, in most countries, small firms with fewer than 20 employees are the most important job generators in the economy. The declining capacity of the formal South African economy to absorb labour has been cited as the reason for the growth in the informal sector. From 1985 to 1990, the formal economy was absorbing only 8 per cent of entrants to the labour market (World Bank, 1993c: 7). However, the job-creation findings in other countries seem to hold over time, with SMEs creating more jobs over all phases of the business cycle except in the latter stages of long upswings. In the United States in the last two decades, about 60 per cent of net new jobs have come from new businesses, almost all of which are small, with the rest coming from expansion of existing firms. OECD findings confirm that the rate of business start-ups is the most significant indicator of job growth (Gray and Gamser, 1994: 6).

Smaller firms account for more than one half of the innovation in the United States and OECD countries, and make markets more competitive by constantly introducing new ideas, products and services. It is this competition among firms that leads to lower prices and better products. One could also argue that small business owners make good citizens. They have a vested interest in the economy and display a preference for doing things their own way. They are independent, they challenge the inappropriate use of authority and ensure that government officials at all levels are responsive to the needs of the community.

Output per worker in smaller firms is often lower than that for larger firms, and wages are accordingly lower. SMMEs in service industries, however, often have higher output per worker than larger firms in the same industries. Gray and Gamser (1994: 6) attribute this to greater innovation occurring in smaller firms. They also argue that SMEs contribute to the efficient use of resources in an economy by responding quickly to changes in demand, thus minimising the cost to society of making output adjustments. Large firms, by contrast, achieve economies of scale by building large plants and running them at constant output levels, building new plants only when they are confident that the upward shift in demand is permanent. Empirically, industries with more variable demand environments are likely to have a greater proportion of total output produced by smaller companies.

MAKING MARKETS WORK BETTER FOR SMALL AND MEDIUM BUSINESS

Surveys of African-owned business in South Africa (GEMINI, 1993; World Bank, 1993b) identified the major constraints to be lack of access to markets, financing difficulties and government policy and regulation. Other factors perceived to impede the progress of emerging enterprise are crime and violence, labour laws and the administration of value-added tax. One could argue that these latter considerations are also matters of policy and regulation.

General Policy Measures

Most governments follow broad macroeconomic policies that apply to business generally, but some of these policies have a particular impact on the small enterprise sector. Because small business is more sensitive to the business cycle, economic instability affects smaller companies more severely, and there are more business closures and start-ups in the SME sector than among larger companies. International data suggest that about 20 per cent of new businesses close in the first year, and less than 50 per cent survive into their fifth year (Gray and Gamser, 1994: 9). Not all the closures are failures in the sense that they are forced into liquidation by creditors. Many closures seem to represent good business decisions, for example, retirement of the owner, or withdrawing resources from one business to put them in another where they will earn a better rate of return. Many entrepreneurs and informal sector operators open and close a number of businesses before they find one that produces the returns and conditions that suit the owner. However, it remains true that more small businesses than large go to the wall in economic downturns, and more small businesses are started in upswings.

This fact, and the finding that job creation is closely linked to new business start-ups, should encourage governments to reconsider *policies affecting the entry of new businesses*, for example, licensing fees and registration requirements. The costs of compliance with regulations also weigh more heavily on the small firm. Large firms tend to have the critical mass necessary to comply with regulations in areas such as health, labour and taxation. Small businesses have less organisational slack, and the costs of compliance relative to turnover and profits are higher. Easy *access to information about laws and regulations* would minimise the cost of doing business.

Stable *fiscal and monetary policy*, that is, reasonable interest rates, reasonable and understandable levels of taxation and a reasonable level of inflation, result in more predictable cash flows from a business, and therefore reduce business risk. The more successful developing countries have interest rates that are in line with world rates, and low rates of inflation. The interest rate, after all, determines the cost of capital in the economy. The lower this is, the more viable and globally competitive investments become. Competitive financial markets are as important for small firms as for large, even though they do not raise funds on capital markets. Active and liquid financial markets, with speculators who are always willing to make the other side of a trade deal, result in the spreading of risk which serves to reduce the overall cost of capital in the economy. Liberal foreign exchange policy also contributes towards reducing the cost of capital by improving access to world capital markets. Policy should also provide for a safe monetary system with proper supervision of financial intermediaries.

Competition policy should be focused on preventing anti-competitive behaviour rather than placing impediments in the way of concentration *per se*. This, together with *trade policy*, often results from the rent-seeking activities of vested interest groups in large industry who have the resources to lobby government for protection against local and imported goods. This results in the inputs to smaller firms being more expensive, making them in turn less competitive with imported goods and very often unviable. This form of tariff protection is considered to be a major reason why South African secondary industry is underdeveloped relative to primary goods industries.

Investment in education and physical infrastructure is particularly important for the development of emerging enterprises, which do not have the individual capacity to import labour or lobby for infrastructural resources. *Well-defined property rights and access to justice under the law* are also important policy variables. Contracts should be made easy to enter into, and recourse to litigation should be readily available against those who break them.

New businesses are very often started at home. Preventing home business through *land-use regulation* can represent a significant barrier to emerging enterprise. In South Africa, there is considerable red tape involved in having zoning laws altered to suit the changing use of land in certain communities.

Specific Policy Support

Three fields of specific policy support for SMEs are outlined below.

Fiscal Policy

Taxation policies can have very large positive and negative effects on SMEs. Generally lower levels of taxation and less complicated tax laws seem to stimulate incentive in successful developing countries. Fiscal policy should be roughly neutral to labour and capital as well as to companies and individuals. This is clearly not the case in South Africa where the company tax rate is 35 per cent, secondary tax on companies 25 per cent, the top marginal rate of personal tax 43 per cent and value-added tax (which allows capital goods, but not labour, inputs as credits) 14 per cent.

Depreciation allowances, permitting faster write-offs of new investment by smaller firms, would prevent some of the liquidity constraints faced by growing businesses. Allowances for training for the self-employed, and business development allowances, could provide incentives for additional investment in these vital components of a growing business. Research has shown that successfully growing firms invest more in training and marketing than those which do not grow. It has also been established that retained earnings are the most common source of expansion finance for small companies (Gray and Gamser, 1994: 29). A lower rate on initial profits for all firms would allow small businesses to retain more earnings.

Small businesses could benefit from an allocation of provincial and local government tax revenue for the development of industrial parks, market information and local business advice. Providing tangible benefits and making compliance easier could be a means of bringing the informal sector into the revenue net; this has proved something of a challenge to South African tax authorities.

Education

The successful developing economies have invested large amounts on universal basic education, tertiary education and vocational training. Apart from the tax incentives mentioned above, government could play a larger role by co-funding apprenticeship programmes with smaller businesses. Investing in the training of employees is a risky business for smaller firms because they often cannot legally enforce a worker's remaining in their employ after the training period. Reducing the cost of the training programme would make training more attractive to the smaller business owner. Short-term subsidies from government could also encourage the growth of industry and trade associations. These could offer industry-specific training programmes, seminars, conventions, and so on, which are primary learning venues for professions around the world. Such subsidies could build capacity among emerging business associations.

Labour and Workplace Regulation

One of the thorniest issues in small business development is that of the apparent trade-off between good working conditions and economic development. The labour movement has worked long and hard to achieve the degree of protection that workers in South Africa presently enjoy, and it would argue that this is not enough. However, in an economy where nearly one half of the economically active population is employed outside the formal sector, or not at all, it seems that labour laws should allow flexibility in wages and working hours, given reasonable safety standards. The Industrial Council system, where agreements between employer bodies and unions are extended to non-parties, is seen as raising barriers to entry and is considered particularly pernicious by many in the small business sector. Gray and Gamser (1994: 35) argue that smaller businesses are often more labour-intensive and therefore produce more jobs for a given level of output, than the more capital-intensive larger firms. In an economy that has not reached full employment, it would seem advantageous to favour smaller businesses and more jobs, even if some of the jobs are less productive and lower-paid than those in big business.

CONCLUSION

There seems little doubt that a vibrant small and medium business sector helps economies to grow by providing competition, innovation and job creation. What is also becoming clear is that successful developing economies have placed less emphasis on specific SMME development but instead have tended to take a stance of 'active neutrality' by creating a generally favourable policy environment for all forms of business. Gray and Gamser (1994: 38) cite a recent World Bank report on the growing East Asian economies which indicates that sound macroeconomic policy reforms took place at an early stage and set the tone for subsequent industry-based initiatives. By contrast, in Eastern Europe, where less attention has been paid to macroeconomic policy, micro-policy initiatives have had poor to mixed results.

The extensive informal sector in South Africa indicates that there is an underlying entrepreneurial spirit which, given effective education and infrastructure, could move to formal business settings. The government will have to deal with this sector for some time, and must be careful not to create a regulatory environment that displaces existing micro-enterprises or eliminates potential business opportunities for low-skilled people with no capital. This will require good local government to ensure that the continued existence of a large informal sector does not lead to abuse of the system and to disrespect for the law and the tax authorities.

23 Health, Education and Productivity

Alan Whiteside

Productivity has become something of a catchphrase in South Africa in recent years, but there is no denying its importance in enhancing the competitiveness of a firm or country. Productivity may be defined, in the widest sense, as representing

> the relationship between physical output and the capital, labour, materials and energy required to produce that output. That is, productivity is a physical output per unit of capital, unit of labour, unit of energy and unit of raw materials. Productivity improvement involves the better and more efficient utilisation by management of all production resources to ensure maximum output at minimum cost. (NPI, 1994: 1).

This paper is concerned with labour productivity and with two factors, namely, the health of a nation and the educational levels of the workforce, which strongly influence that productivity.

HEALTH

There are two common measures of the health of a nation: morbidity (expressed as a percentage of working days lost through illness) and mortality (the death rate). Clearly, productivity is adversely affected by the amount of time that people take off work because they are unwell, and by the premature loss through death of people in the workforce. The normal mortality rate is about 0.2–0.5 per cent of the working-age population.

In most developing countries poverty, communicable diseases (particularly those of childhood) and malnutrition are the main causes of mortality and morbidity. As a country becomes wealthier so the pattern of the disease burden changes, and the prime cause of morbidity and mortality becomes chronic diseases such as circulatory problems

Table 23.1 Demographic and Health Indicators

Country	Life expectancy at birth (years) 1990	Total fertility rate[a] 1990	IMR per 1000 live births[b] 1990	One-year-olds immunised (%) 1988–9
Angola	46	6.4	160	31
Botswana	67	5.0	37	67
Lesotho	56	5.8	97	78
Malawi	46	7.6	147	55
Mozambique	47	6.3	173	44
Namibia	57	5.9	103	41
S. Africa	62	4.3	50	NA
Swaziland	57	6.5	115	78
Zambia	50	7.2	79	73
Zimbabwe	61	5.6	73	75

Notes: a. Number of children a woman would have in a lifetime if she lived until the end of her reproductive years and bore the age-specific national average of children at each corresponding age.
   b. Number of children dying before their first birthday per 1000 live births.

Source: ADB (1993), Vol. 3.

and cancers (World Bank, 1993d). The link between health and development works both ways: a healthy nation will be able to develop faster, while development brings its own rewards in health.

Insufficient attention has been paid until very recently to health as a development issue, although it has long been understood by business that a healthy workforce is a better one. The importance of health for development, however, goes far beyond the well-being of workers. A recent study of the effect of adult ill-health on families concludes that where the mother falls ill or dies, children will have higher mortality rates and perform less well in school (Over et al., 1992). Investing in health clearly has many benefits over and above the obvious one of improving individuals, well-being, but it does have to be the right investment.

Southern Africa's health status varies greatly, as is illustrated in Table 23.1.

Angola, Malawi and Mozambique have a very poor health status with low life expectancies and high infant mortality rates. By contrast, Botswana's health position approaches that of the developing world.

Table 23.2   Health Service Provision Indicators (average annual)

Country	Population per doctor 1984–91	Population per nurse 1984–91	Per capita public health expenditure (US$) 1986–91
Angola	17 790	1020	9
Botswana	5 804	554	64
Lesotho	18 610	1525	13
Malawi	11 330	3110	6
Mozambique	37 960	5760	8
Namibia	5 246	313	68
South Africa	1 773	320	94
Swaziland	15 651	700	16
Zambia	7 150	740	7
Zimbabwe	6 700	1000	18

Source: ADB (1993), Vol. 3.

South Africa rates second in the region, but these data conceal great spatial and racial disparities. Of great concern are the high fertility rates in Southern Africa: the continued rapid growth in population means that, at best, there must be continued massive investment in social services merely to maintain the existing level of services; at worst, already threatened budgets will not keep pace with demand for services.

Namibia and South Africa are the best served by doctors and nurses, and have the highest per capita public expenditure on health; worst off are Malawi, Mozambique and Angola (Table 23.2).

Public spending on health in South Africa approaches that of high-income countries (Table 23.3), but there is great inequality in health services. The better-off (mainly White) population has access to a private health service as good as any in a developed country: 68 per cent of Whites as against only 7 per cent of Africans are members of medical aid schemes. There is also a great disparity between urban and rural areas, but even in the cities services are now deteriorating. In urban areas there is approximately one doctor per 700 people, in rural areas the ratio is 1:1800 while in the former homelands it was estimated that there were between 10 000 and 30 000 people per doctor (ANC, 1994).

Between 25 and 35 per cent of South African children under 5 years of age suffer from chronic malnutrition or stunted growth, and the South African child mortality rate (the number of children per 1000 live births who die before the age of 5 years) in 1993 was 72 (double that to be

Table 23.3 Spending on Health

	Budget[a] (%)	GNP[b] (%)
Low-income countries	3.4	1.3
Middle-income countries	5.1	2.4
High-income countries	12.5	3.5
South Africa	10.3	3.1

Notes: a. Average international proportion of budget allocated to health (1991).
   b. Average international government expenditure on health as a proportion of GNP (1987).

Source: South African Institute of Race Relations, *Fast Facts*, October 1994.

Table 23.4 HIV Prevalence in South Africa, 1992–4 (%)

Region	1992[a]	1993[a]	1994[b]
Cape	0.66	1.33	2.48
OFS	2.87	4.13	7.69
Transvaal	2.16	3.09	7.08
KwaZulu-Natal	4.77	9.62	19.78

Notes: a. Survey results.
   b. Predicted rate.

Source: Department of National Health and Population Development (1994).

expected of a middle-income country) compared with a worldwide average of 34. Government statistics give a fairly clear idea of the disease burden of the country. Heading the list is tuberculosis, with 47 805 cases notified in the first nine months of 1994. A poor second comes malaria with 4184 cases (Department of National Health and Population Development, 1994). Not recorded, however, are the non-notifiable diseases linked with poverty.

There is rapid and widespread growth in the incidence of HIV throughout South Africa, and in some parts incidences of 35 per cent and over have been reported in ante-natal clinic attender surveys. In South Africa the incidence of HIV is lower, but this is due to the later arrival of the epidemic rather than to any innate immunity. Data, as shown in Table 23.4, reflect the spread of the disease. Most HIV carriers will develop the disease during the latent period (6–8 years) and will then die.

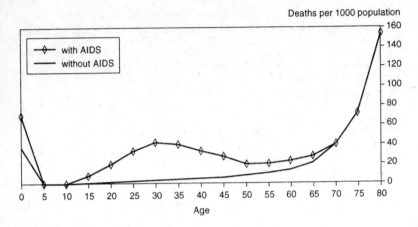

Figure 23.1 Impact of HIV on Age-specific Mortality Rates at 20 per cent Adult Prevalence

Source: Way and Staneki (1994).

There are several reasons why AIDS should be regarded differently from other diseases. It affects adults between 20 and 40 years of age, that is, individuals who do not normally fall ill or require health services, many of whom are in careers in middle management, and most of whom will have children; it is terminal; it is primarily transmitted through sexual intercourse; and it has a long latent period. The result will be an increase in morbidity and mortality rates. The effect on a population is shown on Figure 23.1, while actual recorded mortality rates in Zambia are shown in Table 23.5.

The epidemic will greatly affect the operation of the Zambian economy, the provision of social services and the business environment. It is not yet clear how this will happen, but it will put at risk many of the gains in health and development of the past decades. In this regard, Zambia is a microcosm of the situation in the sub-continent.

The way forward to improve the region's health is through a mixture of primary health care and development. The type of investment in health is of crucial importance: Nikiforuk (1991) argues that medical science has had little to do with improvements in health, and that stronger immune systems, better food, changes in accommodation and clothing, improvements in sanitation and the provision of clean water have been more important. With the threat of AIDS, health care and preventative medicine will take on an even greater importance.

Table 23.5 Crude Mortality Rate in 20 Zambian Companies (%)

1987	1988	1989	1990	1991	1992	1993[a]
0.24	0.48	0.58	0.95	1.26	1.6	2.1

Note: a. Predicted.

Source: Baggaley et al. (1993).

EDUCATION

Education is an important determinant of the quality of the workforce. However, time spent in education is not a sufficient indicator, and it is important to consider also the quality and type of education, scientific and technical training being particularly important. The role of education in successful economic growth and development is widely recognised, and one of the simplest measures of the value of education is the rate of return (Table 23.6).

This table shows that the lowest social rate of return is 8.7 per cent for higher education in the OECD countries; in all other areas and for all levels the rate of return is over 10 per cent. It is interesting to note that throughout the world primary education has the highest social rate of return. Private rates of return are higher than social rates because of the public subsidies given to education. The table also shows that the wealthier the region is, the lower is the rate of return.

In most Southern African countries primary schooling is provided free by the government and is supposed to be compulsory. There are usually some fees at the secondary level but the government is still the main provider. At the tertiary and vocational level fees are levied and are generally paid by the government through scholarships. However, in general the Southern African population is poorly educated, the region scoring badly in most of the UNDP indicators (UNDP, 1994). The levels of tertiary education are particularly poor, especially in science. In general there is a fairly good provision of basic primary education, although its quality is not always as high as would be hoped, and high birth rates mean that the sector needs continued expansion. Secondary education reaches a significantly lower percentage of potential pupils while very few go on to either tertiary or vocational levels. A major shortfall in the system at all levels is the poor quality of mathematics and science education.

The education system in South Africa is characterised by gross in-

Table 23.6 Returns to Investment in Education by Level (%)

| | Social | | | Private | | |
	Primary	Secondary	Higher	Primary	Secondary	Higher
Sub-Saharan Africa	24.3	18.2	11.2	41.3	26.6	27.8
Asia[a]	19.9	13.3	11.7	39.0	18.9	19.9
Europe/Middle East/North Africa[a]	15.5	11.2	10.6	17.4	15.9	21.7
Latin America/Caribbean	17.9	12.8	12.3	26.2	16.8	19.7
OECD	14.4	10.2	8.7	21.7	12.4	12.3
World	18.4	13.1	10.9	29.1	18.1	20.3

Note: a. Non-OECD.

Source: Psacharopoulos (1993).

equality. While Whites have received state-subsidised education of a comparable standard to that in any developed country, the education provided to Africans has been abysmal. This group has also been adversely affected by the political unrest of 1976–94, with frequent boycotts of schools and other educational institutions.

It is evident from Table 23.6 that investment in education makes sound economic sense for developing countries. A study of social rates of return to education in the Durban area confirms this: the overall rate of return was 13.8 per cent for Whites, 14 per cent for Indians, 15.7 per cent for Coloureds and 14.2 per cent for Africans. On the basis of further disaggregation of the rate of return, it was apparent that more resources should be devolved to Coloured, African, Indian and White schooling but in that order, and that in African schooling the emphasis should be on the lower primary level which yields the highest return (Trotter, 1984).

South Africa already invests an above-average proportion of its budget in education. Between 1983 and 1990 the figure stood at 16–18 per cent, while in 1994/5 it increased to 21.5 per cent. Expenditure alone, however, will not provide a panacea: rather, there is a need for reallocation, quality control and reassessment of the type of education to be provided. Of particular concern is the need for emphasis on technical training. Here South Africa's record is abysmal by contrast to the so-called 'winning nations'. For example, the number of apprentices and artisans in South Africa has decreased since 1985 to unacceptably low levels, new indentures declining by 30.4 per cent in 1991–2. Since training of this nature takes place over a cycle of several years, this decrease will only have an effect on the number of persons acquiring artisan status a few years hence. In 1992 the number of persons who completed their artisan training was less than half that in 1985. This trend will have a negative effect on economic growth and productivity.

A recent report states that South African companies are actually disinvesting in human capital. In South Africa the percentage of payroll spent on training is estimated at somewhere between 0.5 and 1.5 per cent compared to an average of 10 per cent in Japan and 5 per cent in the US. Although there may be some discrepancies regarding the basis on which these percentages are calculated, it can be asserted that South African companies are simply not investing enough in human capital (Visser, 1993).

IMPROVING PRODUCTIVITY

Southern Africa is not highly regarded as a competitive region in global terms. Thus, for example, South Africa was ranked only eleventh out of 15 newly emerging industrial countries in the 1993 World Competitiveness Report. South Africa scored particularly badly in domestic economic strength, internationalism, government and people. The other countries of the region are not covered in the report.

Competitiveness is closely related to productivity, the competitiveness of a firm or nation depending on the price of inputs and the efficiency with which they are utilised. The NPI (1994) argues that productivity determines the standard of living and per capita incomes. In order to increase productivity and thus the wealth of the region, therefore, it would make sense for key government segments and the private sector to examine the inputs they can influence, and the obvious area is human capital. A national productivity drive for South Africa has been recommended, consisting of three steps:

1. an awareness campaign, emphasising the need for and benefits of productivity improvements, with the government fully supporting such schemes;
2. a change in the education system which should be revamped away from its present emphasis towards better equipping individuals with an understanding of technology and markets as well as with skills more relevant in a modern economy; and
3. the sharing of improvements in productivity between customer, labour and shareholders.

Productivity in Southern Africa will have to improve if the countries of the region are to become increasingly competitive and avoid marginalisation. There is considerable scope for improving the quality of the region's human capital in terms both of health and education, but this will be a difficult process with few short-term results.

Select Bibliography and References

ADB (1993) *Economic Integration in Southern Africa*. Abidjan: African Development Bank.

ADB (1994a) *African Development Report*. Abidjan: African Development Bank.

ADB (1994b) *Economic Integration in Southern Africa*, 3 vols. Abidjan: African Development Bank.

Ades, A. and H.B. Chua (1993) 'Thy Neighbor's Curse: Regional Instability and Economic Growth'. Mimeo.

ANC (1994) 'A National Health Plan for South Africa'. Johannesburg: African National Congress.

Baggaley, R., D. Chilangwa, P. Godfrey-Faussett and J. Porter (1993) 'Impact of HIV on Zambian Business', Abstract, VIII International Conference on AIDS in Africa, Marrakech.

Barro, R.J. (1991) 'Economic Growth in a Cross Section of Countries', *Quarterly Journal of Economics*, 56(2).

Barro, R.J. and J.W. Lee (1993a) 'International Comparisons of Educational Attainment', *Journal of Monetary Economics,* 32(3).

Barro, R.J. and J.W. Lee (1993b) 'Losers and Winners in Economic Growth'. Paper prepared for the World Bank's Annual Conference on Development Economics, 3–4 May, Washington, D.C.

Biggs, T., G.R. Moody, J.-H. van Leeuwen and E.D. White (1994) 'Africa Can Compete! Export Opportunities and Challenges for Garments and Home Products in the U.S. Market'. Discussion Paper No. 242, Africa Technical Department Series. Washington, D.C.: World Bank.

Block, W. (1982) 'Discrimination Helps the Underprivileged', *Journal of Economic Affairs*, 2(2).

Botswana Confederation of Commerce, Industry and Manpower (BOCCIM) (1994) 'Cost-Benefit Study of Liberalising Foreign Exchange Control Regulations: Botswana'. Gaborone: Phaleng Consultancies (Pty) Ltd.

Bouton, L., C. Jones and M. Kiguel (1994) 'Macroeconomic Reforms and Growth in Africa: Adjustment in Africa Revisited', Policy Research Working Paper. Washington D.C.: World Bank.

Bureau of Market Research (1992) *Defining a Small Enterprise in South Africa*, Report No. 191. Pretoria: Bureau of Market Research.

Caballero, R. and V. Corbo (1990) 'The Effect of Real Exchange Rate Uncertainty on Exports: Empirical Evidence', *The World Bank Economic Review*, 3(2).

Calvo, G. (1978) 'On the Time Consistency of Optimal Policy in a Monetary Economy', *Econometrica*.

Calvo, G. (1991) 'The Perils of Sterilization', *IMF Staff Papers*, 38.

Calvo, G., L. Leiderman and C. Reinhart (1992) 'Capital Inflows and Real Exchange Rate Appreciation in Latin America: The Role of External Factors',

Working Paper WP/92/62. Washington, D.C.: IMF.

Canning, D. and M. Fay (1993) 'The Effect of Transportation Networks on Economic Growth', Discussion Paper Series. New York: Columbia University Department of Economics.

Central Statistical Services (1991) *Statistically Unrecorded Economic Activities of Coloureds, Indians and Blacks: October 1990.* Pretoria: CSS.

Chamber of Mines of South Africa (various years) *Annual Reports*, Johannesburg: Chamber of Mines.

Chua, H. (1993) 'Regional Spillovers and Economic Growth', Discussion Paper No. 700. New Haven: Economic Growth Center, Yale University.

Clarke, L.C. (1993) 'Botswana as a Prospective Financial Centre'. Symposium of the Botswana Society, Gaborone.

Coussy, J. (1992) 'Cost Benefits of Regional Integration in sub-Saharan Africa', Paper presented to workshop on 'Promotion of Regional Cooperation and Integration in sub-Saharan Africa', Florence.

DBSA (1991) *A Regional Profile of the Southern African Population and its Urban and Non-urban Distribution: 1970–1990.* Midrand: Development Bank of South Africa.

DBSA (1994) *South Africa's Nine Provinces: a Human Development Profile.* Halfway House: Development Bank of South Africa.

de Melo, J. and A. Panagariya (1992) *The New Regionalism in Trade Policy.* Washington, D.C.: World Bank and CEPR.

Department of National Health & Population Development (1994) *Epidemiological Comments,* 21(10).

Dornbusch, R. (1989) 'Real Exchange Rates and Macroeconomics: A Selective Survey', *Scandinavian Journal of Economics,* 91(3).

Easterly, W.R. (1993) 'Good Policy or Good Luck? Country Growth Performance and Temporary Shocks', *Journal of Monetary Economics,* 32(3).

Easterly, W.R. and R. Levine (1994) 'Africa's Growth Tragedy', mimeo. Washington, D.C.: World Bank.

Easterly, W.R. and S. Rebelo (1993) 'Fiscal Policy and Economic Growth: an Empirical Investigation', *Journal of Monetary Economics,* 32(3).

Easterly, W.R. and K. Schmidt-Hebbel (1994) 'Synthesis', in W.R. Easterly, C.A. Rodriguez and K. Schmidt-Hebbel (eds.), *Public Sector Deficits and Macroeconomic Performance.* New York: Oxford University Press.

Economic Research Unit (1993) *Special Employment Projects.* Report prepared for the Urban Foundation. Durban: Economic Research Unit, University of Natal.

Edwards, S. (1992) 'Exchange Rates as Nominal Anchors', Working Paper No. 4246. Washington, D.C.: National Bureau of Economic Research.

Edwards, S. (1993) 'Latin America and the Caribbean: A Decade After the Debt Crisis', mimeo Washington, D.C.: World Bank.

Enke, S. (1963) *Economics for Development.* London: Dennis Dobson.

Ernst, D. (1994) 'Network, Transactions, Market Structure and Technology Diffusion – Implications for South–South Cooperation', in L. Mytelka (ed.), *South–South Co-operation in a Global Perspective.* Paris: OECD.

Esterhuysen, P. et al. (1994) *South Africa in sub-Equatorial Africa: Economic Interaction.* Pretoria: Africa Institute of South Africa.

European Community (1988). 'The Economics of 1992: An Assessment of the Potential Economic Effects of Completing the Internal Market of the European Community', *European Economy*, 35.

European Round Table of Industrialists (1993) 'Foreign Direct Investment as a Tool for Economic Development and Cooperation – Suggestions for Future Improvements', in *European Industry: A Partner of the Developing World*. Brussels.

Fallon, P.R. and R. Lucas (1991) 'The Impact of Changes in Job Security Legislation in India and Zimbabwe', *World Bank Economic Review*, 5(3).

Fallon, P. and L.P. da Silva (1994) *South Africa: Economic Performance and Policies*. Washington, D.C.: World Bank.

Fischer, S. (1993) 'The Role of Macroeconomic Factors in Growth', *Journal of Monetary Economics*, 32(3).

Forest, D. (1982) 'Minimum Wages and Youth Unemployment: Would Britain learn from Canada?', *Journal of Economic Affairs*, 2(2).

Gaomab, M. (1994) 'Fiscal Policy and Employment in Namibia', Working Paper No. 43. Windhoek: NEPRU.

GATT (1993) *Trade Policy Review: The Republic of South Africa*, Vols 1 and 2. Geneva: GATT.

GEMINI (1993) *The Structure and Growth of Microenterprises in Southern and Eastern Africa: Evidence from Recent Surveys*. Washington, D.C.

Gerschenkron, A. (1962) *Economic Backwardness in Historical Perspective*. Cambridge, MA: Harvard University Press.

Gerson, J. and S.B. Kahn (1988) 'Factors Determining Real Exchange Rate Changes in South Africa', *South African Journal of Economics*, 56(1).

Goldin, I. et al. (1993) *Trade Liberalisation: Global Economic Implications*. Paris: OECD.

Gray, T. and M. Gamser (1994) *Building an Institutional and Policy Framework to Support Small and Medium Enterprises: Learning from Other Cultures*. Report submitted to the United States Agency for International Development.

Greene, J.E. and P. Isard (1991) *Currency Convertibility and the Transformation of Centrally Planned Economies*. Washington, D.C.: IMF.

Hicks, J.R. (1932) *The Theory of Wages*. London: Macmillan.

Hindson, D. (1994) 'Synthesis of Proceedings'. Report prepared for the KwaZulu-Natal Economic Workshop, Durban.

Hofmeyr, J.F. (1994a) *The Rise in African Wage Movements in South Africa*, Monograph No. 9. Durban: Economic Research Unit, University of Natal.

Hofmeyr, J.F. (1994b) 'The Analysis of African Wage: 1975–1985', *South African Journal of Economics*, 62(3).

Hofmeyr, J.F. and P.N. Wilkins (1995) 'Economic Aspects of the Proposal to Transfer Water from the Tugela to the Vaal Basin'. Unpublished report. Durban: Economic Research Unit, University of Natal.

Holden, M. (1988) *Definitions and Calculations of Real Exchange Rates: An Application to South Africa*, Occasional Paper No. 20. Durban: Economic Research Unit, University of Natal.

Holden, M. (1989) 'Comparative Analysis of Structural Imbalance in the Face of a Debt Crisis', *South African Journal of Economics*, 57(1).

Holden, M. (1990) 'The Growth of Exports and Manufacturing in South Africa from 1947 to 1987', *Development Southern Africa*, 7(3).

Holden, M. (1992) 'The Structure and Incidence of Protection in South Africa', in P. Black and B. Dollery (eds.), *Leading Issues in South African Microeconomics*. Johannesburg: Southern Book Publishers.

Holden, M. (1993) 'Trade Policy and Industrial Restructuring in South Africa', Paper delivered at Western Economic Association Conference, Lake Tahoe.

Holden, P. and S. Rajapatirana (1994) *Unshackling the Private Sector: A Latin American Story*. Washington, D.C.: World Bank.

Husain, I. (1994) 'The Macroeconomics of Adjustment in Sub-Saharan African Countries', Policy Research Working Paper No. 1365. Washington, D.C.: World Bank.

Husain, M. (1994) 'Savings, Economic Growth and Financial Liberalization: 'The Case of Egypt', mimeo. Abidjan: ADB.

IDRC (1993) 'Towards a Science and Technology Policy for a Democratic South Africa', Mission Report. Ottawa: IDRC.

ILO (1994) *Industry on the Move*. Geneva: International Labour Organisation.

IMF (1993) *Direction of Trade Statistics: Yearbook 1993*. Washington, D.C.: International Monetary Fund.

IMF (1994a) *Exchange Arrangements and Exchange Restrictions: Annual Report 1994*. Washington, D.C.: International Monetary Fund.

IMF (1994b) *World Economic Outlook*. Washington, D.C.

International Finance Corporation (1993) 'Trends in Private Investment in Developing Countries 1993', Discussion Paper No. 16. Washington, D.C.: IFC.

James, J. (1992) 'New Technologies, Poverty and Employment: The Future Outlook', World Employment Programme Research Working Paper. Geneva: ILO.

Jebuni, C. (1994) 'Financial Structure, Reforms and Economic Development: Ghana', mimeo. Abidjan: ADB.

Kamarck, A.M. (1967) *The Economics of African Development*. New York: Praeger.

Kane, E. J. (1991) 'Incentive Conflicts in the International Regulatory Agreement on Risk-Based Capital', in S.G. Rhee and R.P. Chang (eds.), *Pacific-Basin Capital Markets Research*, Vol. II. Amsterdam: North-Holland.

Khan, A. R. (1994) *Overcoming Unemployment*. Geneva: ILO.

Killick, T. (1995) 'Economic Flexibility in Africa: Evidence and Causes', in T. Killick (ed.), *The Flexible Economy: Causes and Consequences of the Adaptability of National Economies*. London: Routledge and the Overseas Development Institute.

Killick, T. (1995) *The Flexible Economy: Causes and Consequences of the Adaptability of National Economies*. London: Routledge and the Overseas Development Institute.

Kimaro, S. (1993) 'Economic Cooperation in Southern Africa: A Post-apartheid Perspective', mimeo.

Kimei, C. (1994) 'Financial Structures, Reform and Economic Development: Tanzania', mimeo. Abidjan: ADB.

King, R.G. and R. Levine (1993a) 'Finance and Growth: Schumpeter Might Be Right', *Quarterly Journal of Economics,* 108.

King, R.G. and R. Levine (1993b) 'Finance, Entrepreneurship, and Growth:

Theory and Evidence', *Journal of Monetary Economics,* 32(3).

King, R.G. and R. Levine (1994) 'Capital Fundamentalism, Economic Development and Economic Growth', Policy Research Working Paper No. 1285. Washington, D.C.: World Bank.

Kouri, P. and M. Porter (1974) 'International Capital Flows and Portfolio Equilibrium', *Journal of Political Economy,* 82(3).

Krugman, P. (1987) 'The Narrow Moving Band, the Dutch Disease, and the Competitive Consequences of Mrs. Thatcher: Notes on Trade in the Presence of Dynamic Scale Economies', *Journal of Development Economics,* 27.

Krugman, P. (1994) 'Competitiveness: A Dangerous Obsession!', *Foreign Affairs,* March/April.

Labán, R. and F. Larraín (1994) 'The Chilean Experience with Capital Mobility', in B. Bosworth, R. Dornbusch and R. Labán (eds.), *The Chilean Economy: Policy Lessons and Challenges.* Washington, D.C.: Brookings Institution.

Labán, R. and F. Larraín (1995) 'Continuity, Change, and the Political Economy of Transition in Chile', in R. Dornbusch and S. Edwards (eds.), Reform, *Recovery and Growth: Latin America and the Middle East.* Chicago: University of Chicago Press.

Lahouel, M. (1994) 'Trade and Exchange Rate Policies and Performance of the Tunisian Economy in the Eighties', mimeo. Abidjan: ADB.

Lall, S. (1995) 'Industrial Adaptation and Technological Capabilities in Developing Countries', in T. Killick (ed.), *The Flexible Economy: Causes and Consequences of the Adaptability of National Economies.* London: Routledge for the Overseas Development Institute.

Larraín, F. and R. Vergara (1993) 'Investment and Macroeconomic Adjustment: the Case of East Asia', in L. Servén and A. Solimano (eds.), *From Adjustment to Sustainable Growth: The Role of Capital Formation.* Washington, D.C.: World Bank.

Layard, R., S. Nickell and R. Jackman (1991) *Unemployment: Macroeconomic Performance and the Labour Market.* Oxford: Oxford University Press.

Leith, C. (1992) 'The Static Welfare Economics of a Small Developing Country's Membership in a Customs Union: Botswana in the Southern African Customs Union', *World Development,* 20(7).

Llewellyn, T. and S. Potter (eds.) (1991) *Economic Policies for the 1990s.* Oxford: Blackwell.

Lucas, R. (1988). 'On the Mechanics of Economic Development', *Journal of Monetary Economics,* 22(1).

Lustig, N. et al. (1992) *North American Free Trade Area: Assessing the Impact.* Washington, D.C.: Brookings Institution.

Maasdorp, G. (1993) 'Trade', in G. Maasdorp and A. Whiteside, *Rethinking Economic Cooperation in Southern Africa: Trade and Investment.* Johannesburg: Konrad Adenauer Stiftung.

Maasdorp, G. (1995) 'Models for Regional Cooperation in the Indian Ocean Region: Southern Africa'. Paper to the International Forum on the Indian Ocean Region, Perth.

Masuoka, T. (1990) *Asset and Liability Management in Developing Countries.* Washington, D.C.: World Bank.

Mathieson, D.J. and L. Rojas-Suarez, (1993) *Liberalization of the Capital Account – Experiences and Issues.* Washington, D.C.: IMF.

Matsebula, M.S. (1994) 'Economic Integration in Southern Africa: Benefits and Costs from Swaziland's Viewpoint', Discussion Paper No.3. Abidjan: African Development Bank.

Mauro, P. (1993) 'Corruption, Country Risk and Growth', mimeo.

McFarland, E.L. (1983) 'Benefits to the Republic of South Africa of her Exports to the BLS Countries', in M.A. Oomen, F.K. Inganju and L.D. Ngcongco (eds.), *Botswana's Economy since Independence*. New York: McGraw-Hill.

McGrath, M. and A. Whiteford (1994) 'Disparate Circumstances', *Indicator South Africa*, 11(3).

Michaely, M., D. Papageorgiou and A. Chokski (1991) *Liberalising Foreign Trade: Lessons of Experience in the Developing World*. Oxford: Blackwell.

Miller, M.H. (1994) 'Functional Regulation', *Pacific-Basin Finance Journal*, 2.

Morris, M. (1994) 'Economic Development of Region E: the Assessment Report', mimeo. Durban.

Mytelka, L. (ed.) (1994) *South–South Co-operation in a Global Perspective*. Paris: OECD.

Namibia Central Statistics Office (1994) *Household Income and Expenditure Survey: Preliminary Results*. Windhoek: Government Printer.

Namibia National Planning Commission (1994) *Draft National Development Plan 1*. Windhoek: Government Printer.

NEF (1994) *A Framework for Implementation of a National Public Works Programme*. Midrand: National Economic Forum.

NPI (1994) *Productivity Focus 1994*. Pretoria: National Productivity Institute.

Navaretti, G.B. (1994) 'What Determines Intra-industry Gaps in Technology?' Development Studies Working Papers, No. 77. Oxford: Queen Elizabeth House.

Naya, S. (1994) *The Asian Development Experience: Its Relevance to African Development Problems*. San Francisco: International Center for Economic Growth.

Nikiforuk, A. (1991) *The Fourth Horseman: A Short History of Epidemics, Plagues and Other Scourges*. London: Fourth Estate.

North, D. (1990) *Institutions, Institutional Change and Economic Performance*. New York: Cambridge University Press.

OECD (1991) 'Economic Policy-making since the mid-1960s', *OECD Economic Outlook 1991*.

Oman, C. (1993) *Globalisation and Regionalisation: The Challenge for Developing Countries*. Paris: OECD.

Oshikoya, T. (1994) 'Financial Sector Reforms, Interest Rate Liberalization and Economic Growth in Nigeria', mimeo. Abidjan: ADB.

Oshima, H.T. (1994) 'The Impact of Technological Transformation on Historical Trends in Income Distribution of Asia and the West', *The Developing Economies*, 32(3).

Over, M., R. Ellis, J. Huber and O. Solon (1992) 'The Consequences of Adult Ill-Health', in R. Feacher, T. Kjeastrom, C. Murray, M. Over and M. Phillips (eds.), *The Health of Adults in the Developing World*. New York: Oxford University Press.

Page, S., M. Darenport and A. Hewitt (1991) *The GATT Uruguay Round: Effects on Developing Countries*. London: Overseas Development Institute.

Perez, C. (1994) 'Technical Change and the New Context for Development', in L. Mytelka (ed.), *South–South Co-operation in a Global Perspective.* Paris: OECD.

Petri, P.A. (1994) 'The Lessons of East Asian Success: A Primer for Transitional Economies'. Paper prepared for the International Center for Economic Growth Transitional Economies Conference, Osaka, Japan.

Porter, M. (1990) *The Competitive Advantage of Nations.* New York: Macmillan.

Porter, M. (1994) 'The Nature and Issues of Competitiveness', in *Proceedings of the Third Private Sector Conference.* Francistown: Botswana Confederation of Commerce, Industry and Manpower.

Presidential Task Force on Market Mechanisms (1988) *Report of the Presidential Task Force on Market Mechanisms.* A report submitted to the President of the United States, the Secretary of the Treasury, and the Chairman of the Federal Reserve Board.

Psacharopoulos, G. (1993) 'Returns to Investment in Education: A Global Update', Policy Research Working Papers, UPS 1067. Washington, D.C.: World Bank.

Rhee, S.G. (1992) *Securities Markets and Systemic Risks in Dynamic Asian Economies.* Paris: Organisation for Economic Cooperation and Development.

Rhee, S.G. (1993a) 'Development of Financial Derivative Markets in Six Dynamic Asian Economies'. Report presented at the 1993 OECD/DAE Informal Workshop, Paris.

Rhee, S.G. (1993b) 'Fixed Income Securities Markets of Six Dynamic Asian Economies', in *Emerging Bond Markets in the Dynamic Asian Economies.* Paris: Organisation for Economic Cooperation and Development.

Rhee, S.G. and R. P. Chang (1992) 'The Microstructure of Asian Equity Markets', *Journal of Financial Services Research.*

Riddell, R.C. and A.J. Bebbington (1995) *Developing Country NGOs and Donor Governments.* London: ODA.

Riddell, R.C., A.J. Bebbington and L. Peck (1995) *Promoting Development by Proxy: the Development Impact of Government Support to Swedish NGOs.* Stockholm: Swedish International Development Agency.

Riddell, A.R. and W. Cummings (1994) 'Alternative Policies for the Finance, Control, and Delivery of Basic Education', *International Journal of Educational Research,* 21 (8).

Robson, P. (1993a) *Transnational Corporations and Regional Economic Integration.* London: Routledge.

Robson, P. (1993b) 'The New Regionalism and Developing Countries', *Journal of Common Market Studies,* 31(3).

Rodriguez, C. (1991) 'Situacion Monetaria y Cambiaria en Colombia', mimeo. CEMA, Argentina.

Romer, P. (1986) 'Increasing Returns and Long-Run Growth', *Journal of Political Economy,* 94(4).

RSA (1964) *Statistical Yearbook 1964.* Pretoria: Government Printer.

RSA (1976) *South African Statistics 1976.* Pretoria: Government Printer.

RSA (1992) *South African Labour Statistics 1992.* Pretoria: Government Printer.

RSA (1993) *South African Labour Statistics 1993.* Pretoria: Government Printer.

Ruiters, A. (1994) 'Small and Medium Enterprises in South Africa: A Statistical and Policy Review'. Report submitted to the Sunnyside Group, Johannesburg.

Saasa, O. (1992) *The Zambian Economy in Post-apartheid Africa: a Critical*

Analysis of Policy Options. Lusaka: Institute for African Studies.

Sachs, J. and F. Larraín (1993) *Macroeconomics in the Global Economy*. London: Harvester Wheatsheaf.'

Sader, F. (1993) 'Privatization and Foreign Investment in the Developing World, 1988–1992', WPS 1202. Washington, D.C.: World Bank.

Sato, M. (1993) 'Arguments over Japanese Derivatives'. Speech delivered at the 7th International Association of Options Exchanges & Clearing Houses General Meeting, Nagoya, Japan.

Seddon, D. and J. Belton-Jones (1995) 'The Political Determinants of Economic Flexibility with Special Reference to the East Asian NICs', in T. Killick (ed.), *The Flexible Economy: Causes and Consequences of the Adaptability of National Economies*. London: Routledge and the Overseas Development Institute.

Seers, D. (1972) 'What Are We Trying to Measure?', *Journal of Development Studies*, 8(3).

Semkow, B. W. (1994) 'Whither Capital Market Reform in Taiwan?', *Butterworths Journal of International Banking and Financial Law*.

Serven, L. and A. Solimano (eds.) (1993) 'Striving for Growth after Adjustment: The Role of Capital Formation'. Washington, D.C.: World Bank.

Simelane, V.R. (1994) 'The Impact of Economic Integration on Member Trade: An Empirical Analysis of the PTA for Eastern and Southern Africa'. Unpublished PhD Thesis, University of Connecticut.

Singh, A. (1994) 'Global Economic Changes, Skills and International Competitiveness', *International Labour Review*, 133(2).

Smith, A. (1976) *An Enquiry into the Nature and Causes of the Wealth of Nations*, fifth edition. Chicago: University of Chicago Press.

Summers, L. (1991) 'Research Challenges for Development Economists'. *Finance and Development*, 28(3).

Thomas, W. (1989) 'The Training Challenge for South Africa's Small Business Sector'. Paper to Training for Development workshop, Pretoria.

Thomsen, S. and S. Woolcock (1993) *Direct Investment in European Integration: Competition among Firms and Government*. London: Royal Institute of International Affairs.

Tornell, A. (1990) 'Real vs. Financial Investment: Can Tobin Taxes Eliminate the Irreversibility Distortion?', *Journal of Development Economics*, 32.

Trotter, G. (1984) *A Survey of Education Facilities and Social Rates of Return to Education in the Durban Metropolitan Region*. Durban: Economic Research Unit, University of Natal.

UNDP (1994) *Human Development Report 1994*. New York: Oxford University Press.

UNIDO (1991) *The Potential Role of Official Development Assistance (ODA) Projects in Promoting Industry in the Least Developed Countries (LDCs)*. Vienna: UNIDO.

United Nations (1994) *World Investment Report*. New York: UN.

UNCTAD (1994) *World Investment Report 1994*. Geneva: United Nations Conference on Trade and Development.

Visser, J. (1993) 'Why South Africa isn't a Leading Nation'. Paper delivered to a Skills SA Foundation conference.

Vosloo, W.B. (ed.) (1993) *Strategies for Economic Growth.* Johannesburg: Small Business Development Corporation.

Way, P.O. and K.A. Staneki (1994) *The Impact of HIV/AIDS on World Population.* Washington, D.C.: US Bureau of the Census.

West Indian Commission (1992) *Time for Action.* Black Rock: The Commission.

White, H. and J. Luttik (1994) 'The Countrywide Effects of Aid', Policy Research Working Paper No. 1337. Washington, D.C.: World Bank.

Whiteford, A. and M. McGrath (1994) *Distribution of Income in South Africa.* Pretoria: HSRC.

Williamson, J. (1982) *The Crawling Peg: Past Performance and Future Prospects.* New York: Macmillan.

Winrock International Institute for Agricultural Development (1991) *African Development: Lessons from Asia.* Arlington, Va.

World Bank (1989) *Sub-Saharan Africa. From Crisis to Sustainable Growth: A Long Term Perspective Study.* Washington, D.C.

World Bank (1991 et seq.) *Global Economic Prospects.* Washington D.C.: World Bank.

World Bank (1992) *Global Economic Prospects and the Developing Countries.* Washington, D.C.

World Bank (1993a) *The East Asian Miracle: Economic Growth and Public Policy.* New York: Oxford University Press.

World Bank (1993b) 'Characteristics of and Constraints Facing Black Businesses in South Africa: Survey Results', Discussion Paper 5. Washington, D.C.

World Bank (1993c) 'An Economic Perspective on South Africa'. Washington, D.C.

World Bank (1993d) *World Development Report 1993.* New York: Oxford University Press.

World Bank (1994) *Adjustment in Africa: Reforms, Results, and the Road Ahead.* Washington, D.C.

Index

accelerated growth 150
acquisitions and mergers 36
   European 41
adaptability and global
      economy 101
Africa
   decline 2, 96
   /East Asian income gap 23–4
   environmental degradation 96
   ethnic conflict 25
   ethnic diversity 2, 25–6
   growth lag 25
   health deterioration 96
   marginalisation 3–6
   North-South links 44
   poverty 96
African-Asian cooperation 95
African Development Bank 51
African-owned business 12, 253
agricultural labour 234
aid monies 212
Andean Pact 39, 49
Angola 15, 46, 60, 159
   health 259
   infant mortality 259
apartheid xiv, xv, 4, 10, 13, 61, 69
   and labour 234, 236
APEC 3, 39, 40
Argentina 39, 113–14
   capital flight 113
   Convertibility Law 113
   devaluations 113
   fiscal deficits 113
   fixed exchange rate 119
   foreign exchange control 192
   full convertibility 114
   hyperinflation 113
   inflation 114
   real exchange rate 114
   Tequila effect 121
   trade competitiveness 114
Arnold, M. 9
ASEAN 40, 96

Asia 6, 12
   agricultural development 101
   export-led growth 98
   and FDI 98
   GDP 98
   growth rates 95
   human resource development 102
   import ratios 95
   inflation 99–100
   intra-regional trade 34
   land reform 102
   market-oriented economy 97
   openness 98
   regulatory systems 99
   savings and growth 99
Asian 'economic miracle' 5, 170
   critical determinants of 97–8

balance of payments 8, 151
Bantustans, migration to 64
Big Emerging Markets 9, 196–7
black market premia 21, 23, 25
BLNS 4, 55–7
   common external tariffs 57
   compensation to 4, 56, 57
   exports 56
   primary commodities 56
   revenue-sharing 57
   and South African trade 47
bond markets 140, 144
Botswana 7, 20, 48, 55, 57, 58,
      60, 124, 131, 133, 196
   capital inflows 130
   health 259
   Human Development Index 165
   poverty 165
   pula 132, 135
   reserves 132
brain circulation 65
brain drain 4, 15, 62; see also
      migrant workers
   effects in Botswana, Zambia,
      Zimbabwe 65

brain drain – *continued*
  school-leavers and graduates 13
Brazil 39
  legal system 189
  real exchange rate 113
brokerage 141
Burkina Faso 19
Burrows, H.R. xiv
Burundi 16, 19
business environment 9, ch. 16
  African 178
  Mexican 178

CACM 39
capital account convertibility 124–5
capital accumulation 166
capital-intensive development 247
capital-investment flows 129
capital markets, internationalisation
  7, ch. 12
  stages of 137–41
Caribbean 40
CARICOM 42
CEAO 40
Central European Free Trade
  Area 39
Chad 20
child health 260; *see also* infant
  mortality
Chile 114–16
  Central Bank 115
  crawling peg regime 111
  current account deficit 115
  exchange rate bands 108
  exchange rate, fixed 110
  exchange rate, pegged 114–15
  exchange rate management 115
  legal system 189
  real exchange rate 113, 115
  reserves 120
  Tequila effect 121
China 34, 98
  food production 102
  growth rate 95
civil service, Asian 104
Clarke, L. 7
CMA 1, 51, 58, 131, 135, 156
Colombia 120
  crawling peg regime 111

exchange rate bands 108
  real exchange rate 113
  reserves 121
COMESA 3, 40, 45, 46, 51, 156
commission
  fixed 142
  negotiable 141
communicable diseases 258
communications 59, 181; *see also*
  information technology;
  infrastructure
comparative advantage 57, 58, 168
competition policy 255
competitive advantage 49, 168
competitiveness 6, ch. 15, 265
  African 199
  dynamic/static 36
  and marginalisation 197
  obstacles to 176–7
  and productivity 265–6
computer technology 207
contagion effect 2, 28, 29, 96
core-periphery hypothesis 8, 53–4
corporations, transnational 211
corruption 14, 50
Côte d'Ivoire 20
crawling peg regimes 111
  and inflation 111
credit, short-term 139
Cross-border Initiative 51, 59
curb markets 99, 153
currency convertibility 7, 50, ch.
  11, 128, 135
current account convertibility 123–4

debt capital 130
debt equity 130
debt forgiveness 160
demand management 152
democracy 4, 10, 59
demonstration effect 28, 29
  Asia 96
deregulation 140
derivative market 141
devaluation 152
distance costs 37
division of labour 182–3
dominance dependence 57
donor assistance 8, 51, 172, 180

Durban Economic Research
  Committee xiv
dynamic efficiency effects 54

East Asia 34, 165
  growth 95
  human capital 166
  intra-regional trade 34
  investment 166
Eastern Europe 33
Easterly, W. 2, 5, 6, 12
EC 1992 41
economic development 182
economic efficiency 8
economic growth 13
  Africa 19
  black market premia 21
  financial development 21
  fiscal surplus 21
  global 19
  human capital 21
  infrastructure 21
  national policies 20
  negative 19
  political instability 21
  rate 19
  rent-seeking 21
  sub-Sahara 95
economic integration, global 8
economic reform ch. 19
Economic Research Unit, Natal
  xiv–xv
economies of scale 49
education 12, 102, 103, 210–11,
  255, 256, ch. 23, 263–5
  apprenticeship programmes 256
  and ethnic diversity 25
  industry-specific training 256
  investment in 255
  and productivity 12
  by race 264
  spending on 264
effectiveness 173
empowerment 216
  African 165
Enterprise for the Americas
  Initiative 38, 39, 51
environmental degradation 149
equity capital 8, 13, 130

ethnic conflict 25
ethnic diversity 25–6
European Regional Development
  Fund 49
European Social Fund 49
European Union 38, 39, 41, 51
exchange control 192–3
exchange rate 224
  devaluation 152
  policy 6
exchange rate management 8, 131,
  151
  Latin America 108–16
exogenous shocks 161, 165
  Asia 100
export-led growth 169
external reserves 126
  effective value 128
  gross 127
  liquidity of 128

female employment 236
fertility and population growth 260
financial derivatives market 140
financial intermediation 99
financial liberalisation 153–4, 187
financial services industry 140
fiscal deficit
  money-financed 110
fiscal discipline 186
fiscal incentives 99
fiscal policy 229, 254, 255–6
fiscal restraint 190
fiscal surplus 21
fixed income securities market 140
floating currency 6
flying geese 3, 48, 49, 96
foreign aid 91 *see also* donor
  assistance
foreign currency-denominated
  accounts 125, 131
foreign debt 224
foreign direct investment 3, 9, 10,
  36, 200–2
  Africa 19, 37
  Asia 98
  distance costs 37–8
  East Asia 170
  and foreign capital 36

foreign direct investment – *continued*
  labour costs 37
  Malaysia 19
  market-based 42
  and multinationals 170
  patterns of 36–7
  polarised 2
  preferential trade arrangement 38
  South Africa 13–14, 175, 200
  world flows 36
foreign reserves 7
formal employment 238
Foroma, J. 11

G-7 33
garment production 198–9
GATT 33, 77, 135, 170, 230
  reforms 1994 35, 43, effects on
      developing countries 35
  and South Africa 230
  trading patterns 129
GDP growth 34, 175, 232
GDP/reserves ratio 130
GEIS 228
Ghana 163, 175
  economic reform 150
gold price 223, 227, 234
government/business relations 104
government intervention 103
government regulation 7
Grande Anse Declaration 40
growth failure, transmission of 28
growth, trade-related 53

Hawkins, T. 7, 8
health and productivity 12, ch. 23
  and development 259
health indicators 259
health service provision 260, 261
Hesketh, M. 11–12
HIV/AIDS 5, 12, 261–2
  KwaZulu-Natal 5, 87–8, 89
Hofmeyr, J. 11
Holden, M. 10
Holden, P. 9
Hong Kong 23, 96, 141
  market crash 145
Horwood, O. P. F. xiv
household

composition by race 73
  head of 73, 75
  per capita income 75
  size 73
human capital 21
Human Development Index 164,
    165
human resource development 59
  Asia 102

illegal workers 22, 62
  to South Africa 4
IMF 51, 123–4, 160, 221
  Article VIII status 124, 134
  reserve tranches 126
import-substitution 157
incentive policies 186
income distribution 5, 69
  class-based 71–2
  determinants of 73
  by race 69, 70, 72–3
indigenisation 165
Indonesia 96, 101
  FDI 99
  food production 102
industrialisation 57, 58, 182
inequality 8
infant mortality 19
  African 20, 260–1
inflation 6, 8, 149
  Asia 99–100
  Latin America 107
informal sector employment 231
information superhighway 205
infrastructure 19, 21, 50, 202
  Africa 23
  investment in 255
  social 50
institutional policies 187
interest rates
  controlled 140
  deregulation 140
  policy 228
investment 9, 166, 175
  criteria 168
  cross-border 3, 41
  effective ch. 15
  gross domestic 223
  private sector 175

investment – *continued*
  public sector 175
  transnational 37
investor protection 140, 141

Japan 96, 102, 143
  Finance Ministry 142
  futures market 142
job creation 11
job security 245, 247
jobless growth 170

Kamarck, A.M. 20
Kangueehi, T. 5 ·
Kenya 20, 49, 164, 173, 175
KwaZulu-Natal 5, ch. 8
  crime 88, 89
  dependency rate 85
  economic management 88
  education and training 91
  GGP 86, 87
  HIV/AIDS 5, 87–8, 89
  industry 87
  infrastructure 89
  job creation 89, 91
  labour force participation rate 85
  political instability 88
  political violence 88, 89
  population 85
  Reconstruction and Development
    Programme 89, 90
  resources 87, allocation 86
  tourism 86, 89
  Tugela-Vaal Transfer Scheme
    89–90
  unemployment 5, 85

labour
  costs 50
  free movement of 16
  laws 63
  in mines 62
  organised 63
  segmentation 236
  skilled 61–2
  unskilled 61, 170
labour markets 193
  segmentation of 240–2
labour migration 61, 62

labour regulations 256
land redistribution 165
land use regulation 255
Larraín, F. 6
Latin America 6, 12
  capital flows 6, 108, 118
  exchange rate bands 108
  exchange rate policy 6, 108–16
    fixed 108, 110, flexible 112,
    floating currencies 108,
    managed 110, real 6, ch.
    10, 12, 113
  export competitiveness 107
  financial sector 187
  fiscal deficit 110
  fiscal discipline 186
  foreign debt crisis 108
  foreign exchange reserves 117
  imports 117
  incentives 186
  inflation 107
  institutional policies 187–8
  international reserves 117–19
  legal systems 188
  macroeconomic policies 186
  monetary policy 111–12
  Plan Real 110, 119
  private sector 183, 185
  privatisation 187, 192
  property rights 188
  public sector 183
  reform 184–5
  reserve accumulation 108,
    117
  reserve management ch. 10
  speculative capital 108
  stabilisation 108
  sterilisation 108, 118, 120, and
    operating losses 118–19
  trade blocs 39
  trade liberalisation 40
  trade policy 186
legal system
  Latin America 188
  South Africa 189
Lesotho 48, 55, 60
  CMA 58
  labour migrants 61, 62
  workers' remittances 63

life expectancy 19
  African 20
  maternal 20
liquidity crisis, South Africa 227
Lomé Convention 3, 38, 51, 52
London, A. 7

macroeconomic policy chs. 13 and
  14
  convergence 16
macroeconomic stability 6
  Asia 99
macro-policy 161
  trickle-down effects 162
Malawi 48, 165
  infant mortality 259
  life expectancy 259
Malaysia 2, 96, 102, 140
  FDI in 19
Mali 19
manufacturing growth 34
marginalisation
  Africa 19
  aggregate level 55
  continental 1
  corporate 9
  of economy 6, 159
  and FDI 201
  KwaZulu-Natal ch. 8
  of labour force 242
  Namibia ch. 7
  national 2, 3
  and national politics 214
  of periphery 55
  of poor 159, 163
  and poverty 8
  regional 1, 3
  small country 4, 53–60
  sub-national 2, 5
  and technology 10, ch. 18
  within country 4–5
market growth 166
market integration 41
market transparency 140
Matsebula, M. 4
Mauritius 7, 38, 49
McGrath, M. 5
Mercosur 39
mergers 36

Mexico 6, 39, 119
  Central Bank 116
  crisis 6, 120
  current account deficit 120
  default on debt obligation 184
  exchange rate 113, 116, 119
  exchange rate bands 108
  maquila industries 181
  peso 116–17
  Tequila effect 120
micro-economy 9
micro-enterprises 251
migrant labour 4, ch. 5
  from Lesotho 61, 62
  from Mozambique 61, 62
  to South Africa 234
  mining 234–5
  and migrant labour 61
monetary integration 7, 135
monetary management 130
monetary policy 254
  Latin America 111
monetisation 130
money markets, short-term 141
morbidity/mortality 258, 261;
    see also health indicators
Mozambique 15, 48, 55
  infant mortality 259
  life expectancy 259
  migrant labour 61, 62
Multi-Fibre Arrangement 35
multinationals 8
  and the regional dimension 167

NAFTA 3, 39, 41
Namibia 4, 5, 7, 55, ch. 7
  agriculture 83
  and apartheid 80
  and CMA 58
  consumption 80
  education 81, 82–3
  environmental degradation 84
  exports 79
  GDP 79, 80
  GNP 79
  health system 81, primary 81,
    83
  income differentials 80
  inequality 79–82

Namibia – *continued*
  inflation 80
  infrastructure 83
  pension scheme 82, 83
  population growth 79, 84
  poverty ch. 7, 81, 83
  public expenditure ch. 7
  subsistence farming 81
  unemployment 82
  wealth distribution 80
  Windhoek 80, 81
  women 84
  World Bank Expenditure
    Review 83
Natal Regional Survey xiv
national policies 214
Naya, S. 6
NBFIs 139
new business start-ups 254
  and job creation 254
NGOs 10, 160, 177, 180, 216
niche markets 212
NIEs 33, 96
  and FDI 37
Nigeria 23, 154, 159, 163
North-South links 3
NTBs 35, 50

OECD 35, 42–3, 51, 161–2, 214

Paraguay 39
parastatals 8
per capita income 1, 173, 174, 223
  Africa 149
  BLNS 55
  South Africa 65–6
periphery 49
Peru 188
  foreign exchange 192
  security 193
Philippines 99, 100
polarisation 49
policy choices 5, 20, 254
  competition 255
  fiscal 255–6
  trade 255
political stability 59
political violence 193
population growth 149, 175, 232, 233

portfolio equity 19, 130
portfolio investment, direct 140
poverty 5, 8, 72, 77, 79, 149, 258
  income line 72
  by race 72–3
  reduction 150
preferential trade arrangement 38
primary products, reliance on 10
  Namibia 79
privatisation 187, 192, 211
  rejection of 160
production
  and health 258
  internationalisation of 3, 36
productivity 12, 200, 247, 253,
    258, 265–6
property rights 178, 183, 255
  Latin America 188
  South Africa 189
protectionism 3, 45
PTA Clearing House 46
public expenditure ch. 7
public goods 50
public works projects 91

quality 173
quality-of-life indicators 5, 19
  KwaZulu-Natal 85

Reconstruction and Development
    Programme 11, 14, 162,
    229–30
recovery-induced demand 33
Regional Economic
    Integration 155–6
regional institutions 50
regional integration 212
regionalism 3, 34, 38
  and credibility 42, 44
  open 40
regulatory structures 145
rent-seeking 28, 50
  and bureaucracy 15
  competitive 25
  and interest groups 255
reserve management policy 6, 7,
    ch. 10, 132
resource allocation 10
resources, natural 168

Rhee, G. 7
Riddell, R. 10
risk-hedging 141
risk perception 50
  KwaZulu-Natal 5
Robson, P. 3
Rwanda 16, 60

Saasa, O. 4
SACU 1, 3, 4, 40, 45, 46, 56
  monetary union 58, 135
SADC 3, 45, 46, 51
  GDP 163
  free movement of labour
    protocol 16
  trade protocol 40
SAPs 6, 15, 16, 155, 159, 167
savings 153, 223
  and growth 23, 99
  and investment 183
sectoral cooperation 58
security 193
securities
  equity-linked 140
  government-issued 139
  and industry 139
  market 142–3
Seers, D. 148
self-employment 251
skilled labour 4, 61, 64, 234; *see
  also* brain drain
skills shortage 13, 91
skills training 243
Simelane, V. 4
Singapore 40, 96, 100, 141
Single European Market 41
small firm advantage 212
SMEs ch. 22
SMMEs 12, 212, ch. 22
  contribution to GDP 252
  definition 251
  job creation 252
  in KwaZulu-Natal 90–1
  micro-enterprises 252
  output 253
Social Charter on the Fundamental
    Rights of Workers 63
social instability, African 149
South Africa

affirmative action 13, 15
business environment 189
capital flight 228
capital flows 223
coloured population 72
corruption 14, 15
crime and violence 13, 14, 193,
    238
debt indicators 224
debt standstill 229
development problems 48
disinvestment 227
economic growth 11, 69–70
economic reform ch. 19
education 15, 154, 264–5
emigration 13–14, 15,
    farmers 65
exchange rate 224
FDI 200
firm size 251
GDP 222, 232
GDP/external debt ratio 149
GEIS 228
gross reserves 127
import surcharge 228
income distribution 5
Indian population 70, 72
informal sector 70, 252
intra-regional trade 47
job creation 11, 252
labour market ch. 20,
    segmentation 11, 240–2,
    unionised 239, 240
labour shortage 234
labour surplus 11
majority rule 13
migrant labour 61
per capita income 149
population growth 232
poverty 5
property rights 189
PWPs 243–4
RDP 162, 221, 229–30
sanctions 10, 47, and labour
    migration 64
savings and investment 223
structural adjustment 228
unemployment 11, 14, 48, 70,
    193, 231

South Africa – *continued*
  and United States ch. 17
  unionisation 11, 14–15, 193
  wage differentials 11, 232, and
    mining 235, and
    unionisation 239
  wage movements 11
South Korea 96, 100, 140
  bank assets 144–5
  bond market 145
  corporate debt 145
  government bonds 144
  finance ministry 143
  land reform 102
  Securities and Exchange
    Commission 142–3
South-South cooperation and
  trade 43, 52
special drawing rights 126, 133
spillover effects 29, 48, 49
state marketing boards 176
static efficiency gains 54
stock market rescue funds 143
strike activity 193; *see also* trade
  unions
structural adjustment programmes
  10, 37, 50, 159–60, 161, 167, 228
  Asia 101
subsidies, targeted 160
supply-side shocks 162
sustainable development 8, ch. 9,
  150, 164
Swaziland 7, 16, 48, 55, 61, 196
  CMA 58

Taiwan 96, 98, 101, 102, 140
  Central Bank of China 146
  global depository receipts 146
  securities 146
  Securities and Exchange
    Commission 145
  Stock Exchange 146
Tanzania 46, 154, 159
tariff barriers 49
tariff reductions 35, 50
task-level efficiency 199
tax administration 8
technological revolution 10, 12
technology 181, ch. 18

introduction of 205
  marginalisation 208, causes
    of 205–9, reducing 209–13
  skill requirements 205
  and unemployment 205
telecommunications 59
Thailand 96, 100, 143
Tlhase, I. 5
tourism 48, 59, 89, 167
trade creation 54
  benefits 42
trade diversion 54
  costs 42
trade integration 45, 46
trade, intra-regional 46, 47
trade liberalisation 10
  gains 42
  Latin America 40
  multilateral 34
trade patterns, Southern Africa
  128–9
trade policy 186, 255
trade reform 190–1
trade unions 14, 193, 235, 238
  African 236
  mass-based 238
  and wage-setting 237
trading blocs 39, 49
training levies 211
transmission mechanisms 151
transport 59
Trotter, G.J. xiv

UEMOA 39, 40
Uganda 164
underemployment 238–9
unemployment 8, 193, 237
Unger, M. 8
United States ch. 17
Uruguay 39

wage legislation 11, 12
wage movements 232–7
  union-driven 239
wage rates 50
  market clearing 15
Whiteside, A. 12
Wilkins, N. 5
worker incentives 199

workers' remittances 63
workplace regulation 257
World Bank 29, 34, 51, 106, 151,
  160, 165, 185, 221
  Asia 101
  Long-term Perspective
    Study 163
world recession 33
WTO 3, 12–13, 35, 45, 51

Zaire 16, 51, 159
Zambia 4, 16, 55
  brain drain 64, 65
  excess liquidity 131
  HIV/AIDS 262
  market liberalisation 132

reserve money 130
Zimbabwe 7, 11, 15, 16, 48, 60,
  131, 159, 165, 196, ch. 21
  capital-intensive production 247,
    tax incentives for 247
  Economic Structural Adjustment
    Programme 163
  informal sector 246
  investor confidence 11, 248–9
  job security 245, 247
  labour legislation ch. 21
  minimum wages 11, 245–6, 247,
    248
  productivity 247
  unemployment 246, youth
    247